GOD, NATURE, AND THE CAUSE

HAMMAAD

God, Nature, and the Cause

ESSAYS ON ISLAM AND SCIENCE

Basil Altaie

كلام للبحوث والإعلام
KALAM RESEARCH & MEDIA

ISLAMIC ANALYTIC THEOLOGY INITIATIVE SERIES

KALAM RESEARCH & MEDIA
P.O. Box 78000, TwoFour54, Media Zone, Abu Dhabi, UAE
www.kalamresearch.com

ISBN 978-9948-02-527-6 (PAPERBACK)
ISBN 978-9948-02-536-8 (HARDBACK)

The publication of this volume was possible with the support of the
JOHN TEMPLETON FOUNDATION

Design by Sohail Nakhooda
Typesetting by Integra, India
Printed in the USA

For Adam
Ola, Asmaa and Zara

CONTENTS

PREFACE

SINCE THE TIME WHEN MUHAMMAD IQBAL published his book *The Reconstruction of Religious Thought in Islam* in 1930, many authors have proposed their views on possible ventures that may lead to the sought-after reconstruction of Islamic religious thought. The aim is always to target the development of Muslim society and inspire Muslims to contribute positively to the life of the rest of the world. In a limited number of regions, such as Turkey and Malaysia, these targets have been only partially achieved over the last few decades, but the heart of the Islamic world, Arabia, is still far from achieving such goals. To the contrary, the dominating dogma and backwardness in this part of the Islamic world has helped develop violent movements managed by mysterious agendas to spread destruction and terror in the world under the name of Islam. Had it not been for a deeply rooted ill-informed understanding of Islam, such terrorist movements could not have flourished. Moreover, most of those reconstruction proposals have found no outlets for their application, because of the absence of support from the ruling regimes or the ignorance of the religious clerics themselves, who are very keen on adopting old tenets and old approaches. In this respect, we should not underestimate the influence of those old approaches, not only because of their glorious fame, which is much exaggerated, but also because of their systematic consistency. In addition, it would not be an easy task to change the dogma of any society dominated by ignorance and rational illiteracy. That is why we need to pay attention to the role that science and scientific development can play in transforming the public mind, which constitutes a vital element in the success of any social transformation.

The question of the impact that science and scientific development have on the beliefs of the modern Muslim is one vital inquiry which needs to be pursued. An accurate judgment on this issue would certainly require field data to be collected from different Muslim societies, classified according to their social and economic groupings, and subjected to precise quantitative analysis. Obviously, such data is not available now; nevertheless, without such a study, one can crudely conclude that the development of modern science has very little influence on the beliefs or religious practices of modern Muslims. However, we can probe into a more theoretical assessment of the relation between modern science and the basis of Islamic belief through investigating the rational Islamic approach to theological beliefs and natural facts.

The aim of this collection of essays is to analyze the possibility of developing a modern Islamic worldview of natural philosophy, which is construed from the basics of Islamic belief and constructed on the basis of Islamic *kalām*. *Kalām* was the venture through which Muslims during the eighth and the ninth centuries (the second and the third centuries after the Prophet Muhammad, peace be upon him) rationally rehearsed the basis of their beliefs in an attempt to establish a logical approach for defending those beliefs. In this, they practiced many debates, exchanging their ideas and opinions about the fundamental questions concerning the theories of knowledge, divinity, human free will, predestination, and the natural world. The part of *kalām* dealing with questions of natural philosophy was called *daqīq al-kalām*, while the other, larger, part dealing with questions of the divine attributes, punishment and reward, and the Day of Resurrection was called *jalīl al-kalām*. However, it was unfortunate that, within a few decades, *kalām* faced social as well as religious problems as it became part of the political conflict between different systems of thought.

One may think that *kalām* is outdated and that it was settled long ago as merely being a monumental part of Islamic cultural history, and thus that it can have no practical role to play in our modern times. Actually, this is not the case; investigating *kalām* on the part of natural philosophy by reverting to its original sources shows that this venture in Islamic thought is capable of accommodating the philosophical basis of modern natural sciences, particularly the physical sciences. *Kalām* has much to offer in respect of contemporary natural philosophy, especially on the question of the cosmological argument. William Lane Craig, for example, has taken one useful argument—the "Kalām Cosmological Argument"—from the legacy of the old *kalām* to present it in our modern time as a strong philosophical argument for the beginning of the world. In addition, the basic doctrines and principles of *daqīq al-kalām* are very much in conformity with the vision of modern physical theories and the modern understanding of the natural world through quantum mechanics and the theory of relativity. Nonetheless, the old part of theological *kalām*—that is, *jalīl al-kalām*—does not seem to offer a similar degree of richness and practical applicability on the social and theological areas of our knowledge and practices. For this reason, *kalām* needs to be reformed to allow all of its advanced features to facilitate a new construct that would, hopefully, play an important role in the transformation of Islamic thought and Muslim societies. Much of the ugly side of belief that has spread hatred and atrocities has no rational or instructive foundation in Islam. It was only the application of false narrations and misinterpretations of the facts and goals of the religion, which were produced through the irrational system of belief of some Muslims. In the absence of a profound system for deducing Sharia law, fanatics can construe the kind of Sharia that manifests their psychological disorder and malady.

Two factors make *kalām* a vital approach that could prove to be successful in the development of modern Islamic thought, which in turn can positively contribute to the progress of society. The first is that it was born and grown within Islamic culture; it was not inferior in any respect, rather it stemmed from the stream of revelations and the spirit of the Islamic mind and culture. The second is that it is very much in harmony with the underlying principles of contemporary scientific trends and therefore it is an inspiration for both science and Islam.

In this volume, I present chapters dealing with "God, Nature, and the Cause", through which I discuss questions related to divine action, the laws of nature, causality, and the concept of spacetime, all from an Islamic perspective. The aim is to present the views of the original rational Islamic approach to the philosophical theology of nature, which was called *daqīq al-kalām*. For this purpose, and since many readers are unfamiliar with Islamic *kalām*, I introduce the basic doctrines of this approach in the first chapter of the book. In this, I present what I have extracted as the principles of the Islamic worldview concerning the main topics of natural philosophy. These principles have been cultivated from a large field of thought and writing by those rational thinkers who looked at the world and saw it enlightened with the light of the Creator, those who were called the *mutakallimūn*.

In Chapter Two I discuss the concepts of a law of nature and a law of physics in order to clarify a common misconception about them. Causality in Islamic thought has been considered in Chapter Three, and in Chapter Four the question of divine action is discussed and a proposal from an Islamic perspective is presented. In Chapter Five the concepts of space and time within *kalām* are discussed and compared with the modern concept, and in Chapter Six I present two examples where the concepts of space and time in *kalām* and philosophy are exposed. Finally, in Chapter Seven I outline my proposal for a neo-*kalām* that might initiate a modern transformation in Islamic thought and enable Muslims to revive their role in contributing positively to the peace and welfare of mankind.

ACKNOWLEDGMENTS

I WOULD LIKE TO PRESENT my deepest thanks to the management at Kalam Research & Media for their unlimited support in making the writing and publishing of this book possible. I would also like to thank the anonymous reviewers who presented some useful suggestions that have enhanced the content of the book.

BASIL ALTAIE
May 2016

CHAPTER ONE

Daqīq al-Kalām: A Possible Role in Science and Religion Debates

Probably no chapter in the history of the cosmological argument is as significant—or as universally ignored—as that of the Arabic theologians and philosophers. Although we find in them the origin and development of two of the most important versions of the cosmological argument, namely the argument from temporality and the argument from contingency, the contribution of these Islamic thinkers is virtually ignored in western anthologies and books on the subject.

William Lane Craig[1]

CURRENT DEBATES IN SCIENCE and religion raise several important questions about our understanding of the role played by religion in intellectual life. Concerns over these questions and their impact on individuals and societies differ from one culture to another. In the West, during this age of advancements in science and technology, and after the steady decline in religious domination of society, people are much more open to those questions. They discuss more freely the fundamentals of religious belief, which had usually been accepted on faith. In the East, and especially in the Muslim world, there are always limitations imposed by society and by the domination of religion over the mentality of most people. People in the Muslim world are almost confined to an inflexible set of thoughts, rituals, and beliefs. This kind of stagnation prevents people from posing the right questions and sometimes inhibits their quest for a proper and courageous understanding of their goals. This state of stagnation has dominated Muslim societies for a long time, nearly half a millennium now. It was created, as far as I can see, under special circumstances, which could have opened up the

Islamic intellect toward accepting a rational reanimation of the social mind, rather than confine it to the state of languishment and decline that we now have. This seems contrary to the spirit of the original Muslim intellectuals and lawmakers.

As early as the beginning of the eighth century, a striving cultural movement among Muslim intellectuals was initiated. The aim was to develop a system of thought that could accommodate different perspectives and opinions concerning the religious legitimacy of certain positions. Moreover, the aim was to develop a systematic methodology of deduction that would formulate an official religious position on matters concerning the everyday life of both the individual and the society. This was the first development of official Sharia law in Islam. Such a development needed an intellectual foundation capable of providing the necessary support and authentication for the deductions made. Muslims initially found two sources for this foundation: the Qur'an and the traditions of the Prophet Muhammad (peace be upon him). These were sufficient to deal with most problems and needs of Muslims in the first century after the Prophet's passing. But, as time went on, and as large areas of the world came under Muslim rule, new situations presented themselves and a wider scope of vision was required. This culminated in introducing a rational approach into the system of deduction, and perhaps it was Imam Abū Ḥanīfa al-Nuʿmān who established this methodology in Islamic jurisprudence.

Abū Ḥanīfa (699–767) adopted the methodology of *qiyās* (analogy) to deduce Sharia law and, as a result, this required an advanced intellectual background for proper analogies to be presented. However, sometimes analogies could not be found or did not help; in such cases, Abū Ḥanīfa would resort to reasoning to decide on the correct course of action to take, and to discard the wrong, and this was called *istiḥsān* (preference). Here, in this part of the process of deduction, the intellect played a most important role in arriving at a religious position on acts or matters of belief; a whole process called *ijtihād* (original interpretation) was adopted, which could be considered an instrument for innovation.

The methodology of Abū Ḥanīfa was adapted by Imam al-Shāfiʿī (767–820) to bring it closer to the Prophet's legacy, and those of his Companions; more and more authentication of the sources used for innovative deductions was required and this instigated the compilation of the traditions (hadiths) of the Prophet and his Companions, and hard work was done to authenticate them. However, this authentication process was not free of religious or political bias. Moreover, many fraudulent parties took the opportunity to generate false stories and narrations for a variety of reasons and aims, and some of these stories were integrated into the body of Islamic literature and still exist today.

Next, Imam Aḥmad ibn Ḥanbal (780–855) adopted a more hardline approach to Sharia law, relying solely on a literal understanding of Qur'anic stipulations and the Prophetic narrations and leaving no place for rational deduction. The Muslim public then had to wait many years before further innovative thinking (*ijtihād*) occurred when Ibn Taymiyya (1263–1328) arrived on the scene to assert the Hanbali approach, making some notable philosophical accomplishments which were later to be ignored by Sheikh Muḥammad ibn ʿAbd al-Wahhāb (1703–92), who had reestablished the doctrine of Aḥmad ibn Ḥanbal, albeit lacking in vigor and revealing a decline in intellectual values.

Many later deductions of Islamic religious culture depended on the conditions of that period—meaning, the eighth and ninth centuries—but there were also strong intellectual movements that adopted rational considerations of the Islamic sources and fundamentals of belief in an endeavor to establish a system of Islamic thought that could provide for the development of the proper tools for *ijtihād*. In addition, these movements constructed a worldview concerning the big questions about the purpose of our existence, the creation of the world, the role of man and the possible existence of free will, and understanding the construct of nature by which events are phenomenally occurring. This was *kalām*, an important chapter in the development of Islamic thought which is much ignored by historians of thought and philosophers focusing on the cosmological argument.

In this chapter, I will introduce *daqīq al-kalām*, the main part of *kalām* that deals with questions of natural philosophy, which is easier to tackle and perhaps the element of *kalām* most untouched by religious or political bias. However, since we are mainly concerned here with the basis of the relationship between science and religion, and since this topic was of paramount importance in Islamic *kalām*, I would rather start furnishing the reader with some terminological preliminaries and related matters, which will help to introduce the subject. The content of this chapter will form the intellectual basis for the chapters that follow and will facilitate understanding of those chapters.

Science and Belief

In Arabic, the word *ʿilm* points to knowledge of a specific discipline. The verb *ʿalima* means "to acquire knowledge" and "to get to know [something]". Al-Jurjānī defined *ʿilm* as "the confirmed belief that conforms to reality".[2] There is another word which could be synonymous to *ʿilm*, this is *khabar*, which points to a report not accompanied by any evidence of either its truth or its falsehood. Al-Jurjānī specified *khabar* as being something that is "contingent on being true or false".[3] So, ʿ*ilm* is the knowledge that is associated with reason or other confirmed sources of belief, whereas *khabar* is a piece of information that is to be believed. Such knowledge, ʿ*ilm*, has two sources in Islam: the first is the divine revelations, which began with Allah providing the first man (Adam) a priori information: "And He taught Adam all the names (of everything)" (Qur'an 2:31). This information constituted the names by which all things in the world are identified. The names were not necessarily given in any specific language, rather such information was meant to prepare the human mind for comprehending the world. It is a sort of a priori knowledge, or "read only" memory, that helped install the operating system of the human mind. The second source for ʿ*ilm* is the intellect (ʿ*aql*) itself, which follows certain rules of logic acquired from the natural world through contemplation and practical experience.

On the other hand, the word "science", as defined by *Merriam-Webster*, can mean the "knowledge about or study of the natural world based on facts learned through experiments and observations".[4] In this meaning, science becomes more specific knowledge that is acquired through experimentation and reason. It is to be found more in activities that investigate the world.

The word ʿ*ilm* is mentioned in the Qur'an more than eighty times in many verses and it covers all of the above meanings, including science in the modern meaning of the term. The Qur'an has encouraged people to look through the earth and the heavens and contemplate the construction of the world and its creation, and reflect on the Creator. In several places, the Qur'an encourages mankind to consider the existence of the world and its properties, and the need for a creator:

> He in Whose Hand is the dominion, and He is Able to do all things. Who has created death and life, that He may test you which of you is best in (their) deed. And He is the All-Mighty, the Oft-Forgiving. Who has created the seven heavens one above another, you can see no fault in the creations of the Most Beneficent. Then look again: "Can you see any rifts (inconsistencies)?" Then look again and yet again, your sight will return to you in a state of humiliation and worn out. (67:1–4)[5]

This is an important verse, which is presented here as an example of the rational arguments given in the Qur'an and which has attracted the attention of the Nobel Laureate Professor Abdus Salam.[6] In this verse, the Qur'an metaphorically presents us with three states of the mind: the first is the "wondering mind" that looks through the heavens and admires the perfection of creation; the second is the "skeptical mind" that looks for inconsistencies in creation; the third is the "humbled mind" that can see no fault but a perfect and consistent system and, consequently, has no alternative but to admire the glory of the creation and the greatness of the Creator. Such a state might have been experienced by many of the great minds in mankind's history. Obviously, such questions are presented as a challenge for the human mind, since reason is the correct approach for discovery. So, although the aim of those motivations is teleological, the Qur'an has left it open for the human mind to grasp the facts of nature so as to support the belief, or disbelief, in the truth revealed by the Lord:

> Say: "The truth is from your Lord". Then whosoever wills, let him believe, and whosoever wills, let him disbelieve. (18:29)

The first revealed verses of the Qur'an began with the request[7] to "read". The verse clearly attracts the attention of mankind to the creation and to the importance of documenting the discovered facts by writing with the pen:

> Read! Read in the Name of your Lord, Who has created (all that exists), Has created man from a clot. Read! And your Lord is the Most Generous Who has taught by the pen, Has taught man that which he knew not. (96:1–4)

The claim here is that the proper Islamic approach for acquiring knowledge about the natural world should be through reason. This is supported by many verses of the Qur'an, where we see that the word of Allah is pointing us to think and to reason. In fact, the word *ʿaql* is always used in the Qur'an as a verb, never as noun. This may point to the Qur'an's attitude toward reason: that it is an active agent. The word "see" can be regarded in a similar way and to see is to contemplate and reflect:

> Say: Travel through the Earth and see how Allah has originated creation; so will Allah produce a later creation: for Allah has power over all things. (29:20)

This is why *naḍar* (study and thinking) was one of the most praised and required duties of Muslims. This is why most books of *kalām* start with reviewing the rules of *naḍar*. To acquire knowledge is an important aid to understanding the world and, according to the Qur'an, a proper understanding of the world leads to acknowledging Allah and His creation in the best way:

> And such are the examples that We set forth for mankind, but only those understand them who have knowledge. (29:43)

Primarily the Qur'an assumes that there is no conflict between scientific truth and divine revelation; facts gathered from the natural world always point to the transcendental power which is behind all the phenomena of the world:

> And those who have been given knowledge see that what is revealed to you from your Lord is the truth, and guides to the Path of the Exalted in Might, Owner of all praise. (32:6)

Of course, this harmony between "proper science" and revelation is set forth on the basis that what we discover by contemplating the world is going to be addressed by the same rules that we have applied to our quest. This means that, when we assume there should be a cause for something happening or that has happened, we should also be ready to ask the question about the ultimate cause of all causes.

The Prophet Muhammad also encouraged his followers to learn and look for wisdom, and to acquire knowledge from whichever source it came. "Seek knowledge even in China" is a saying that is attributed to the holy Prophet. Following this line of teaching, Muslims, once they had settled on their system of public governance, went to investigate nature and seek knowledge from all the available sources at the time.

It was Khālid ibn Yazīd (d. 704), the grandson of the first Umayyad caliph (Muʿāwiya), who refused the position of caliph and favored spending his time and effort seeking scientific knowledge and working on translating scientific texts. His favored science was chemistry. His curiosity pushed him to investigate what was known of this science at the time. Khālid was perhaps the first prominent Muslim to undertake scientific investigation himself. Subsequently, translators were hired to work on translating the scientific works of the Greeks and other nations into Arabic. This was a great step toward acquiring knowledge from original sources.

During this period, in the second Hijri century, pioneers of Islamic thought also started to develop their own methodologies for investigating the facts of Islam to do with *ʿaqīda* (Islamic creed) and Sharia (Islamic law) through the Qur'an and the teachings of the Prophet. This initiated the establishment of the "Islamic sciences", which started with commentaries on the Qur'an and documenting the legacy of the Prophet by collecting his narrations and authenticating his biography.

Writing commentaries on the Qur'an required the formalizing of the Arabic language. For this aim to be achieved, Arabic grammar had to be systematized according to a set of rules. Al-Khālīl ibn Aḥmad al-Farāhīdī (d. 786) devised a lexicon of words by starting with sets of Arabic letters and experimenting with all possible combinations and permutations, out of which he generated a huge collection of meaningful Arabic words. This was published in his book *al-ʿAyn*, which is the original source for Arabic dictionaries. After that, Arabic language studies followed and it was Sībawayh (d. 796) who completed the first written book (which he called *al-Kitāb fī al-naḥw*) on the grammar of the Arabic language.[8]

Two schools of grammar appeared and, even as early as those times, debates were held under the auspices of prominent state officials to discuss linguistic, philosophical, and scientific questions. This started a new intellectual tradition by which many debates were held and a fruitful exchange of thought resulted. In Baghdad, for example, the Abbasid vizier, Yaḥyā ibn Khālid, held a debate on standard Arabic usage between Sībawayh, representing the Basra school, and al-Kisāʾī al-Kūfī (d. 804), the leading figure in the rival Kufa school.[9] Such debates and discussions enriched Arabic and were a good approach in authenticating the sources and establishing proper rules for Arabic grammar. Such authentic references became essential tools for those working on commentaries of the Qur'an and the hadiths.

On the other hand, it was ʿUmar ibn ʿAbd al-ʿAzīz (d. 720), the eighth Umayyad caliph, who ordered the collecting and documenting of the narrations of the Prophet. This happened about ninety years after the Prophet's passing. Later, some other scholars started their own projects of hadith collection and documentation. By that time, a number of the second generation of the Prophet's followers were still alive and were taken as main sources for the narrations. However, since the authenticity of the narrations needed to be verified, a novel approach was adopted, which included the strict requirement that the chain of narrators should be continuous and that each person in the chain should be established as just and truthful, otherwise the narration could be ignored. To achieve this requirement, a number of Muslim scholars devoted their efforts to documenting and researching biographies of the hadith narrators. The first of such biographies was perhaps written by Ibn Saʿad al-Fahmī of Egypt (d. 791), then many others followed. Specialists of biographies went on to set rules according to which the authenticity of narrators could be evaluated. This endeavor developed one of the novel and original Islamic sciences called *al-jarḥ wa al-taʿdīl* (rules to impeach and condone), upon which scholars who were specialized in collecting and authenticating hadiths heavily relied to classify a hadith of the Prophet and categorize it according to different levels of authenticity. Muslim historians followed a similar approach in documenting historical events and narrations, but surely the authentication process was not as rigorous as that established for the hadith literature.

Influence of the Greeks

The translation of the Greek legacy in philosophy, medicine, and astronomy—mainly the works of Plato, Aristotle, Plotinus, Proclus, Galen, Euclid, Pythagoras, Ptolemy, as well as many others—provided Muslims with original sources for their investigation of nature. Greek ideas were accepted and adopted in areas that had no direct connection to their theology, as far as they did not contradict the basics of the Islamic creed. It is well known that some Muslim philosophers were influenced by the Greek philosophies. For example, this inspiration can be seen in the philosophy of al-Fārābī (c. 872–950), who was heavily influenced by Plotinus, and the influence of Aristotle, Plato, and Plotinus on Ibn Sīnā (Avicenna; 980–1037) was immense. It was not until about a century after Ibn Sīnā that the predominance of Aristotle's philosophy was exposed in the work of Ibn Rushd (Averroës; 1126–98), who offered the best explanations for Aristotle's metaphysics and preserved much of the Aristotelian legacy. The point that marked dissociation was when some early philosophers of Islam tried to adopt Greek philosophical thoughts concerning the eternity of the world. Al-Kindī (c. 801–73) was perhaps the first Muslim philosopher who argued that the world is not eternal and that God is, simply, One. Everything in the world is temporal, according to al-Kindī:

> We say that the true, first act is the bringing-to-be of beings from non-being. It is clear that this act is proper to God, the Exalted, who is the end of every cause. For, the bringing-to-be of beings from non-being belongs to no other. And this act is a proper characteristic [called] by the name "origination".[10]

Al-Kindī's existing scientific corpus is sizable and includes treatises on medicine, music, astrology, and mathematics. Franz Rosenthal[11] has given a full account of these works and recently Peter Adamson[12] has published the works of al-Kindī and his contemporaries.

Following this period, great intellectual works were published in Baghdad and Basra, through which a revolution in thought took place that was supported by the caliphs of the early Abbasid reign. The second caliph, Abu Jaʿfar al-Manṣūr (d. 775), ordered the acquisition of works of medicine and astronomy from Indic and Greek sources. Hārūn al-Rashīd (d. 809) continued to care for Arabic literature and history, and his son al-Maʾmūn (d. 833) went further by establishing a state-funded organization called the "House of Wisdom" to take care of translating texts of all sorts from Greek, Sanskrit, Persian, and Syriac into Arabic. This caused a huge transformation in Muslim society and produced a very active environment of cultural exchange. Heated debates on religious and philosophical issues were taking place in the royal palace of al-Maʾmūn and in his presence. An atmosphere of respect and appreciation was overwhelming in those debates. On one occasion, al-Maʾmūn is said to have blamed one of the contestants for humiliating his opponent while debating the subject of Muslim state leadership (*imāma*).

The general environment of freedom of thought, which was safeguarded by the state, allowed for the generation of new and original ideas. This atmosphere marked a turning point in the cultural history of Islam that continued for several decades, and which could have flourished further had it not been corrupted by politics. The good part of it was the employment of a rational approach as the basis for deducing Sharia rules. This was the era of *kalām*, where many Muslim scholars contributed their thoughts in the establishment of a rational knowledge system that could produce the necessary methodology for a proper understanding of the truth of Islam. However, soon this enlightened movement suffered a setback. Debates between the Muʿtazila and the scholars of hadith turned into clashes, as the former used the political force of the state to impose their belief that the Qur'an was created, a dilemma which was called the problem of the "Creation of the Qur'an". Many religious scholars were imprisoned and tortured for not accepting the notion that the Qur'an had been created. This caused social unrest, as violence erupted throughout major cities between the opponents and the proponents of this notion. As was mentioned above, during this same period Aḥmad ibn Ḥanbal, the famous Imam, laid down the basis of what he considered to be the proper tenets of the Sunna. This basis marked a milestone in the development of Islamic thought and has left its imprint up until the present day, seen in contemporary Sunni Islam.

In the centuries that followed, Muslims absorbed the natural sciences which were known to the Greeks and they went on developing this knowledge. The main point to indicate here is the introduction of experimentation and an interest in observation. Muslim astronomers built several small observatories in Baghdad, Damascus, and Cairo. At the time of the Mongols, the famous Maragheh Observatory was erected, which included a huge library in which many famous astronomers of the time worked. Muslims were able to contribute original observational techniques and calculations as well as develop astronomical instruments, despite being unable to supersede the geocentric Ptolemaic model. In chemistry, Muslim scientists left a great legacy of experimentation and developed many techniques for the purification and isolation of compounds, as well as amalgamation. In mathematics and geometry, several great minds appeared who contributed original works to mathematical calculations. Many of these achievements are still hidden from history. In optics, genuine discoveries were made in both the theoretical and practical aspects: fine mirrors were produced and the idea of lenses was discussed. The laws of motion, including the role of force in accelerating the body, were discussed by some scientists and philosophers, despite the philosophers who were adopting Aristotelian views and explanations. In fact, many of the contributions of Muslim scientists were essential ingredients for the European scientific renaissance during the sixteenth and seventeenth centuries.

The Rise of *Kalām*

Kalām is one of the genuine Islamic sciences and it is the philosophical expression of Islam's worldview, especially its ontological, epistemological, and metaphysical components. It was through *kalām* that Muslims developed their own philosophical worldview to rival Greek philosophy and, irrespective of some claims attributing some of its notions to the Greeks, the original *kalām* remains solely an Islamic invention.

In Arabic, *kalām* means "speech" or "a sequence of words". However, it also means "discourse" and this is the meaning which was intended in the case of Islamic *kalām*. The term *kalām* describes a specific discourse which was applied to a particular system of thought which had arisen in Islam prior to the discovery of philosophy. Its exponents, called simply *mutakallimūn*, were contrasted with those who, beginning with al-Kindī, were called simply "philosophers".[13] In its philosophical context, *kalām* is a collection of concepts, assumptions, principles, and problems that were used to explain the relationship between God and the physical world in accordance with the basics of Islamic creed.

Classically, *kalām* was considered to form the foundation of jurisprudence *(fiqh)*, which constitutes the basis for Sharia, which comprises Islamic rulings on life. The reason for this is that Sharia comprises a deductive system of rules and instructions which needs logical foundation in order to be fully justified and established. *Kalām* was further classified into *jalīl al-kalām* and *daqīq al-kalām*. The former is the aspect dealing with problems related to the divine attributes, the resurrection of the dead, the vision of God, and the questions related to divine knowledge, will, and power. These subjects lead on to the question of human free will, as held by one school of *kalām*, and the counter-proposal of self-acquisition (*kasb*) of actions that was suggested by another school. The prominent groups that contributed to *jalīl al-kalām* were the Muʿtazila, the Ashʿaris, the Murjiʾa, the Shiʿa, and the Khawārij. The Batinis, such as the Ismailis, have also been considered to be schools of Islamic *kalām*.[14] The Murjiʾa, Shiʿa, and Khawārij did not have much to say about natural philosophy, while the Ismailis summarized their views in the "Letters of Ikhwān al-Ṣafā'", which is a re-expression of Neoplatonic philosophy.

On the other hand, *daqīq al-kalām* deals with problems of natural philosophy, most prominent among which is the question of the creation of the world, its structure, temporal development, and the meaning of causality. This has led to discussing the concepts of space, time, motion, force, and many other aspects of the physical world. Using Ian Barbour's terminology,[15] one might say that *jalīl al-kalām* could be called "natural theology", whereas *daqīq al-kalām* is the "theology of nature".

Despite the fact that the subject of *kalām* has been somewhat neglected, I feel that this movement has much to offer the subjects of natural philosophy and the arguments in the current debate between science and religion, and therefore it is well worth studying. It will be shown that *daqīq al-kalām* can provide a basis for a contemporary philosophy of science which resolves many of the philosophical questions of modern physics as well as some questions in science and religion. Many of the arguments of *daqīq al-kalām* are still current and have sound conceptual values in contemporary science and the philosophy of modern science, the "Kalām Cosmological Argument" which was re-devised by William Craig,[16] is just one contemporary example in a whole field of ideas, concepts, and arguments that can be utilized by the modern philosophy of science. However, the subject is in such a state now that it cannot lend itself to an effective role unless it is purified, reformulated, and harmonized to fit the themes of modern philosophy. Much work and a painstaking effort must be expended before *daqīq al-kalām* is fit for a contemporary role.

For the sake of acquainting the reader with the necessary background in *kalām*, I will outline those views that have a sound value in present-day natural philosophy. These will include my own rearrangement and designation of the basic doctrines and principles of *kalām*. I will try to summarize their main contributions to natural philosophy, which were historically covered under *daqīq al-kalām*, after which I will move briefly through some vital problems where I feel some genuine research work is currently needed in order to identify the possible scope for deploying *kalām* in contemporary science–religion dialogue.

Reasons for the Rise of *Kalām*

Historically, one can say that two basic motivations drove the emergence of *kalām*. The first was internal: different opinions expressed by Muslim theologians on the fate of "sinners" initiated an argument that developed into a whole tradition of thought. For example, some theologians suggested that a Muslim sinner was a non-believer and should be considered a *kāfir* (one who negates Islamic belief); other theologians suggested that he should be considered only "corrupt" (*fāsiq*), a middle position which lay between the status of *kāfir* and believer. One other problem was the understanding of the divine attributes. According to Ibn Khaldūn, *kalām* originated when the articles of faith, especially the divine attributes, were discussed. At first Muslims were drawing their understanding directly from the plain verses of the Qur'an and the hadiths, taking the problematic verses, which were called *mutashābih*, at face value. Later, as they went into more detail, they looked for interpretations of those verses; consequently, as Ibn Khaldūn says, "some differences occurred which caused them to go into argumentation and debates thus introducing intellectual evidences in addition to the evidences derived from tradition, and in this way the *kalām* originated".[17]

The second reason for *kalām*'s emergence was the reaction of Muslims to the new ideas they faced when they came into contact with different nations and civilizations, particularly the classical Mediterranean and the Indic. This contact, at a time when Muslims were the dominating power in the world, created a dialogue between civilizations, rather than Samuel Huntington's "clash of civilizations". It is known that Abū al-Hudhayl al-ʿAllāf and his nephew Ibrāhīm al-Naẓẓām were very active in presenting arguments in support of Islamic doctrine. They used to hold debates with others who subscribed to non-Islamic beliefs such as Manāniyya and Diṣāniyya, sometimes in the presence of Caliph al-Maʾmūn himself. These debates in natural philosophy included arguments that were drawn from their reflections on the natural world based on views from the Qur'an. Such arguments were later developed to form the main body of the principles of *daqīq al-kalām*. Generally, no one can specify a given source for the development of those principles upon which most of the *mutakallimūn* agreed, but as we study the views and arguments of *kalām* we can designate a common pattern of thought.

The Two Main Schools of *Kalām*

The *mutakallimūn* (the practitioners of *kalām*) formed two main schools: the Muʿtazila, which was the first to be formed, and the Ashʿarīyya *(Ashʿaris)*. Prominent leaders of the Muʿtazili school included Wāṣil ibn ʿAṭāʾ (d. 748), ʿAmr ibn ʿUbayd (d. 761), Abū al-Hudhayl al-ʿAllāf (d. 840), Ibrāhīm al-Naẓẓām (d. 835), and al-Jāḥiẓ (d. 868). Most of the original contributions of the leaders of *kalām* have been lost, but some of their main ideas and arguments have been preserved through the writings of their students or opponents. Valuable monographs and critiques from some prominent leaders of the Muʿtazila still exist; most prominent among these were Abū al-Husayn al-Khayyāṭ (d. 912) and Abū al-Qāsim al-Balkhī (d. 931), sometimes called al-Kaʿbi, Abū ʿAlī al-Jubbāʾī (d. 915), and his son Abū Hāshim al-Jubbāʾī (d. 933). Some of the original works of these prominent Muʿtazila were preserved through the monographs written by their students and followers, such as Abū Rashīd al-Naysābūrī (d. 1024) and Qāḍī ʿAbd al-Jabbār al-Hamadāni (d. 1024), who wrote an extensive survey of the Muʿtazili system that preserved much of their original thought, and his student al-Ḥasan ibn Mattawayh (d. 1059), who wrote a book preserving a good deal of the opinions of early Muʿtazila on the subject areas of *daqīq al-kalām*.

The Ashʿari school was formed by Abū al-Ḥasan al-Ashʿarī (d. 935), who broke away from the Muʿtazila and formed a new school of thought within the parameters of *kalām*. Beside al-Ashʿarī, the most prominent contributors to the school which bore his name were Abū Bakr al-Bāqillānī (d. 1012) and, later, Abū al-Maʿālī al-Juwaynī (d. 1085), who wrote some excellent monographs on *daqīq al-kalām* and *jalīl al-kalām*. However, one can say that the most efficient utilization of *kalām* was made by Abū Ḥāmid al-Ghazālī (d. 1111), whose contributions represent the most mature writings produced among the Ashʿaris. In later times, the Ashʿari *kalām* was reformulated by Fakhr al-Dīn al-Rāzī (d. 1209), who introduced some philosophical arguments into classical *kalām* and was followed by Sayf al-Dīn al-āmidī (d. 1233), ʿAdūd al-Dīn al-ʿIjī (d. 1355), and Saʿd al-Dīn al-Taftazānī (d. 1390).

The *mutakallimūn* considered the Qur'an to be the prime source for their views about the world and, accordingly, they derived and formulated their doctrines about the natural world to be in conformity with the stipulations of the Qur'an. *Daqīq al-kalām* investigated some of the basic concepts, such as space, time, matter, force, speed, heat, colors, smells (gases), and so on. So it is quite legitimate to revisit this discipline seeking common understanding, not necessarily with physics as such but perhaps with the philosophical realization of the concept taken in its scientific context. This policy is supported by the fact that the resources of *kalām* are quite different from those of classical natural philosophies, including the philosophy of the Greeks. This is the main reason why we find that some concepts of *kalām* are different in their meanings and implications from their counterparts in either Greek or Indian philosophies.

In no way do I claim here that *kalām* forms an integrated body of thought or that it can be found complete with one individual *mutakallim*, or that it forms a complete modern philosophy of nature. Rather, I will try to uncover aspects of those thoughts of the *mutakallimūn* which might serve as possible candidates for integration into the contemporary philosophy of natural sciences, in an endeavor to provide a form of a philosophical feedback to the theory of nature. For example, the principle of continual re-creation can be utilized to better understand the state of indeterminacy of measurement in the physical world. In addition, the notion of "discrete time", which was proposed by the *mutakallimūn* as part of the general principle of the discreteness (atomism) of nature, can be utilized in constructing an "all-discrete"[18] theory of nature that may contribute to resolving some current fundamental theoretical problems related to the unification of natural physical forces. On the other hand, some questions that have already been considered by *jalīl al-kalām* do resonate with primary issues in the contemporary debates in science and religion that are taking place in the West. Questions concerning the knowledge of God, His action in the physical world, His control of the future, and the degree of freedom enjoyed by humans and the natural world were some of the main issues that were debated by the *mutakallimūn*.

Sources and Methodology of *Kalām*

The *mutakallimūn* considered the Qur'an to be their main inspiration for acquiring knowledge about the world. In this respect, they were very keen on understanding the natural world within the prescribed doctrines provided by the Qur'an. This includes the oneness of the Creator, Allah, His omniscience and omnipotence. Although they did not refer explicitly to verses of the Qur'an, it was clear that their main principles for viewing nature needed to conform with the stipulations in the Qur'an. This meant that they had to follow a rational sequence of deductions starting with the divine revelations, which had to be interpreted rationally, and then try to understand nature accordingly. Richard Walzer summarized this by saying that "*Mutakallimūn* followed a methodology that is distinct from that of the philosophers in that they take the truth of Islam as their starting point".[19] William Craig has also taken the same view, saying that the "main difference between a *mutakallim* (practitioner of *kalām*) and a *failasūf* (philosopher) lies in the methodological approach to the object of their study: while the practitioner of *Kalām* takes the truth of Islam as his starting-point, the man of philosophy, though he may take pleasure in the rediscovery of Qur'anic principles, does not make them his starting-point, but follows a 'method of research independent of dogma, without, however, rejecting the dogma or ignoring it in its sources'".[20] One might classify the *kalām* approach as being apologetic, but this is perhaps not the right assessment, since they were reflecting on the teachings of the Qur'an rather than blindly defending it. Their works show that they had, sometimes, widely differing views on the same problems and, in most of their arguments, they were trying to be rationally consistent and at the same time conform with Qur'anic stipulations.

For this reason, I can say that the main approach of the *mutakallimūn* in understanding the world can be presented as follows:

God → Reason → the World

This is entirely the opposite of the approach of the Greek philosophers, which can be presented by this sequence:

the World → Reason → God

On the other hand, Muslim philosophers essentially followed the same approach as the Greeks. They started from a rational comprehension of nature and then tried to reconcile it with Islamic teachings. In this approach, I do find that they were rather apologetic, since they were trying to defend the philosophical truth by recasting it in an Islamic mold.

In order to clarify the above assertion, I here give some important examples. The *mutakallimūn* projected a notion of the creation of the world, which is clearly stipulated in the Qur'an, in their doctrine on temporality, by which they asserted that everything in the world was created by God and that the whole world should have a starting point *with* space and time.[21] The theory which they approved of was that which is commonly known as "creation ex nihilo", which they described as being "not from something" (*lā min shay'*).[22] However, in order to justify the process of creation ex nihilo and the finiteness of the world, they had to assume that everything in the world is composed of a finite number of non-divisible parts, each of which is composed of a substrate (a substance in the Aristotelian sense) called a *jawhar*, and a number of "accidents"[23] that occupy the *jawhar*, which are, naturally, called *aʿrāḍ* (singular *ʿaraḍ*).[24] The *ʿaraḍ* stands for the properties of the non-divisible part. These concepts founded the doctrine of Islamic atomism, of which Shlomo Pines[25] and Harry Wolfson[26] have given detailed accounts.

The *mutakallimūn* assumed that once God has created an atom, He goes on re-creating the *ʿaraḍ*, which allows for the development of the world according to His will. Once God ceases to re-create, that *ʿaraḍ* vanishes. In this way, the *mutakallimūn* envisioned the process by which God sustains the universe. Indeed, this would give the Divine full choice over any part or property in the world. Beyond this, something which might come as a result of the re-creation process, as we will see later in this book, the world would appear to be indeterministic.[27] This was how the *mutakallimūn* assessed the general character of events taking place in nature: it was not the natural deterministic causality that led to the occurrence of an event once conditions became conducive, but the choice of God and His will that would decide for all events despite their being affected by a certain seemingly fixed set of rules or laws. A law is an expression of a causal relationship but, according to *kalām*, this relationship, is unnecessary and it is God who is allowing for this relationship to be effective; thus, causal relationships are thought to be indeterministic. Accordingly, the results of the actions of the laws of nature (fire burning cotton, for example) are undetermined. Through this understanding, the *mutakallimūn* were able to develop a new concept of causality. This topic will be discussed in the next chapter.

Philosophy and *Kalām*

The reconciliatory approach of Muslim philosophers was started with al-Kindī and was further developed by al-Fārābī and Ibn Sīnā, who adopted a mainly Neoplatonic approach. This approach of the early Muslim philosophers in recognizing divine attributes and God's action in the world was refuted by al-Ghazālī in his book *Tahāfut al-falāsifa* (*The Incoherence of the Philosophers*).[28] Ibn Rushd later championed the defense of Aristotle's doctrines, trying to refute the arguments of al-Ghazālī in his book *Tahāfut al-tahāfut* (*The Incoherence of the Incoherence*).[29] However, in his other book, *Faṣl al-maqāl* (*Decisive treatise*), Ibn Rushd strove to show that Islam could accommodate the views of Greek philosophy through certain reinterpretations of some verses of the Qur'an.[30] Ibn Rushd was more truthful than others in defending philosophy, as he set out philosophical truths to be considered on a prime level and according to which stipulations of the Qur'an should be reinterpreted. Yet, this defense ultimately proved to be unsuccessful, since the arguments presented by al-Ghazālī were already strong and effective enough in persuading the intellectual elite of the inadequacy of the philosophical approach. The fact that at the time of al-Ghazālī *kalām* was still under siege and frequently out of favor with many religious scholars and jurists caused one school of Islamic thought (the Hanbali) to move in the direction of a more fundamentalist approach, one that was later to breed thinkers like Aḥmad ibn Taymiyya. The birth of such trends that minimized the role of a rational approach in understanding both the Qur'an and the world did not aid the growth of reason-based theology or science in the Islamic world.

The Main Principles of *Daqīq al-Kalām*

Even though the *mutakallimūn* expounded diverse views according to their schools of affiliation, one finds that in general they subscribed to certain common basic principles that they adopted in order to understand nature.

Maimonides had identified twelve propositions, which he said were "common to all *mutakallimūn* however different their individual opinions and methods may be".[31] These propositions he found to be necessary for *mutakallimūn* to establish their doctrines. Having investigated these propositions some time ago and studied their structure, as well as the implications of their being used in *kalām* arguments, I have rearticulated these doctrines using modern terminology into five principles. These are as follows:[32]

(1) *Temporality of the world.* According to the *mutakallimūn*, the world is not eternal, but was created at some finite point in the past. Space and time had neither meaning nor existence before the creation of the world. Despite the fact that some of the *mutakallimūn* believed that the original creation took place out of a pre-existing form of matter, the dominant view of *kalām* in this respect was that the creation took place *ex nihilo*, that is to say out of nothing. Accordingly, they considered every constituent part of the world to be temporal.

(2) *Discreteness of natural structures.* The *mutakallimūn* believed that all entities in the world are composed of a finite number of fundamental components, each called *jawhar* (the substrate or substance),[33] which is indivisible and has no parts. The *jawhar* was thought to be an abstract entity that acquires its physical properties and value when occupied by a character called an *ʿaraḍ* (accident).[34] These accidents are ever-changing qualities. Discreteness applies not only to material bodies but to space, time, motion, energy (heat), and all other properties of matter.[35] Since the *jawhar* cannot stand on its own, as it would then be unidentified, without being associated with at least one *ʿaraḍ*, it can therefore be considered as an abstract entity and this is a basic character which makes it different from the Greek and Indian atom. Some authors have tried in vain to relate the Islamic concept of the atom with those of the Greeks or the Indians;[36] however, rigorous investigations have shown that it is unlikely that the Muslims took this idea from elsewhere; the Islamic atom possesses genuinely different properties.[37]

(3) *Continual re-creation and an ever-changing world.* Because God is the absolutely able creator of the world and because He is living and always acting to sustain the universe, the *mutakallimūn* envisaged that the world would have to be re-created in every moment.[38] This re-creation occurs with the accidents, not with the substances, but since the substances cannot be realized without being attached to accidents, therefore the re-creation of the accidents effectively governs the ontological status of the substances too. With such a process, God stands to be the sustainer of the world. This principle is very important for two reasons: first, it establishes an indeterminate world; second, it

?

what?
how?

finds a resonance in contemporary quantum physics. Regarding the second, it is astonishing to consider that this theory would explain why, in the quantum world, we see a range of possible values for physical parameters and what we measure is an average of all possible values being expressed by the so-called "expectation value". With this vision, the principle of re-creation may provide yet another explanation for why our physical measurements detect only the average of possible values. This proposal will be investigated in more technical detail in Chapter Four of this book.

(4) *Indeterminism of the world.* Since God possesses the absolute free will, and since He is the creator and the sustainer of the world, He is then at liberty to take any action He wishes with respect to the state of the world or its control. Consequently, the laws of nature that we recognize have to be probabilistic not deterministic, so that physical values are to be contingent and undetermined.[39] From such a theological stance, the *mutakallimūn* deduced the indeterminacy of the world. This resulted in rejecting the existence of deterministic causality,[40] because nature, according to the *mutakallimūn*, cannot possess any sort of will. The *mutakallimūn* also rejected the Greeks' four basic elements[41] and the alleged existence of any kind of self-acting property belonging to those elements. This is a very central argument in *kalām* for the proof of the need for God; if nature is blind, no productive development would be expected.

(5) *Integrity of space and time.* The *mutakallimūn* had the understanding that space has no meaning on its own. Without there being a body, we cannot realize the existence of space. So is the case with time, which cannot be realized without the existence of motion, which needs a body to be affected.[42] This connection between space and time is deeply rooted in the Arabic language itself.[43] Therefore, neither absolute space nor absolute time exists.[44] This understanding enabled them to visualize motion as being discrete, so that the trajectory of moving bodies are thought to be composed of neighboring "rest points", *waqafāt*.[45] Accordingly, a body is seen moving faster than another only because the number of rest points along its trajectory is small compared with those along the trajectory of the other. In another theory, the Muʿtazili al-Naẓẓām believed that motion on the microscopic level takes place in discrete jumps called *ṭafra*. That is to say, the body moves in discrete steps or leaps. The famous historian of modern physics Max Jammer considered this understanding of al-Naẓẓām as being the oldest realization of a quantum motion; he says: "In fact al-Naẓẓām's notion of leap, his designation of an analyzable inter-phenomenon, may be regarded as an early forerunner of Bohr's conception of quantum jumps."[46] This proposal by al-Naẓẓām may also solve the old Zeno paradox.[47]

Philosophy and Contemporary Science

The emergence of the theory of relativity and quantum physics at the dawn of the last century, and their magnificent success in resolving many problems in theoretical physics in addition to opening new horizons for science and technology, took most philosophers by surprise. Consequently, some radically new concepts emerged with which the philosophies of the eighteenth and nineteenth centuries were entirely unfamiliar. The most prominent concepts were the integrity of spacetime proposed by relativity theory and the concept of quantum measurement uncertainty, which was required by quantum physics. The second concept meant that it would be impossible to determine any natural development with complete certainty, a concept that jeopardized the Laplacian doctrine of the determinism of the natural world, which is one of the main pillars of classical natural philosophy. Moreover, the concepts of the reality and objectivity of the world were now questionable. The impact of these ideas was so strong that it pushed philosophers to pause for some time before talking about a new paradigm. Some philosophers continued to deal with the topic of natural philosophy using the very same paradigm of the classical philosophy of science. However, any inspection of the status quo of contemporary science makes it clear that no viable philosophical framework for modern science can be acknowledged other than empiricism. The basic reason behind this is that the classical European enlightenment philosophies could not deal with the conceptual development of modern physics in the twentieth century. In fact, the Western philosophical heritage is essentially incompatible with the theoretical developments of the theory of relativity and quantum physics. This is because Western philosophies were based on the fundamental doctrines and thinking methodology of the Greeks, which comprised a philosophical system that had at its main core some fundamental principles which inclined to a stagnated view of a self-sustaining deterministic nature. This concept was shown by experiments to be invalid when the microscopic world was investigated. For this reason, I conjecture that the modern Western philosophies, with their roots still in Athens, are unable to structure a consistent framework; instead, modern philosophers of the twentieth century, such as Karl Popper, ended up simply denying the need for a framework.[48] One might conclude that in general the Western mind has never acknowledged philosophically the development of the abstract concepts of quantum physics; most philosophers of science, including Popper himself, specifically critiqued the Copenhagen school's interpretation of quantum measurements.[49] On the other hand, some new theories were developed claiming a hidden deterministic underlying truth in the apparently indeterministic world. These theories, which were called "Hidden Variables

Theories", are still struggling to defy the natural reality of indeterminism. This issue will be discussed in more detail in other chapters of this book in connection with other related questions in science and religion (see Chapter Three under Causality in Quantum Mechanics and Chapter Four under Human Freedom). In any case, the achievements of quantum physics are well established now and quantum theory has proved to be a consistent theory despite the possibility that it might be incomplete.

More recently, a more appropriate concept named "natural realism" was developed to reform the philosophical propositions of empiricism and to shape a more consistent viable philosophy of modern science. However, as current views in the West remain bound to the classical philosophical doctrines of determinism and necessity instead of contingency, we cannot see that any progress can be made on the theoretical level. Quantum theory will remain imprisoned in a box of empirically generated concepts while experiments and technological applications of the basic theory continue developing without any new horizon, a horizon which is badly needed for new discoveries and a further extension of our vision.

We need to understand the true implications of twentieth-century physics as much as we need to understand its philosophical implications. Many of the concepts proposed by quantum theory and the mathematical structure of quantum mechanics are still in need of deeper understanding and interpretation. The meaning of an "operator" in quantum mechanics is obscure, as is the meaning of "unpredictability of measurements". The role played by the observer in measurements as proposed by the Copenhagen school does not seem to be widely accepted; moreover, the alternative multiverse interpretation does not seem to be convincing, either. Both interpretations create a problem with the reality of our world. Therefore, a better alternative should be proposed by which we can have a more realistic interpretation of the experimental results and, at the same time, establish the reality and objectivity of the world. Mathematical entities called "imaginary quantities" in physics, although representing unmeasurable quantities, are also worth studying at the philosophical level in order to understand much of their practical naturalistic meaning.[50]

In theoretical physics, most of us play the game of generating equations that sometimes do not have clear explanations. An example of this is string theory, which is a very beautiful theory that shows an element of re-creation through the continuous vibration of the string, but unfortunately this theory has made no prediction to make it a viable scientific theory. In general, with relativity and curved spacetime physics, we are not yet ready to understand the full meaning and implications of a space-like universe, for example. Such understanding is needed to describe the inside of a black hole, for example, and to finally realize the fate of the universe in one version of the cosmic destiny. For this reason, many of the black hole physicists were taken by surprise by the declaration by Stephen Hawking that information is not completely lost when a particle falls into a black hole.[51] In cosmology, and despite the eminence of the big bang theory, we are still far from deciding whether the universe did have a start in time or whether it has an infinite extension into the past. The point singularity that contains all matter and energy that exists in our universe stands not only as an epistemological challenge but as an ontological dilemma too. In general, while science is firm and strong on the practical side of the story, it is still far from reaching a resolution on the theoretical side. That is why we should not overspeculate on this matter; instead, we should have some fixed basic principles and doctrines, some sort of an epistemic paradigm, while finding our way through the issue of the relationship between science and religion.

Theological Questions Facing Science

Classical "theology of nature" was based on Aristotelian physics. Modern natural philosophy of the eighteenth and nineteenth centuries was based on Newtonian mechanics and his law of universal gravitation. This was later complemented by the laws of thermodynamics and optics, which acquired sophisticated form after the establishment of Maxwell's electromagnetic theory. The most general feature of the philosophies that relied on Newtonian physics was mechanistic determinism. Now that Newton's and Maxwell's physics have become on the conceptual level obsolete, we are in need of a new theology of nature that can accommodate the conceptual discoveries of modern physics, namely relativity theory and quantum mechanics. Such accommodation will be genuine only if the philosophical theology we are looking for enjoys a thoughtful environment that operates in harmony with the basic conceptual trends of modern physics. These should include the basic facts of the natural world as they have been found through the discoveries of modern physics of the twentieth century and characterized by some particular features: temporality, indeterminism, and holism. These features have been verified experimentally and many applications of modern technology are based on these features. Evidently, there is a clash between concepts of modern physics and the philosophical trend of identifying natural reality and objectivity. That is to say, we have a conflict between what scientific investigation is suggesting and the available philosophical vision.

The characteristic features of modern physics mentioned above can perhaps be accommodated by *daqīq al-kalām*. This claim is supported by the fact that the principles of *daqīq al-kalām*, which I have outlined above, are in clear conformity with the quantum description of matter and discreteness, and the relativistic description of spacetime in its feature of integrity. The discreteness of spacetime, which is a much sought-after feature that has not been achieved yet in physics, is already a basic part of the *kalām* view.

Over the last thirty years or so there has been a growing interest in discussing issues in science and religion. The Vatican Observatory has expressed interest in this issue and has funded a series of studies by renowned figures of science and philosophy, who have contributed some original works in this field. These contributions are published in five volumes.[52] Several authors were concerned with the question of how to reconcile religious views about God and the world, including divine action and the laws of nature, with scientific facts. Some authors believe that no such reconciliation can be achieved; others have expressed opinions suggesting that there could be a successful reconciliation, often quoting Albert Einstein saying, "religion without science is blind and science without religion is lame". Some others even questioned the necessity of such reconciliation and whether it has any value within our age of science. Yet, those studies tried to propose solutions for major problems which are thought to have common intersections between science and religion, such as divine action, the objectivity of the world, free will, omnipotence, the emergence of the soul, spiritual experience, intelligibility of the universe, the mind of God and its relation to the laws of physics, the creation of the universe and the anthropic principle, and many other topics. Most of the contributions on these issues express scattered views, which sometimes look like ad hoc suggestions to solving specific isolated problems. In most cases, such proposals show no common thread to connect the ideas. A unified philosophical base is necessary to enable consistent conclusions to be drawn. The absence of such a basis does not allow those views to culminate into a philosophy and, in the absence of a philosophy, one has no pilot.

I would suggest that *daqīq al-kalām* can provide a strong basis for developing a consistent and viable philosophy which acknowledges modern science. Moreover, if properly restructured and utilized, *daqīq al-kalām* can pave the way for profound reformation in Islamic thought, as well as other intellectual systems active in the modern world. Islamic *kalām* has the potential to restructure our understanding of nature, reality, the world's relation to God, human destiny, and the purpose of living. For these reasons, I find it to be the best available candidate for a new understanding of the natural world and its relationship with the divine.

Despite being Islamic in origin, *daqīq al-kalām* is a neutral proposition for understanding the world. The fact that its basic principles are independent of religious belief, except for those agreed by all monotheistic religions, makes it a neutral tool to be considered by other religious or even non-religious philosophers to tackle questions concerning the relationship between science and religious belief. The American philosopher and Christian theologian William Lane Craig has already adopted one of the principles of *daqīq al-kalām*, the principle of temporality, in his argument about the existence of a creator. He has clearly acknowledged the Islamic source of his argument and has set it under the title: "The Kalām Cosmological Argument".[53] Consequently, there is nothing preventing us from developing these arguments in defense of theistic beliefs in general. However, over issues of pure theology, such as God's attributes, the unity of God, the punishment of sinners, and the reward of the believers, problems might surely arise between the different religious beliefs. These issues are subjects of *jalīl al-kalām* and different religious sects will have their own systems of thought.

An Overview

In the following chapters of this book, I will discuss some currently hot issues in science and religion, adopting the arguments of *kalām* as foundations for my views. The aim is to explore how to deal with these issues and to present what Islamic *kalām* might have to say about them. Let me present here a short synopsis of what I have to say later.

In Chapter Two, I discuss the concepts of the laws of physics and the laws of nature, where it is noted that there is some confusion concerning these two concepts. This confusion is causing serious misunderstanding over the reality of the laws of physics and the actual value of scientific laws and theories. The laws of nature are defined as being those phenomena which we see happening in nature, while laws of physics are our own rational description of those laws. An example is the phenomenon of gravity, which is a law of nature, and Newton's law of gravity. A law of nature describes ontology, while a law of physics is an epistemology that we might be able to express as a mathematical law. This later includes identifying the variables contributing to the phenomena and recognizing their mutual relationships. While laws of nature are identified as being indeterministic, a fact which is drawn from what we know about quantum measurements, the laws of physics are deterministic, being described by differential equations. But, the question arises over why there should be a law in the first place? This is the question behind Einstein's perplexity about a conceivable universe. It is noted that our own existence with such a complex structure is sufficient evidence for law and order in the universe. It is also noted that the laws of nature are in need of vitalization and coordination through being in operation. Their own indeterminacy suggests the need for an operator driving these laws. Such an operator cannot be just another law of nature, since such a character would render the law a part of nature abiding by its properties, thus needing another operator and so on ad infinitum. Consequently, such an operator should be acting beyond space-time, not belonging to our physical universe. In addition, an analysis of the conditions and content of the scientific theory is presented in this chapter and the relations between physics and mathematics are elaborated on by providing several examples from classical and modern physics. The chapter concludes with a discussion about the state of the laws of physics in the first moment of the existence of the universe and the mind of God.

In Chapter Three, I discuss the concept of causality, presenting the views of *kalām* and using many of the arguments inspired by *daqīq al-kalām,* where it has long been understood that Muslims deny causality and causal relationships. It is shown that this is a matter that needs to be subjected to scrutiny and it is shown that Muslims did not deny causal relationships, but have in fact denied deterministic causality. To start, some important terms are defined for reasons of clarity and then an in-depth analysis of the phenomenology of cause is considered. Cause from the perspective of the Qur'an is presented through several quoted verses, where it is shown that the Qur'an does not deny causal relationships, but simply deterministic causality. This enables the concept of causality in Islamic *kalām* to be introduced, where it is also shown that, as far as the natural world is concerned, *deterministic causality* is denied and that the *mutakallimūn* have always thought of causal relationships as being necessary to effect law and order in the world, even though the creator is at liberty at any moment to invalidate the effects of natural laws, and by this the *mutakallimūn* allow for miracles to happen. The Muʿtazila devised a sophisticated concept of causality by which they identified four types of causal relationships: adherence (*iʿtimād*), conjunction (*iqtirān*), generation (*tawlīd*), and custom (*ʿāda*). The Ashʿaris, on the other hand, were satisfied with attributing causality to what we are accustomed to seeing of the behavior of nature, which is why they called it *ʿāda*. The concept of causality according to al-Ghazālī is also considered in this chapter and it is shown that, contrary to the myth that al-Ghazālī never denied causality as such, he denied only that causes could act autonomously by the power of their nature. The innate properties of matter are impotent, in his opinion, and cannot produce effective action. In conjunction with this, Ibn Rushd's criticism of Ashʿari understanding of causality is also presented. After this historical coverage, the concept of Laplace's determinism of the natural world is presented and it is shown that this concept and the related argument of determinism is no longer valid, since the concepts and laws of classical physics have failed to provide an accurate description of nature. New concepts driven by the theory of relativity and quantum mechanics are discussed and it is shown that the *kalām* understanding of the concept is not far from what these theories of modern physics have suggested. The question of the first cause and the problem of the initial conditions of the universe are also discussed, where it is argued that an ultimate cause has to be assumed for the creation of the universe. Such a cause goes beyond spacetime and matter, and inevitably is supernatural.

In Chapter Four, the question of divine action is discussed, which is one of the basic conflicts between science and religion. The question which needs an answer in physics is: How would an indeterministic nature, as presented by quantum mechanics, be able to derive itself spontaneously? The immediate answer to this is that an external agent might be required to drive the development of such a system. The requirement that the agent should be external rests on the argument that, if it were integral to the world itself, then it would certainly abide by the laws which are at work in the world; consequently, such an agent would need another agent to drive it. Then, the question would arise over how such an agent would be able to effect actions in our physical world? Within the current scientific and religious debates, many models have been suggested to explain divine action. Perhaps the best review of ideas and opinions on this subject is compiled in the work of Christoph Lameter,[54] in which it is shown that the quantum explanation currently stands as the most reasonable one. However, this explanation is associated with the problem of measurement in quantum mechanics, which is fundamentally an epistemological problem that is due to an unrecognized missing ontological agent that might be at play within the quantum domain. In this chapter, I have described this problem in its simplified technical context, and have presented the most well-known available suggestions for its interpretation, all of which suffer from loopholes. In a new vision of the problem, I have suggested that the problem of quantum measurement might be solved by utilizing the principle of re-creation. We assume that all constituents of a system are subject to re-creation with certain frequency, depending on their total energy. This assumption enables us to explain quantum measurement and many of the quantum phenomena in a clearer way. We also understand the physical basis of the Heisenberg uncertainty principle more clearly. The notion of re-creation can also explain quantum entanglement and be used to develop the concept of cosmic wholeness. Some of the criticisms made of the quantum divine action are also addressed.

In Chapter Five, I consider the concepts of space and time according to some of the theistic philosophical views and Islamic *kalām*. The main point is to expose *kalām*'s understanding of spacetime as being one of an integrated entity. Besides this, the notion of jump (*tafra*) suggested by al-Naẓẓām is presented and the concept of discrete motion, as suggested other *mutakallimūn*, is also presented. Perhaps the most important notion that might have a key application in current physics is the notion of discrete time, a concept which is essential for the development of modern physics and for the cosmology of the very early universe.

Two examples demonstrating the advanced views and arguments of al-Ghazālī are presented in Chapter Six: one discussion concerning the size of the universe and the possibility of it being larger or smaller than we think, and another about the corruption of the Sun. This is an example of the challenges that were put forward by al-Ghazālī to refute the Aristotelian view on metaphysical questions.

I conclude the book with a discussion of the possibilities for a "neo-*kalām*" theory to become a tool for provoking a genuine transformation in Islamic thought and society. In this final chapter, I discuss the obstacles which are expected to hinder such a transformation, outlining a long-term road map for achieving this transformation.

CHAPTER TWO

Laws of Nature and Laws of Physics

The concept of a law of Nature cannot be made sense of without God.

Nancy Cartwright

I had no need of this hypothesis.

Pierre Laplace to Napoleon Bonaparte

IN MANY CONTEMPORARY SCIENCE and religion debates, it is noted that there is some confusion concerning two concepts: the laws of nature and the laws of physics. This is causing serious misunderstanding about the reality of the laws of physics and the actual meaning of scientific laws and theories. It is generally thought that laws of physics represent the actual phenomena which they are describing. This may have been an inherited concept from classical Greek philosophy, since it is known that the word φυσικς (physics) as used by Aristotle means "nature". The word nature means the intrinsic property of something that is capable of causing an effect.[1] On the other hand, the concept of a "law of nature" needs to be clarified so that we can understand its actual meaning, and what it means to be a) natural and b) a law. We can realize the importance of this topic once we understand, for example, the deep philosophical implications of quantum indeterminism and once we know whether that is an objective fact, something which is a reality in the world, or whether it is an artifact of the theory. In cosmology, we need to know whether cosmic inflation is a natural historical cosmic necessity that actually happened during the evolution of the universe—which, if it did, elevates it to the level of being a law of nature—or whether it is just a model that was devised to explain some problems with the big bang theory. A further example is whether we can consider natural selection to be a law of nature for the evolution of living creatures or just a mere suggestion for a possible mechanism, or part of a mechanism, that biological evolution requires. Such questions are indeed of high importance in science and religion debates and in evaluating the content of a scientific theory.

The discussion presented by Paul Davies in his book *The Mind of God* about the "laws of nature" is a typical example of the confusion over laws of nature and laws of physics. Davies sometimes uses the term "laws of nature" to mean what we would describe as natural phenomena, and uses the term "laws of physics" to point to the phenomena themselves. This kind of confusion may lead to absurdities and to the faulty identification of the entities at play when discussing such vital questions as the creation of the universe in a philosophical context. For example, he says that, "given the laws of physics, the universe can create itself".[2] This is a typical example of what I call confusion or misunderstanding by mixing the two concepts into one common meaning. This belief that the laws of physics are descriptions of natural phenomena was the case until the beginning of the twentieth century, when relativity theory came to replace Newtonian mechanics and his law of universal gravitation with more accurate formulations, and when quantum mechanics uncovered the fact that the classical laws of physics were only an approximate formulation of natural phenomena. This confusion might have been brought about by the common origin of the words "nature" and "physics", as both terms historically expressed the same meaning. The confusion causes misunderstanding over the reality of the laws of physics and this leads us to give such laws the status of being in existence "out there" with exaggerated supremacy and sovereignty.

On arguing for the initial conditions of the universe, or the laws operating at initial conditions, Paul Davies suggests that:

> Laws of initial conditions strongly support the Platonic idea that the laws are "out there" transcending the physical universe. It is sometimes argued that the laws of physics came into being with the universe. If that was so, then those laws cannot explain the origin of the universe, because the laws would not exist until the universe existed.[3]

The correct expression for the above paragraph is to say that the laws which are actually "out there" are the laws of nature, for which we do not know with absolute certainty their mathematical construct or the logic behind their operation. These laws of nature came into being with the universe and we do not know how they could have existed before the birth of the universe.

Richard Dawkins is another example of an author who puts forward speculations drawn from Darwin's theory of evolution and tries to present them as being laws of nature. Whereas evolution *is* a law of nature, being an observed fact, Darwin's theory of biological evolution is not. It could be considered to be a law of biology, however. It is not a problem of terminology that I am dealing with here; it is a bit more than that. Thus, I feel the need to clarify the two concepts to enable us to use them in their proper contexts more accurately.

What is a Law of Nature?

A law of nature is a regular phenomenon that occurs once certain conditions are present. We need not know the details of the process that leads to the natural phenomenon, but the phenomenon needs to be repeated with some regularity in order for it to be designated as a law. For example, a stone could fall once dropped from my hand, which is holding it; this is the law of gravity acting naturally. We know that cotton burns once thrown into fire and that vapor condenses once set on a cold surface. We need not know the mechanism by which such a law acts to observe a law of nature at work; for example, we need not know the mechanism by which cotton begins burning, as this will be part of our identification of the factors contributing to this phenomenon and the relation between such factors, which is usually described by the laws of physics and chemistry. History of thought tells us that humans have given different explanations for the same natural phenomena over the ages, depending on their intellectual level and the dominating culture of their age.

Perhaps the earliest of all the laws of nature that man has discovered is the phenomenon of generating fire by hitting two stones against each other. More sophisticated laws of nature were discovered once man had recognized numbers and was able to calculate things. At this point, man started identifying laws of nature which were periodic; for example, the recurrence of solar and lunar eclipses, which is an indication of an order in the universe. This is one of the earliest laws of nature to attract the attention of humans. By observing this phenomenon over a long period of time, the Babylonians were able to identify the periodicity of the occurrence of these eclipses. They found that eclipses come in cycles, each composed of 223 synodic months (29.5306 days each). Eclipses of each cycle recur during the next cycle with a geographical separation of about 116 degrees of arc. Accordingly, the Babylonians were able to tabulate the eclipses of one cycle, which was later called the "saros cycle", and could predict all other eclipses to come. This was one of the earliest discoveries of a law of nature. It is known that the pre-Socratic Greek philosopher Thales of Miletus used this knowledge to resolve a battle between two fighting armies.

More sophistication in recognizing nature was shown when man was able to construct theories from which he could deduce new predictions. Theories were basically proposed in order to explain natural phenomena. That is to say that after man was able to *describe* laws of nature, such as the occurrence of eclipses, he began to *explain* how such laws worked. At this point, *reasoning* started and *causes* were identified for what happened. The early interest of man was directed toward the sky as he wondered how the stars, the Sun, the Moon, and the planets were moving periodically around Earth. Perhaps it was a trivial law of nature to know that Earth should be at the center of all, for everywhere you look you see the sky. According to this model, different celestial objects were located at different distances from Earth according to their observed periods of rotation, measured with reference to the band of fixed stars called the zodiac. The Moon was found to be the fastest with the shortest rotation period of about 27.3 days, so it was placed nearest to Earth; then it was Mercury with a rotation period of 88 days, and next was Venus, which covers the trip in 225 days, and then comes the Sun in the fourth orb, which was observed to cover the zodiac within about 365 days. The red planet Mars was found to cover the zodiac within 680 days and the bright planet Jupiter was known to cover a period of about twelve years. The slowest of all was Saturn, which took about thirty years. Ancient and medieval thinkers, however, considered the celestial orbs of the planets to be thick spheres of rarefied matter, nested one within the other, each one in complete contact with the sphere above it and the sphere below it.[4] And, since it was observed that the stars were fixed and did not change their positions relative to one another, it was argued that they must be located on a single starry sphere called the "sphere of fixed stars".[5] Perhaps the reason why man thought that the celestial objects were fixed in material spheres was to understand why such objects did not fall to Earth, since it was common to see an object fall when set free. Then, in order to explain the apparent motion of these celestial objects within different periods, another metaphysical explanation was introduced where the position of each of these concentric spheres was changed by its own god, an unchanging divine mover which moved its sphere simply by virtue of being loved by it.[6] With such an explanation, man started to construct models for the laws of nature.

What is a Law of Physics?

A law of physics, or a scientific law according to the *Oxford English Dictionary*, is "a theoretical principle deduced from particular facts, applicable to a defined group or class of phenomena, and expressible by the statement that a particular phenomenon always occurs if certain conditions be present".[7]

A law of physics is a well-stated relationship by which parameters affecting the happening of any phenomena are identified clearly in conjunction with other parameters. For example, Newton's law of gravity is a well-stated expression for describing the force of gravity between two masses and the distance separating them. It says that the force of gravity between two bodies of a given mass is directly proportional to the product of those masses and is inversely proportional to the square of the distance between their centers. This statement is a quantitative identification which can be used to calculate the force of gravity between two bodies or more, yet it does not tell us that, once the bodies are set free, they will move toward each other. This needs another law to be effected.

God and the Law

During the seventeenth century, the notion of "laws of nature" crystallized; René Descartes (1596–1650) was perhaps the first in the West[8] to discuss the existence of laws or rules of nature. In his *Principles of Philosophy*, he explained three laws concerning the natural motion of bodies and a conservation rule to conserve the quantity of motion as measured by size multiplied by speed. The claim of conservation, and all the other laws, were grounded explicitly in the activity of a transcendent god on his creation.[9] Descartes had a version of the doctrine of continual re-creation, similar to what the Ashʿaris believed: that the sustainment of the creation is thought to be performed. Daniel Garber[10] tells us that the idea of a law of inanimate nature remained quite distinctively Cartesian throughout much of the seventeenth century. The notion of a law of nature cannot be found, for example, in the works of other reformers of the period, such as Francis Bacon (1561–1626) or Galileo Galilei (1564–1642).

In contrast, Thomas Hobbes (1588–1679) did not think that God had any role to play in natural philosophy. In order to explain how a law of nature worked, he resorted to geometry. The way in which Hobbes interpreted nature through geometry was to say that a body at rest would remain at rest because of a possibility to move in any and all directions; since there is no preferred direction for motion, the body would have to remain at rest. A similar argument applied to a body in constant motion. In fact, this was a rhetorical statement rather than a sound scientific argument. This kind of understanding is obviously denying the need for an agent to activate such events.

The geometrical argument is similar to saying that a free stone falls on the ground just because there is a gravitational force between the stone and the earth. But here we are ignoring the question of how gravity works. If you are a free, rational thinker, you would ask such questions, but, if you would like to ignore them, you could always attribute the action of gravity to another cause: the existence of mass according to Newton or the presence of a curvature of spacetime according to Einstein. Hobbes denied divine intervention, as he could not visualize how something non-physical could affect the physical. This we can see in the following paragraph:

> The subject of [natural] Philosophy, or the matter it treats of, is every body of which we can conceive any generation, and which we may, by any consideration thereof, compare with other bodies, or which is capable of composition and resolution; that is to say, every body of whose generation or properties we can have any knowledge . . . Therefore, where there is no generation or property, there is no philosophy. Therefore it excludes Theology, I mean the doctrine of God, eternal, ingenerable, incomprehensible, and in whom there is nothing neither to divide nor compound, nor any generation to be conceived.[11]

Most of the efforts in science are directed toward knowing *how* nature works rather than knowing *why* nature is behaving like this or that. For this reason, and in the absence of sensible answers to the questions "how?" and "why?", it would be reasonable to adopt the empiricists' view that there is no law of nature, otherwise the laws of nature cannot be made sense of without God. In fact, the question of how a non-physical entity could affect a physical entity is one of the challenging questions at present in science and religion debates.

The modern sciences, mainly physics and biology, have weakened belief in God by assuming that the universe can be explained by a collection of laws that can be expressed in logical or mathematical forms. This eventually means that the universe is logically intelligible on the basis of deterministic causality. Classical celestial mechanics, for example, have verified this deterministic causality to the extent that they allowed Pierre Laplace (1749–1827) to claim that, once the initial conditions for any system are known, one can predict all subsequent developments of the system without the need to invoke the intervention of the divine; he says:

> We ought to regard the present state of the universe as the effect of its antecedent state and as the cause of the state that is to follow. An intelligence knowing *all* the forces acting in nature at a given instant, as well as the momentary positions of *all* things in the universe, would be able to comprehend in one single formula the motions of the largest bodies as well as the lightest atoms in the world, provided that its intellect were sufficiently powerful to subject *all* data to analysis; to it nothing would be uncertain, the future as well as the past would be present to its eyes. The perfection that the human mind has been able to give to astronomy affords but a feeble outline of such intelligence.[12]

The view that the world is developing independently of the notion of God culminated later in the declaration by Friedrich Nietzsche (1844–1900) that God is dead. This same belief in deterministic causality may have motivated Albert Einstein to ask whether God had any choice in creating the universe.

The proper scientific investigation of the world started with considering facts of nature as being empirical outcomes of experiments and observations. In this trend, which started with Galileo, the scientific quest to understand the world adopted the principle of seeking explanations for its phenomena by identifying their *natural* causes. Galileo realized that a proper investigation should concentrate on discovering the actual variables involved in the natural behavior of the world and finding the relations between these variables. He studied the motion of freely falling bodies, the swing of a pendulum, and then looked at the sky using his simple telescope. He achieved great discoveries in every track that he followed. This experience enabled him and the generations that followed to obtain a new insight into the world by which mankind was transformed into the age of modern science, the "proper science". The Galilean revolution did not come out from nowhere all of a sudden; the history of thought tells us that there were many previous advances in the methodology of the scientific quest that had paved the way for such a consideration.

The real transformation in the history of science and the physical law came with Sir Isaac Newton, who had studied the works of Galileo and realized the value of symbolizing variables and understood the implications of generalizing the formulations obtained from experiments and observations. Sir Isaac Newton (1642–1727) formulated the three laws of motion and the law of universal gravitation. Newton was an abstract thinker who invented differential calculus, by which he contributed a great deal to the advancement of science and humanity. Despite subscribing to personal religious beliefs, Newton did not include any metaphysical assumptions in his laws. The one comment he made about readjustment of the comet orbs was a remark rather than a serious scientific position. Newton declared that "religion and Philosophy are to be preserved distinct. We are not to introduce divine revelations into Philosophy, nor philosophical opinions into religion".[13] I find that the Newtonian approach to science and religion is the best option that one can adopt where a person subscribes to a religious belief. Science, being in one's intellectual background, may help to refine personal beliefs and inspire greater confidence based on rational attitudes rather than dogma.

After Newton, more sophistication was achieved in formulating the laws of motion and the law of universal gravitation. These refinements and upgrades were brought in by Laplace, Lagrange, Poisson, Euler, and many others who constructed classical mechanics. The laws of classical physics formulated as such were deterministic, as the associated natural phenomena belong to the macroscopic world, which seems to follow deterministic causal relationships. This trend served as inspiration for the thinkers of the eighteenth-century Enlightenment. Consequently, the Enlightenment philosophers subjected religion to an unprecedented rational scrutiny, many of them rejecting Christianity for deism and a few even turning to atheism.

The Laws of Modern Physics

The modern physics of the twentieth century probed the natural world at the microscopic level. New concepts were introduced and a new logic had to be generated. The part was no longer necessarily smaller than the whole, nor did the particle have to be a highly localized entity. The character of the physical law took a sharp turn at the beginning of the twentieth century toward abstraction. Mathematical formulations became more and more representative of the physical system. This allowed for a broadened scope of interpretations and controversy on explaining the implications of the laws of physics. For example, the introduction of wave–particle duality by Louis de Broglie brought in Heisenberg's uncertainty principle and the probabilistic character of the natural phenomena. In essence, laws of nature turned out to be indeterministic, whereas the laws of physics remained deterministic.

There are some aspects of the laws of physics that cannot correlate with the laws of nature, for example, time reversal. This is something that is exclusively assigned to some fundamental laws of physics, but not to the laws of nature. Time reversal does not actually take place in nature because it would contradict the second law of thermodynamics. Time reversal mainly arises in those physical laws which contain a second derivative with respect to time. An example of this is the Maxwell equations of electromagnetism. Another example of a physical law that exhibits time reversal is the Klein–Gordon equation, which is an equation of motion describing the behavior of particles moving at very high velocities (relativistic particles). If the physical law is a first-order differential equation in both space and time, then time reversibility can be achieved in conjugation with space and, if the particle is charged, then it might be possible to have the physical law exhibiting charge conjugation, time reversibility, and space inversion. This is called CPT (Charge conjugation, Parity, Time reversal) symmetry. For some time, particle physicists were fascinated by CPT symmetry, as it seemed to help solve some problems, but later such high hopes proved to be exaggerated. Nature is consistent and will never contradict itself. Consequently, one can say that time reversibility is an artifact of our mathematical formulation.

A good law of physics in my opinion is one with rich content, one that is simple and economical, and elegant in form. Elegance may include some sort of symmetry. An example of this is Einstein's field equation, where we have the whole of spacetime and its material content being expressed in one compact form composed of three terms, two on the left-hand side describing the geometry of spacetime and the third on the right describing the matter–energy content. This form can be decomposed into sixteen second-order partial differential equations (PDEs) describing the gravitational field on one side as a curved four-dimentional spacetime composed of three spatial dimensions and one time dimension. We are all familiar with curved surfaces like the surface of a ball, for example, but we are not accustomed to thinking about curved time. It is rather beautiful to see how time curves when we decompose the Einstein field equations. This is what popular science writers call "time warp". The Dirac equation is another example of a physical law that enjoys richness, simplicity, and elegance. This is a first-order partial differential equation written in a compact form using matrices. Originally, it was invented to describe the state of the electron, which is why Dirac called it the "equation of the electron", but later it was discovered that the same equation describes positrons too. Changing the mass in the equation allows it to describe the proton, neutron, neutrinos, and all spin-½ particles. The Dirac equation can be decomposed into four separate equations, two of them describing an electron with negative and positive energy states, and the other two describing a positron with positive and negative energy states. The Dirac equation is perhaps the most beautiful law of physics, although it is not the richest.

The power of a scientific theory is mainly embodied in its ability to generate verifiable predictions. A theory which can only explain phenomena is still useful, but certainly is considered to be at a lower level in the hierarchy of scientific theories. This surely applies to theories of physics. It is through the practical verifications of its theoretical predictions that we know that a theory is correct, or that it at least presents a better description of the world than its predecessors. Relativity theory, for example, contains all the predictions of Newtonian mechanics and his law of gravity plus several other predictions which have been verified by direct and indirect observations. This is what makes Einstein's theory of relativity superior to Newton's theory.

One other important characteristic of a scientific theory is that it must be consistent. This means that it should not be possible to use the assumptions of a theory to reach conclusions that contradict its other results. Results obtained from a theory should be unique and, if different versions of the same theory were to be discovered, then this would result in a lack of confidence.

This happened with string theory, for example, which, although it gained much popularity, could not provide verifiable predictions despite its basic simplicity and elegance. Five string theories were found, not one (later interpreted to be five versions of one and the same theory). However, this remains a controversial question.[14]

A theory should not depend on many undefined parameters. For example, the theory of cosmic inflation was devised in order to remedy some serious loopholes in the standard big bang theory of the origin and development of the early universe, but it could not specify a well-defined potential for driving the proposed inflation, which is a fundamental parameter. This problem was counted as one of the shortcomings of the cosmic inflation theory. One more example is the standard model of elementary particles, where the values of the masses are not well known, they are only set by hand. This, we hope, will be rectified in order to have a consistent and complete theory for particle physics.

Science has now become the accumulation of consistent knowledge that has two very important properties. The first is the capability of self-correction and the second is the property of correspondence by which new theories converge with those they replace, producing the same results once set to the special conditions described by the old theory or physical law. For example, Einstein's general relativity has provided us with a law of gravity that replaced Newton's law of universal gravitation. However, the law provided by Einstein reduces to the same expression as Newton's law of gravity in the case of weak gravitational field. Therefore, Newton's gravity becomes a special case of Einstein's gravity. This same property applies to quantum mechanics, where we find that the laws of quantum mechanics reduce to the corresponding laws of classical mechanics once the action (energy multiplied by time or distance multiplied by momentum) of the physical system becomes much larger than the value of Planck's constant.

At this moment in history, physics is in crisis. There are many unsolved problems and, toward the end of the twentieth century, the theories of physics became more and more speculative. Mathematical machines produced many abstract speculations with poor physical content and very few verifiable profiles. Most important is the quantum measurement problem, which has found no resolution and is hindering the advancement of quantum physics. In addition, there are problems concerning the unification of quantum mechanics and gravity. Because gravity is being described by a non-linear theory, there seems to be no way of unifying it with the linear theory of quantum mechanics. To understand gravity at the quantum level, it is necessary to understand the beginning of the universe and the singularity at the center of the black hole, and several other situations.

We also encounter problems associated with the standard model of cosmology: the big bang model. Some of the problems have been solved by suggesting the era of cosmic inflation, but some physicists believe that the inflation hypothesis itself is suffering from fundamental theoretical problems. Some other non-inflationary models have been suggested too, but mainstream research in cosmology still follows the big bang model.

Our description of the world remains approximate as long as we are in this world, and in no way can we dream of obtaining an absolute theory in the near future. This fact of life, which we encounter every time we go into deep analysis of our scientific knowledge, pushes us to believe in an extrapolated case where an omnipotent and omniscient agent has to exist for this universe to be. It might be that some people would not agree with the notion of God as represented by the main religions; however, a belief in the necessity of an omnipotent and omniscient agent for the universe to exist does not necessarily mean that we should believe in the God defined by religions. On the other hand, the scientific quest need not refer to the action of such an agent in any detailed description of causation or explanation of events in nature. It remains a matter of personal or communal belief how to account for the role of an omnipotent and omniscient agent.

Logic, Mathematics, and Reality

Away from the standard definitions, and in a simple word, I can describe "logic" as being a collection of basic axioms deduced from known first principles that constitute a set of rules for reasoning and deduction. The most direct and simple logical rule says that the whole is larger than its parts. On identifying the parts of a whole, we are identifying countable entities which belong to the whole. This kind of identification is made possible by the characteristics of our natural world. Computability of the parts is a fundamental characteristic of the world which makes it possible to construct counting machines, which may have started with the Babylonian mathematical tables that were in use a long time ago. Perhaps it is for this reason that the Oxford mathematical physicist David Deutsch considers computability to be an empirical property which depends on the way the world happens to be rather than on some necessary logical truth:

> The reason why we find it possible to construct, say, electronic calculators, and indeed why we can perform mental arithmetic, cannot be found in mathematics and logic. The reason is that the laws of physics happen to permit the existence of physical models for the operation of arithmetic such as addition, subtraction and multiplication. If they did not, these familiar operations would be noncomputable functions.[15]

Here again, I may point out that Deutsch should have used the term "laws of nature" instead of "laws of physics", since it is the laws of nature that are allowing such a computability and not the laws of physics. This is one more example of a physicist and mathematician misusing terms.

This kind of understanding of computability helps one realize why we are able to comprehend the world as a computable and physical system, a world which is explicable in terms of numbers and reasons. This is where the laws of nature and the laws of physics meet; it is in the arena of mathematics that we can describe the physical world most accurately. This is perhaps what made Galileo realize that the world is written in the language of mathematics. It is through the laws of physics that we realize the world is reasonable, comprehensible, and, to some extent, predictable. It is true to say that, "there is evidently a crucial *concordance* between, on the one hand, the laws of physics and, on the other hand, the computability of the mathematical functions that describe *those same laws*".[16] But, it is not true to say that the nature of the laws of physics permits certain mathematical operations to be computable—such as addition and multiplication—for, if it were so, then the laws of mathematics would be a subset of the laws of physics, whereas in fact it is the other way around. Plato's mathematical forms were transcendent; how could it be so unless the laws of mathematics enjoy a kind of superiority over the laws of physics? It is more likely that it is the laws of nature which permit certain mathematical operations, and not the laws of physics.

Babylonians where known to have developed a mathematical system that enabled them to solve numerical equations of the third order. They were able to calculate many parameters of nature, such as the length of the year, taken from different reference points and with very high accuracy. The invention of the sexagesimal system was a great help to Babylonian astronomers and mathematicians, who used the system very efficiently and were able to obtain their results with very high accuracy. Otto Neugebauer, the Austrian-American mathematician and historian of science, described the Babylonian computational efficiency with the following words:

> The system of tables alone, as it existed in 1800 B.C. would put the Babylonians ahead of all numerical computers in antiquity. Between 350 and 400 A.D. Theon Alexandrinus wrote pages of explanations in his commentaries to Ptolemy's sexagesimal computations in the Almagest. A scribe of the administration of an estate of a Babylonian temple 2000 years before Theon would have rightly wondered about so many words for such a simple technique.[17]

Many of the theorems of geometry and geometrical relations were known to Babylonians and, according to Neugebauer, "the Pythagorean theorem was known to the Babylonians more than a thousand years before Pythagoras".[18]

Mathematical systems can be very helpful not only in obtaining accurate prescriptive results, but also in exposing the secrets of the laws of nature. For example, tensor calculus greatly helped Einstein in formulating gravity as a spacetime curvature, by which Einstein was able to recognize Newton's law of gravity as only an approximate formula, making its use suitable for only weak gravitational fields. Tensor calculus enabled Einstein to recognize that the gravitational field in a four-dimensional spacetime has ten components rather than one. This is a fascinating example of the revealing power of mathematical systems. Vector calculus enabled James Clark Maxwell to formulate his electromagnetic theory in a neat and vivid form.

These examples make one feel that mathematics does have its version of reality. The fact that tensor calculus can help me to uncover that a gravitational field has more components than believed as I describe it in a linear vector form is astonishing. However, mathematics cannot stand alone as a tool to probe nature. Physics is also needed to provide us with insight into the underlying meaning and content of mathematical formulations. Mathematics cannot identify on its own the axes of a coordinate system, let alone label such coordinates for describing spacetime, for example. Mathematics is a machine that is able to generate new expressions for describing relationships between symbols satisfying a certain set of axioms and conditions. A good mathematician is someone who can drive this machine efficiently. It is the physicist who identifies those symbols and uses them to describe variables of physical systems. In doing so, he then can deduce the relations between those variables and, accordingly, discover the related physical law. The beauty of mathematics appears when we obtain general solutions for our physical problem, by which we describe the problem in its mathematical form. Then come physical conditions, which are normally introduced to the general mathematical solution as boundary conditions, to assign the physical limits imposed by the real situation specified by the problem.

Here the fundamental question arises: is it physical law that is embodied in mathematics or is it mathematics that is embodied in the natural phenomena (the laws of nature)? One can ask this question in another way: can we say that mathematics is the underlying structure of the world? Many examples can be provided in support of an affirmative answer. On the other hand, there are many consistent mathematical laws which find no place in natural phenomena. It is not possible to explain the world on the basis of mathematical consistency alone, as there are many consistent mathematical forms that do not find a place in the real world. Steven Weinberg was puzzled by this and considered it a dilemma that atheism is suffering from.[19] In addition, one may say that the world of mathematics is quite open to any development and that it is unlimited, except by the required consistency. Indeed, this is where the natural world meets with the world of mathematics. This might sound like Platonic philosophy of course, but it is the result of any free critical thinking. How, then, can we get Weinberg out of the fix he finds himself in? The answer might be somewhere in the distant future, as we have not yet discovered everything in the world. Mathematics, I gather, is the language of the world, but it is physical assumptions that might lead mathematics to acquire meaningful expression, or likewise to produce nonsense. This means that the extent of mathematics as a venture is as broad as the world is open, and not the other way round. The world is designed in such a way that allows mathematically solvable formulae to describe it in a consistent way, and that is what we call the "laws of physics".

However, as the world is so open, to the extent that we do not even know its limits, we cannot say for sure to what degree of conformity our mathematical formulation would comply with the reality of the natural world (the laws of nature). For this reason, it would be reasonable to assume that many of our mathematical formulations which are now thought to be redundant might find their way into certain future applications by which they could represent some states of the natural world. For example, we now deal mostly with what we call a "time-like world" in which physical causality in the conventional chronological order of cause and effect applies, but there is no reason why a different kind of world, a space-like world in which the chronological order of cause and effect is reversed, should not exist. Such a world may exist within the same space and time in which we are living; it is only another region of the spacetime. In fact, the spacetime diagrams invented by Herman Minkowski contain such regions and the theory of general relativity accommodates such a space-like world. This kind of space-like universe is not well understood yet, but it is said that the spacetime inside the event horizon of a black hole is space-like. The laws of physics are basically the same with only some physical quantities having interchangeable roles, such as space and time, and in these cases changes are measured according to variations of space, not variations of time. This means that the status of things may not change as time passes, but would change as we changed places. That is why different trajectories (so-called "geodesics") in a space-like universe would have different destinies and fates. A space-like world is a new world that we are not accustomed to; nevertheless, it is an alternative to our world. Some of the laws of physics would not change when going to a space-like universe, but some other laws may. For example, Maxwell's laws of electromagnetism would not change, but the electric and magnetic charges would exchange roles. We would not be able to see a single electric charge (electric monopole), but instead we would be accustomed to seeing the magnetic monopoles. Were we to move from our time-like world into a space-like world, we would find that the laws of nature have changed even if some laws of physics remain the same.

In the light of the above discussion, we can firmly conclude that mathematics obtains its realistic status through the laws of physics and that the laws of physics are constructed to express the relations between the parameters which contribute to natural phenomena. The laws of nature thus allow for the employment of mathematical constructions to describe them, at least in an approximate form following our own comprehension, and this is what makes these laws describe an approximate reality on the technical level. But, on the conceptual level, no ultimate truth can ever be claimed, no matter how long science is in progress. The good thing is that we are on the right track; every day we improve our calculations and refine our concepts about the laws of nature, but no ultimate status can be reached as long as there is time. Therefore, the dream of an ultimate theory for everything is far-fetched.

Conservation Laws

Conservation laws are the most important safeguards for the consistency of our physical world. These are the main pillars of physics without which no physical world can be comprehended. If there were no conservation laws then we would not be sure of anything, our physics would be vague, and the world would be running miraculously. The fact that some physical quantities are known to be conserved in natural processes makes us confident of the validity of physics. This is why Descartes placed so much emphasis on the importance of conservation law. However, no conservation law is known to be absolute. The conservation of physical quantities is known to apply within certain limits.

Despite the suggestion of conservation laws being made by Descartes and Leibniz as early as the seventeenth century, the deep implications of the notion were not well established until the late 1930s. When it was discovered in the early thirties that the neutron disintegrated into a proton plus and an electron, it was found that the total mass energy of these two particles did not add up to the total mass energy of a neutron. So, Niels Bohr proposed that the conservation of energy might, on average, only be working statistically.[20] However, it was later suggested that another particle is released during the disintegration of the neutron. But, since the electric charge is conserved, and because the neutron has zero charge, the proton has a +1 charge and the electron has −1 charge; therefore, the suggested particle should be neutral. It was called the "neutrino". The story of the discovery of the neutrino is one of the fascinating pieces in the history of modern physics. This discovery reveals many evidences of the success of theoretical physics, which consolidate the fact that this universe is ruled according to certain laws which are based on rigorous logic. The exciting part is the discovery that the neutrino must have a spin-½, which makes it a member of the family of fermions. This was achieved with full reliance on the law of conservation of spin angular momentum. The fuel of the Sun was only discovered with the help of the law of conservation of mass-energy without which the huge energy radiated by the Sun could not be explained.

It is fascinating to know that conservation laws are profoundly related to the symmetry of physical systems. Symmetry is known to mean equality, so when we say, for example, that the human body is symmetrical with respect to right and left, it means that every feature of our right side resembles the corresponding feature of our left side. When we say that an unmarked ball is symmetrical when rotating around any axis passing through its center, we mean that it remains the same at any angle during such rotations. But, once we mark the surface of the ball with scars, then it will not retain the same symmetry. The scars will cause a break in the symmetry. Similarly, an unmarked square is symmetrical under rotation by 90 degrees about an axis passing through its center, but a marked one will not have the same symmetrical properties. Here again, the mark causes a break in the symmetry. All symmetries correspond to certain conservation laws and many conservation laws in elementary particle physics were discovered through studying their symmetry groups.

Light preserves the symmetry of the spacetime it moves through. According to the theory of general relativity, time becomes dilated near massive bodies owing to the bending of time that is caused by gravity. This might be understood as if the light, while moving through spacetime, makes units of distance along its path (the wavelength) larger and larger as it approaches the massive body in order to keep the pace at a constant value. This implies that light (and all electromagnetic radiation) is a property of spacetime; it is the unit by which space and time is measured simultaneously. Accordingly, the speed of light in a vacuum must be constant with respect to all other observers, because otherwise the invariance of spacetime will be lost and, consequently, each point in space or time will have its own physics. Therefore, one can say that the constancy of the velocity of light is the most fundamental law of nature.

Why Should There Be a Law?

Why should the world behave in a way that is comprehensible through mathematics and the laws of physics? The laws of nature (the recurrence of natural phenomena) are clear evidence of an ordered world. But why *should* there be law and order in the universe? In fact, we do not know the origin of the laws of nature, which we describe by the laws of physics; we do not know why the world follows such laws unless we adopt a teleological explanation. This is what provoked Albert Einstein to say that "the most incomprehensible thing about the universe is that it is comprehensible".[21] So, it is we human beings with our advanced consciousness who are giving the world its meaning. But why is a teleological explanation not welcomed by many scientists?

Suppose we live in a world that does not seem to follow any set of laws. We might call such a world "chaotic". However, I am not intending to discuss chaos here, which might be described by highly non-linear laws. Instead, what I mean is a world in which some things are produced suddenly and may disappear suddenly too; a world without any fixed measure or rules and without any regularity. Such a world would not be productive and no material construct could be seen in it. The fact that we are here with such a complex composition is sufficient evidence for the existence of law and order in our world. But does this mean that our existence becomes inevitable, given the laws of physics? Can the laws of physics stand as sufficient cause for our existence? This is by no means a trivial argument. It could be accepted that the laws of physics become sufficient cause for our existence if we can prove that these laws have the power, intelligence, planning, and hindsight to act and produce the results they are acting for. But, which of these laws or sets of laws has the character that would qualify it for such a status? One might say that such a question will be answered once we discover the so-called "theory of everything", that we will discover the mother of all laws of physics, which can explain everything in one shot. But would such a law then belong to the laws of physics? If so, then it would have to have the fundamental characteristics of those laws, among which is the inherent inaccuracy in describing the world, and in this case it would not qualify as the ultimate answer. Otherwise, such a law would have to transcend all of our knowledge and, as such, it would not belong to the realm of physics. On the other hand, mathematically Gödel's incompleteness theorem prevents us from obtaining an absolute, complete proof from any set of axioms. Therefore, if an ultimate law were to exist, it would have to be something that could transcend our mathematics as well as our physics. In fact, this is the essential stumbling block in the atheistic argument for a universe with sufficient cause ascribed to any law of physics at all. In a letter to Solovine, Einstein wrote:

> You find it strange that I consider the comprehensibility of the world (to the extent that we are authorized to speak of such comprehensibility) as a miracle or as an eternal mystery. Well, a priori, one should expect a chaotic world, which cannot be grasped by the mind in any way . . . the kind of order created by Newton's theory of gravitation, for example, is wholly different. Even if a man proposes the axioms of the theory, the success of such a project presupposes a high degree of ordering of the objective world, and this could not be expected a priori. That is the "miracle" which is constantly reinforced as our knowledge expands.[22]

The above questions and analysis lead us to conclude that, no matter how our theories are refined, the ultimate reality cannot be comprehended without resorting to some super, transcendental power that has the will and knowledge to produce such a magnificent world. Such a power might not be a personal being, as described by the holy scriptures of religion, but it would certainly have to enjoy independence from our physical world. If not independent of the world, such a power would have to be either a part or the whole of the world. Accordingly, this power would have to abide by the laws of the world, which would then bring such a superior power to a lower status and restrict it from being able to control the world. This is the reason why Spinoza's god is not valid.

The Cosmological Argument

The cosmological argument ascribes the creation of the universe and all its contents to a supernatural agent: God. Among these is the Kalām Cosmological Argument, which was recently reformulated by William Craig. On the contrary, it is argued that the laws of physics provide enough reasons for the existence of the universe without the need to refer to any supernatural agent. Stephen Hawking[23] and, more recently, Lawrence Krauss[24] have spread such a claim in their popular books written for laymen. The main argument is based on the assumption that vacuum quantum fluctuations, the so-called "virtual states", can be turned spontaneously into real matter and energy, that is to say, real states. This can only be achieved if an external field of force existed, which would enable virtual states of the vacuum to be converted into real states. In a real situation, the field of force would have to be strong enough to achieve such an operation. The question is, from where can such a field of force be produced if we have nothing? Stephen Hawking argued that it could be the force of gravity. But how can a strong field of gravity be produced in a vacuum? No way, since the vacuum fluctuations could only produce a feeble force that would not be strong enough to convert virtual states into real ones. Consequently, a spontaneous generation of real states out of a vacuum is deemed to be impossible.

On the other hand, and through a somewhat philosophical argument, given the fact that vacuum fluctuations are a contingency, they are therefore certainly subjects of the initiation and sustainment that keep such virtual states popping up and down within a time duration below Heisenberg's uncertainty limit. Who, then, would do that and what kind of a law would work to sustain the state of the quantum vacuum? What kind of law governed the initial conditions of the universe before it came into being? Certainly neither Hawking nor Krauss, nor any other physicist, can answer such a question. This point will be discussed further below.

The Cosmic Singularity

On discussing the beginning and the fate of the universe, it is usually claimed that cosmic singularity is unavoidable.[25] Usually, this claim is supported by a reference to the work of Roger Penrose and Stephen Hawking[26] in which they proved a theorem which shows that, in the classic general theory of relativity, cosmic singularity is unavoidable. But, this misses the fact that, in that work of Penrose and Hawking, quantum effects were ignored and therefore such a result cannot be confirmed as representing the actual conditions for the beginning or the fate of the universe. In fact, in discussing this matter, some physicists claim that once space has infinitely shrunk, it must literally disappear and consequently time and matter will disappear too. This claim is not well established in detailed physical terms, since we need a full theory of quantum gravity in order to provide the mechanism for the big crunch or the big bang. To date, such a theory is not available. An alternative detailed mechanism, which might be more realistic, is provided by what I have called the "non-singular quantum model of the early universe".[27] In this model, matter is produced from the vacuum energy that is produced by the unfolding of the curvature of spacetime. So, practically, we start at the moment when a highly curved spacetime existed, producing intense Casimir energy out of the vacuum fluctuations; this energy was converted into matter through the era of matter generation (where massive particles are produced by a condensing of the energy, maybe through the mechanism of a Bose–Einstein condensate, which takes place at very high temperatures). At this moment, the first matter was born and the first law of the interaction of matter with radiation was set at work. In this model, the material content of the universe is generated gradually out of an unfolding of the spacetime curvature which was given a priori, not in one shot as stipulated by the standard big bang model.

For this reason, we have no singularity at the beginning of the universe. Some details of the model need to be worked out further in order to understand the full details of the mechanism of matter generation and the conversion of energy into massive particles. This model is free from all the known problems that are associated with the standard big bang model and, therefore, needs no inflation era to remedy those problems.

Laws of Physics at the First Moment

All physicists agree that the laws of physics ceased to work at the first moment of existence of the universe. The problem of the initial conditions for the birth of the universe is one of the stumbling blocks in gaining a full understanding of the universe's very early moments. Great minds like those of Penrose, Hawking, Hartle, Wheeler, and many others have been concerned with this problem, but no conclusive answer has been obtained. Whereas all the laws of physics just ceased, the laws of nature were at work. This is because the laws of nature were controlling the actions that were occurring. It is because of this that I say that the laws of physics are what we know about events and processes taking place in this world, but the laws of nature are those which might be unknown to us and yet are still at work. This humble understanding of the world is what we may all adopt in order to avoid the blindness of dogma and the arrogance that dominates thinking at times.

It is true that our understanding of the laws of physics is an approach to our understanding of the laws of nature, but at all times our understanding and formulations remain limited by our mental capabilities and comprehension. We cannot claim at any point that we have reached the ultimate understanding of anything at all in the world, so how can we be so confident that we can deny the existence of other agents at work? One thing we have to show in any argument is the logical sequence of reason. Arguments referring to a supernatural agent as being the reason for what happens in nature are not scientific arguments because they cannot explain the events. A supernatural agent is part of a person's beliefs and cannot be proved to exist until one's comprehension adjusts to accommodate facts within a certain framework. However, if one were to attempt to understand this existence and to appreciate such a level of consciousness and comprehension, it would make sense to consider an extended sort of world which goes beyond what we know through conventional logical arguments that adopt cause and effect and employ material existence as the only means of deduction. When we go beyond this kind of logic, we can transcend into a form of logic that allows for other versions of comprehension to be realized. However, here we need to be careful not to fall into the fallacy of illusion. When we go beyond our standard logic and comprehension into a transcendent state, we should always have a connection to our formal logic and rational comprehension, yet we should be free from the materialistic dogma which captivates us inside the horizon of a physical world. So, a subtle balance is needed for a factual understanding of the world as a whole and a humble comprehension that allows for other factors to be at play, to seek a comprehensive picture of what is at work. This might be an approach that achieves Einstein's dream to "catch God at work".[28]

Given the main attributes of God, it is not difficult to realize that He cannot be considered part of the world. A Spinoza type of god, to which Einstein had subscribed, is an extrapolation of the cosmic law and order. This could only be the case if there were a coordinating power within the cosmos itself, a far-fetched requirement to be part of our physical world. Therefore, it seems that in no way can we escape transcendence if we are to seek an explanation for the existence and development of the world.

So why should we seek to prove the existence of God simply through the laws of physics, which are part of our comprehension of the world, and ignore the fact that the world goes beyond our knowledge? Is this not what we cultivate by contemplating the events of this world? Is it not this that we learn from the development of scientific thought through the ages? We cannot disprove the existence of God by tracing what we know of the laws of physics. But can we prove the existence of God otherwise? The blunt answer is no, for God is an entity that goes beyond our standard logic; therefore, it is hard to see how we can, using such arguments. However, once the world is assumed to be His creation, we can always contemplate it and reflect on the attributes of God in an approach to comprehend Him as best as we can. This is how we can approach God and seek His company. But, again, it is a matter of faith and submission.

The laws of physics are deterministic, for example the Schrödinger equation, whereas the laws of nature are probabilistic. We cannot predict the occurrence of any phenomenon with absolute certainty; this is the outcome of quantum physics by which deterministic causality is invalidated. The reason why the laws of physics are deterministic is because they are formulated on the basis of mathematical logic, which has no room for indeterminism. However, indeterminism does not rule out causality, it rules out deterministic causality.

The Mind of God

A final question is whether the laws of physics that we are devising or discovering reflect the mind of God? The answer might be obtained when we answer the question of whether scientific theories express facts and realities or whether they are expressions of our own minds and imaginations? Theories suggest expressions for the laws of physics to expose quantitative relationships between variables. However, some philosophers like Nancy Cartwright think that these laws might sometimes lie.[29] She asserts the fact that, despite the explanatory power of theoretical laws, these laws do not describe reality. Indeed it is the case and this is exactly one major difference between a law of nature and the corresponding descriptive law of physics.

The history of modern science tells us that scientific theories change over time and, although a correspondence is established sometimes between the results of calculations based on new theories and the old ones, it is found that the concepts are liable to change. We now have two famous and well-studied examples: quantum theory versus classical radiation physics, and relativity theory versus Newtonian mechanics and gravitational theory. We have seen how the classical particle concept has changed and how the wave–particle duality concept replaced the old one and constitutes the substratum of quantum theory. Moreover, the determinism of classical physics was replaced by the indeterminism of quantum systems. These new concepts completely changed the philosophy of a law of nature. A deterministic world may not need God if the laws operate independently, but an indeterministic world would surely need an external agent to decide the results and coordinate the actions of different, sometimes conflicting, laws. A universe abiding by deterministic laws can enforce a kind of self-ruling; the entire universe can run in a self-contained manner. On the contrary, if indeterminism underlies the structure of the laws of nature, then surely the need for an external ruler becomes inevitable. That is why Einstein could not accept the notion that God plays dice.[30] Here, reason conflicts with nature, which does not necessarily follow the laws that our minds have devised, but follows the laws that were devised by the Creator.

The laws of physics by which we describe natural events are actually devised by our minds, the mind of Paul Davies for example, but not by the "mind of God". So, in one way or another, we are discovering the human mind and its workings and not how the mind of God works. This fact may easily be recognized once we remember that people thought for more than 200 years that Newton's law of gravity was the law of God controlling the solar system. Then it turned out that neither the mathematical formulation of Newton's law nor his concept of gravity were right, despite the fact that astronomers successfully used it to calculate the orbits of the planets in the sky precisely, and even to predict the existence of other planets which were duly discovered later. That is why no one can catch God at work, not even the great Einstein himself.[31]

Different conflicting and stand-alone laws cannot act by themselves to produce the organizational qualities or the delicacy of nature. These laws need some coordinating mechanism, which would be, in essence, yet another law of nature. Otherwise we have to resort to an external agent that does not abide by the characteristics of nature itself. In no way can we find a single law unifying all the laws in nature, simply because such a law would contain the mechanism and control necessary for the coordination of all the other laws; that is a self-defeating goal, because such a goal, in replicating itself ad infinitum, must ever elude us. Therefore, the role of an external agent that does not follow nature is deemed necessary to resolve such a dilemma, an agent that acts outside of space and time and does not necessarily abide by our logic and comprehension.

Physicists and other scientists need to revise the ways they think about God in order to be able to seriously comprehend the possibility of having an external power, will, or wisdom, or whatever initiates, controls, and sustains the universe. God needs to be thought of as an abstract entity that exists and acts beyond physical space and time. Otherwise, if we think of God as an entity within and as part of our physical world, and characterize Him according to our scientific standards, then we surely will be "led to conclude that adding God would just make things more complicated, and this hypothesis should be rejected by scientific standards", as Sean Carroll puts it.[32] God is not physical; were it so, He would be contained within the universe. He would then be subject to the laws of the universe and would need a supernatural power to coordinate His acts and sustain His will and power.

In one important paper,[33] the philosopher of science Nancy Cartwright has argued that the concept of a law of nature cannot be made sense of without God. Cartwright did not mean to defend a theistic view, rather she argues that assuming that laws of nature are prescriptive and not merely descriptive, and supposing that the laws that are responsible for what occurs in nature, would require God. Cartwright suggests an alternative by which the order of nature can be maintained without immediate reliance on God by accepting the proposal of empiricism. Nothing in the empirical world makes anything happen, rather nature is a collection of events one after another. In this vision, there is still a realization of the regularities among these events and recognition of the causal relationships, nevertheless Cartwright points out that there is no way in which these laws can be said to govern events in nature. This vision is based on the Hume's teachings. In one version of the views, the blue-blood empiricism, some regularities are thought to necessarily hold.

This view echoes the original ideas of al-Ghazālī concerning his rejection of the presence of a deterministic causality. Indeed, al-Ghazālī saw the regularity of events occurring in nature as being a sort of "custom", explaining that these laws are written in the book of nature and, as Cartwright asserts, "there is no sense in which they can be responsible for what happens".[34] Cartwright concludes that, without God, God's plans, and God's will, there can be no laws of nature for an empiricist.

In the next chapter, I will discuss the question of the laws of nature from an Islamic point of view under the subject of causality, where I will show how some Muslims, namely the *mutakallimūn*, understood causal relationships in the world and the action of the Creator in sustaining the world.

CHAPTER THREE

Causality: An Islamic Perspective

And when they [the philosophers] mean by "Nature" that which happens from the burning fire, it is what we consider to happen out of the adherences (iʿtimādāt) *which generate dissociations.*[1]

Qāḍī ʿAbd al-Jabbār

IN THE PREVIOUS CHAPTER, I considered the differences between what we call laws of nature and laws of physics, and I have shown that such a differentiation is vital for a clear understanding of the role of human mind in comprehending the world. From another perspective, we can identify laws in nature as being effects that take place due to related causes. In essence, the laws that are identified as laws of physics describe such causal relationships, since causation is a relation between one entity (the cause) and another (the effect), where the second is understood as a consequence of the first.

The study of causality has gained importance through being a basic concept for understanding the relations between the parameters that contribute to any natural phenomenon. It is the most basic expression for the relation between those factors that are at play in the phenomenon. To understand the causes means to identify the essential parameters and conditions that contribute to the occurrence of the phenomenon. In the analysis of many of the phenomena taking place in the world—for example, the free fall of a stone toward the center of the earth, the igniting of a material as it nears a source of heat, or the recovery from illness after taking medicine—events indicate that those essential parameters and conditions are causes of the occurrence of the related effects. So here we have to identify two levels by which causality must be comprehended. The first is to identify the essential parameters that help bring about the phenomenon as being the causes of the related effects, and the second is to attribute the observed effects in the phenomenon to those parameters and conditions (causes) uniquely, namely, to consider them the actual creators of the phenomenon. On the first level, we need not assume any mindful prevalence throughout, except what might be necessary for the organization of the process, but on the second level we have to ascribe some mindful control embodied in those causes and a purpose for the phenomenon (the effect). It is not sufficient to claim that it is the nature of cause to lead to the related effect unless the term "nature" is fully understood, as well as the mechanism by which the specific cause produces the related effect unambiguously.

In this chapter, I will investigate the concept of causality from an Islamic perspective discussed in a scientific, more specifically a physical, context. This topic has become one of the hot issues that need to be resolved to have a proper understanding of the relationship between science and Islam. Besides the old writings of some Orientalists, several authors have recently accused Islamic traditional thought of being confused on the question of causality. It is customary to say that Muslim thinkers deny causality and causal relationships, and some prominent contemporary scientists and researchers are blaming Muslim traditional scholars such as al-Ghazālī for denying causality and for causing a setback in Islamic scientific development. Some of these accusations might be correct, but they cannot be taken as a general position on the state of the "Islamic mind". Therefore, it is of importance to clarify the situation both in its theological context, as it is in the understanding of prominent Muslim scholars, and in its modern scientific context, as provided by the available theories of physics and related experimental results.

Much has been said and written recently about the question of the first cause and the need for a creator. Most of this was initiated by a revived interest in the question of harmony between science and religion, a field of thought that has initiated rich debate about both science and religion. The question of the first cause, and whether the universe was caused to exist, is part of the subject matter of the "Kalām Cosmological Argument" formulated by William Craig in his book.[2] For this issue to be enriched regarding its relation to causality, an elaboration of the meaning and qualification of a cause, from an Islamic perspective, is certainly needed. Again, such an elaboration cannot be made without consideration of this question in the scientific inquiry on the origin of the universe in its scientific context.

I make no attempt to consider the historical development of the problem of causality or to consider the views of philosophers and thinkers other than those Muslim scholars who were concerned with the subject, since such matters can already be found in standard works. This topic on causality is very much related to the system of belief in Islam, so I aim to provide an Islamic view which I believe is in agreement with the stipulations of the Qur'an, and to recast those stipulations in a modern scientific and philosophical context. The goal here is to demonstrate how the question of causality can be more accurately understood so as to comply with what we have learned over the many ages of investigating the world.

Some Basic Definitions and Concepts

There are a number of terms that are related to the concept of causality, which can be defined in slightly different ways using different terminologies. Below I will present some of the basic definitions and concepts relating to causality and causal determinism. Since these terms are mostly philosophical, it is expected that there will be different expressions for them embedded within different philosophical views. I will define terms as they are to be used subsequently in the text in order to avoid confusion. For this reason, no specific references for these definitions are given.

Cause

The cause here is understood to be an ontological entity to which an event can be attributed. This may include a direct cause, an indirect cause, a prime cause, a secondary cause, and so on.

Causal Relation

Causal relation is an expression describing the relation between a set of factors or entities (causes) that are found to be present in conjunction with a phenomenon (the effect).

Nature

This is a very important term that will be used extensively in this chapter and, therefore, it is important to establish its definition. I use the term "nature" to mean either of the following:

(1) the innate properties of things (in Arabic, *ṭabʿ*);

(2) the phenomena observed in the physical world or the whole of the physical world itself.

Misplacement of these two meanings for the term "nature" may result in much confusion and distortions of the intended meaning.

Predictability

This term refers to the expectation of an outcome or an event. The prediction should be based on certain logical consequences set according to certain knowledge; otherwise it will be mere unfounded prophecy. Predictability is directly related to expectation. Expectations are made according to certain experiences. Experience needs memory, at the least, but not necessarily comprehension; this implies that there should be history.

Predictability is one of the most desired features of modern scientific theory, since it is a good test of the theory. Predictability does not entail determinism, for there are highly predictable systems that are indeterminate. For example, quantum systems are highly predictable though indeterminate, whereas chaotic systems are completely unpredictable while being fully deterministic.

Determinism

In the *Stanford Encyclopedia of Philosophy*, it is said that "the world is governed by (or is under the sway of) determinism if and only if, given a specified way things are at a time *t*, the way things go thereafter is fixed as a matter of natural law".[3] This description of the term "determinism" requires a law that determines an occurrence. This alleged law is called "natural" and here we face the problem of whether it is a law of nature that is specifying the deterministic behavior or whether it is something else. We also can question whether such a "natural" law exists or not. These questions will be discussed below, but, nevertheless, I feel that this description is accurate enough to describe the concept of determinism. To a great extent, the macroscopic world that we deal with in everyday life is deterministic.

Causal Determinism

Again, in the *Stanford Encyclopedia of Philosophy*, we read that this concept points to "the idea that every event is necessitated by antecedent events and conditions together with the laws of nature". Here we can question whether such an association between events is such a necessity that nature could not function without it, and whether such an association fully determines the causal relationships. The laws of physics describe such relationships and specify the variables and the invariables involved in natural phenomena. This is why the laws of physics are deterministic even though they might be describing indeterministic phenomena. For example, the Schrödinger equation describes deterministic causal relations, while the related phenomena (solutions to the equation) include entities that obey probabilistic distribution.

The Phenomenology of Cause

Determinism means that an event described by a physical law must occur once the set of necessary and sufficient conditions is available. For example, the necessary conditions for two bodies to attract each other according to Newton's theory of gravity require that both should have a mass and that they should be separated by a finite distance. However, these conditions are not necessary in Einstein's theory of gravity, since a massless object can feel gravity as it passes by a massive object. The difference between the two theories lies in describing the force of gravity as a field emanating from a mass according to Newton or a spacetime curvature according to Einstein. Once curved spacetime becomes available, light rays will follow curved paths called "geodesics" of spacetime and will curve their paths around sources of mass. The curvature of time is shown in the elongating of the light beam's wavelength (it gets redder). Two massless particles (e.g., photons) do not attract each other, nor does a photon (a quantum of light) attracted by the Sun suffer free-fall acceleration. A photon approaching the Sun will get redder. This is the gravitational redshift law of nature. Here we say that the redshift of the light is caused by the mass of the Sun and, accordingly, one can calculate the mass of any object causing such an effect. This is what astrophysicists usually do to calculate the masses of dim stars. One can say that the photon approaching the Sun is actually feeling the Sun's gravity and that its wavelength is becoming longer.

The sufficient condition for a cause is something else. It is not an easy task to define the sufficient conditions for any cause, since there may always be something unknown which contributes to that set of conditions. I have mentioned that the necessary condition for two bodies to attract each other is that the two bodies must have individual masses according to the Newtonian picture of gravity. However, this is not a sufficient condition, even within Newton's picture. We need to add to this condition that the two bodies should be electrically and magnetically neutral. For example, if the bodies are charged with similar electrical charges, then they will repel each other and their gravitational attraction will be affected. Similarly, if the two bodies are magnetically charged, then magnetic force will affect their gravitational attraction too; Newton's gravity cannot be properly verified then. There might always be other conditions that will prove to be effective on a large or small scale. The theory of special relativity has shown us that Newtonian mechanics ignores some effects that are only observable at high speeds and the theory of general relativity has shown us that there are also certain effects that are ignored by Newton's law of gravitation; these effects become very important in strong gravitational fields. In addition, it is known that quantum physics has revealed important facts about the microscopic world that were not described by classical physics. The theory of relativity and quantum physics have drastically changed the concepts and the mathematical formulations of classical physics. New theories imply new conditions and the new concepts suggest new causes for the phenomena.

The development of scientific knowledge tells us that, without assuming the presence of causal relationships, we cannot deduce anything or explain any of the phenomena of nature. Without causality, the universe becomes a chaotic one where nothing is predictable. However, the most important question in this topic is: Do causes produce their effects directly? Is the cause just a representation of the reason for what happens, without being effective itself, or is the cause actually the agent that is producing the resulting effect?

A cause might be attributed to an innate property (nature) of an object. The question here is: Does that property constitute a sufficient cause for the occurrence of the effect? This question has been asked by the *mutakallimūn*, for example by al-Bāqillānī in his book *Tamhīd al-awā'il*, which I will come back to later. If this is the fact, as al-Bāqillānī says, then "the mere availability of irrigation should achieve the growth of plants at all times endlessly, which is not the case".[4] But, one could say that this is not the case because it is a sort of "effect and response" relationship that is needed to expose a cause. Thus, here we have two parts at play: the related innate property and the object it is acting upon. Heat, for example, is an innate property, but it does not burn iron as it does paper or cotton. The burning of cotton needs heat and dry cotton. Once the heat is sufficient to set fire to it, the cotton will be ignited and will start to burn by the oxidizing of carbon molecules in its cellulose fibers. If the cotton is replaced by solid wood, a feeble fire may not be able to ignite it.

We can analyze the above example with further details. We have two levels of analysis: microscopic and macroscopic. At the microscopic level, we consider the interaction between the heat source and the cotton molecules, where the heat, in the form of photons or electromagnetic radiation, is absorbed by the carbon atoms (C) in the presence of oxygen molecules (O_2), available in the air, causing the electrons in the outer shell of the carbon atom to combine with electrons in the outer shells of two oxygen atoms. This combination produces one carbon dioxide (CO_2) molecule, generating at the same time an excess amount of heat, light, and some ash, part of the constituents of the cotton. The burning soon becomes spontaneously sustained by self-generated heat, the basic condition required to burn the rest of the cotton, which is the sufficient amount of heat required to excite the carbon atoms and allow them to combine with the oxygen atoms from the air to form the compound CO_2. This self-sustained reaction continues as long as the conditions do not change. For example, the air may become scarce for some reason or the cotton may get wet and become difficult to ignite, and so on. In any case, there is no reason why the fire will extinguish unless there is a reason that forces it to do so.

The question is: What causes the cotton to burn? Is it the heat of an external source which ignites it? Or is it a property of the cotton that it has a low ignition temperature? Is it because the burning of cotton is an exothermic reaction that produces enough heat to cause a self-sustained ignition? Is it the availability of oxygen in the air? Or is it that oxygen can combine with carbon to form a CO_2 molecule? We can also ask whether it was caused by the atomic structure of either the carbon or the oxygen, or of both. In fact, we can ask an endless number of questions concerning the actual cause of fire burning cotton. And it will turn out that many factors play a part in causing this process on the microscopic level.

On the macroscopic level, it would seem that fire + air + cotton are the only essential factors for the burning to take place. The fire might be considered the most essential cause for the burning, since it is the source of the heat, but nonetheless there are several factors at play in the process of burning cotton and each is as essential as the fire itself. This example explains how many factors contribute to the cause of any process in nature. It would be difficult to identify one, and only one, of such factors as the cause. Philosophers admit that it is practically impossible to prove causality, and this is a part of their academic teachings.

This is why it was thought that the occurrence of any event is always associated with apparent conditions. The full conditions cannot all be known while our knowledge about the world is incomplete. From this point of view, it is impossible to say for certain that the cause of any event is fully known, unless all the related parameters are known.

The above simple analysis and discussion is the kind of factual presentation that has to be complemented with philosophical analysis of the problem. First, we notice that chronological order is a fundamental aspect of causality. Effect occurs chronologically after the cause, not the other way around. This may suggest that the effect is generated by the cause, but this is no proof. It could be that such a chronological order presents some conjugation between what has been considered as a cause and the events that happen. An example is to say that climatic seasons are caused by the changes occurring in the celestial map of fixed stars. The ancient Arabs would assign climatic events such as rain, cold spells, or wind to the appearance or disappearance of constellations from the night sky. Through observing the cyclical commencement of climatic seasons over a long period of time, Arabs were able to identify a relation between the appearance of a certain constellation and these events. Since their knowledge of the sky was dominated by astrological beliefs, they concluded that the appearance of constellations must be the cause for the climatic seasons. But, we all know now that this was completely false. There is no causal relationship between climatic seasons and the sky map; such a coincidence is a kind of conjugation that occurs because of the motion of Earth around the Sun. As Earth moves around the Sun, the view of the sky changes so that different constellations appear in the night sky with the different climatic seasons. In fact, this very example is indirect evidence to show that Earth makes a full rotation around the Sun in one full tropical year. Incidentally, one might be surprised to know that the Prophet Muhammad (peace be upon him) warned his followers and prevented them from attributing the cause of such climatic events, rain specifically, to the appearance of certain constellations in the sky and asked them to attribute it to Allah and take it to be some of His blessings.[5]

One might say that the belief of those Arabs was flawed in its basic principles, since it was not possible to prove it scientifically. But, what kind of proof can one provide for it to be an effect, other than the verification of the event as it repeats itself regularly over the ages? Well, maybe one needs to prove theoretically that there is a relation between the configuration of the stars in the sky and the events on Earth. But was this not the case with the full astrological organ that dominated scientific thinking at that time? In fact, astrology was part of the teaching curricula in astronomy and the astrological effect of celestial bodies, including the constellations, was a fundamental part of Greek philosophical doctrines. Was it not the case that Ptolemy, the great astronomer of the Greeks, wrote one of his most important works on astrology? Indeed, as suggested by James Sanders, many beliefs, even those which are scientific, are contextual by nature.[6]

The Cause in the Qur'an

The Qur'an is the principal source for Muslims and, in the early days of Islam, the followers of the Prophet (the *Sahāba*, or "Companions") understood the Qur'an literally and accordingly they adopted this understanding, which was carried over to the second and third generations of Muslims. It was only about a century later that Muslim theologians and thinkers started discussing commentaries of the Qur'an and introduced their interpretations of some verses and wording to conform with rational understanding. Basically, the Qur'an attributes all the events and processes happening in the world, such as rain, wind, disasters, plant growth, the flight of birds, and all acts in the world, to Allah. Here are a few related verses:

> It is He Who sends down water (rain) from the sky, and with it We bring forth vegetation of all kinds, and out of it We bring forth green stalks, from which We bring forth thick clustered grain. And out of the date-palm and its spathe come

> forth clusters of dates hanging low and near, and gardens of grapes, olives and pomegranates, each similar (in kind) yet different (in variety and taste). Look at their fruits when they begin to bear, and the ripeness thereof. Verily! In these things there are signs for people who believe. (6:99)

There are two points addressed in this verse: the clear affiliation of events with the prime cause, Allah, and the request for humans to pay attention to these signs of divine action. In another verse we read:

> Allah is He Who raised the heavens without any pillars that ye can see; is firmly established on the throne (of authority); He has subjected the Sun and the Moon each one runs (its course) for a term appointed. (13:2)

Also in the same context of natural events we read:

> Have you not seen how your Lord spread the shadow? If He willed, He could have made it still then We have made the Sun its guide. (25:45)

One might take this verse as evidence for the claim that Allah could rule the universe miraculously in accordance with His wishes, as it would be impossible to make the shadow still unless the Sun were at a fixed point in the sky. Such an act would need a miracle, as it seems to go against the natural course of celestial objects. But this is not the case at all. In fact, the shadow can be brought to a standstill without ordering Earth to be stationary. To obtain such a state, it would be sufficient to prolong the period of Earth's rotation around its axis (the day) to one full year, or to reduce the period of its rotation around the Sun to only twenty-four hours. But perhaps the first option would be better, for a solar day to become a solar year, since the second would mean breaking the laws of mechanics. In this situation, Earth could be said to be in a locked orbit around the Sun. This is an expected situation for some planets that are now being discovered in other solar systems. In a locked orbit, half the globe would be facing the Sun and the other half would be facing away from it; the Sun would appear at a fixed point in the sky and, consequently, a shadow over Earth would be constant. This reminds me of another two verses in the Qur'an related to this hypothetical situation, which say:

> Say: Tell me! If Allah made night continuous for you till the Day of Resurrection, which God other than Allah could bring you light? Will you not then hear? (28:71)

> Say: Tell me! If Allah made day continuous for you till the Day of Resurrection, which God other than Allah could bring you night wherein you rest? Will you not then see? (28:72)

In these two verses, Allah is telling us that He could have made the length of the night and the day so prolonged as to continue until the end of life on Earth, which is the Day of Resurrection. But how can this be done without a miracle? In fact, this situation is quite possible and could happen without dispensing a miracle. If Earth were in a locked orbit, then half the globe would be illuminated by the Sun and the second half would be in darkness. Note that Allah does not just mention the day but the night too, since both are complementary, half the globe would be in daytime and the other half in nighttime. So, as we see through the above two examples, Allah need not perform miracles to rule the universe, and the examples given in the Qur'an are given for contemplation and to provoke thinking about the phenomena in the world.

In another verse, we can clearly see the attribution of life and death to Allah, this is one example of the domination of Allah over everything that goes beyond the power and abilities of the human:

> Allah is He Who created you, then provided food for you, then will cause you to die, then (again) He will give you life (on the Day of Resurrection). (30:40)

We also read:

> See you not that Allah merges the night into the day, and merges the day into the night, and has subjected the Sun and the Moon, each running its course for a term appointed; and that Allah is All-aware of what you do. (31:29)

In this verse, once again, the Qur'an stresses the role of Allah on a cosmological scale, but here we have to pay attention to the statement "and has subjected the Sun and the Moon, each running its course for a term appointed", from where one can take the meaning that there is a course that these objects follow for a certain term. Whether this course, or track, is autonomous or whether it is divinely maintained is not clear from this verse:

> See you not, that Allah sends down water (rain) from the sky, and causes it to penetrate the Earth, (and then makes it to spring up) as water-springs and afterward thereby produces crops of different colors, and afterward they wither and you see them turn yellow, then He makes them dry to become chaff. Verily, in this, is a Reminder for men of understanding. (39:21)

In other verses, the Qur'an points to angels as being Allah's messengers, who are sometimes being directed to undertake certain duties, to execute the orders of Allah. For example, angels execute the order of Allah on death:

> The angel of death, who is set over you, will take your souls, then you shall be brought to your Lord. (32:11)

In addition, it is mentioned that the angels called upon Mary with a message from Allah concerning her privileged status:

> And when the angels said: O Mary, surely Allah has chosen thee and purified thee and chosen thee above the women of the world. (3:42)

We also read in the Qur'an that angels were sent to fight side by side with the believers in support of their fight against the non-believers at the Battle of Badr:

> (Remember) when you sought help of your Lord and He answered you (saying): "I will help you with a thousand of the angels each behind the other (following one another) in succession". (8:9)

It is also understood from the Qur'an that angels are always being employed to do their duties in Heaven (21:103) and in Hell (74:31). It is known that angels were sent to Lūṭ's (Lot's) city to destroy it and on their way they passed by Ibrahim (Abraham) and told him of the good news that he would have a son (11:69–83). Therefore, we can confidently conclude that the angels are servers who carry out the orders of Allah; accordingly, they are a means through which Allah executes His orders. The nature of the angels and how they work remain mysteries, but certainly something to be resolved by theologians one day.

My point here is to conclude that the Qur'an does not object to the existence of secondary causes, only that such secondary causes are to be understood as the means of execution, no more; meaning that they cannot make decisions of their own or object to a divine order. Here it might be important to point to a mistake made by Harry Wolfson when he states that "in one instance an angel is said to have disobeyed God's command (2:28–32; 38:71–74)".[7] In fact, in Islamic tradition, it was not an angel who disobeyed the divine order, but the devil, who was a *jinn* (see Qur'an 18:50). Angels are obedient creatures that can by no means disobey Allah, since they were originally created to obey:

> Over which are (appointed) angels stern (and) severe, who disobey not, (from executing) the Commands they receive from Allah, but do that which they are commanded. (66:6)

Most Muslim theologians and thinkers followed the basic presentation of the Qur'an concerning the understanding of causality and asserted the belief that Allah is the only cause in the world and anything that happens in it. It is notable that scholars from both schools of *kalām*, the Ashʿaris and most of the Muʿtazila (excepting two characters), approved of this understanding and took it as part of the basic beliefs of Islam. Wolfson[8] has discussed this point in great detail and has resolved some questions of historical interest. The reason for such an insistence on this concept is the fact that the beliefs of Islam require one not to assign any partner to Allah in His creation and ruling of the world. This is the absolute essence of *tawḥīd*. If any kind of partner is assigned, whether implicit or explicit, then the person believing such is no longer a Muslim. This is why Muslims could not tolerate the assumption that nature can act on its own, or that causes can effect events intrinsically by their very nature. This leads to *shirk* (idolatry or polytheism), which would disqualify one from being a Muslim. This may explain why a great thinker like al-Ghazālī could not accept causal nature or deterministic causality, but insisted on the absolute freedom of the divine to effect whatever imaginable in the world, including turning a book into a "beardless slave boy".[9]

When taken as part of public belief, the denial of deterministic causality became a factor that hindered scientific thinking. Spread through the masses, such a belief was effectively denying the existence of a law that controls the working of the world's phenomena. This aborted rational thinking and encouraged laziness and a belief in the utopian state of the Islamic mind. Many of the verses in the Qur'an that encourage scientific thinking were ignored and it was thought that the universe ran miraculously. This was a very dangerous transformation in the Islamic media away from subjects that intelligent theologians should have taken into consideration. What made the situation worse were the restrictions that have been imposed on theological studies and religious innovations (*ijtihād*) since the fifteenth century. No innovative studies were allowed, except those that were in line with the traditional belief system. These restrictions, among other factors, arrested the Islamic mind and wasted Islamic genius. Indeed, this was one of the fundamental reasons for a decline in Islamic civilization. This period of decline in the Islamic world has extended from the fifteenth century onward.

Really?

Causality According to Traditional *Kalām*

I have discussed the question of causality according to traditional *kalām* in my book *Daqīq al-kalām*,[10] which was published in Arabic, and I have shown that the early *mutakallimūn* were seriously engaged with this problem, which was one of the main issues in their endeavor to explain and understand the world according to Islamic beliefs. In addition, in a joint article,[11] some colleagues and I examined the concept of causality in *kalām* and in modern physics, and we showed that there are some aspects where the *kalām* view shares the modern scientific view on this topic.

The *mutakallimūn* adopted the stipulations of the Qur'an directly with respect to their belief in divine omnipotence and omniscience. They accepted that Allah is the only actual cause effecting changes in the world; He is the Creator and the Generator of all events. They had differing opinions on the efficacy of the intrinsic nature of things and its role in effecting a cause. In principle, the *mutakallimūn* rejected the idea that the innate properties of an object constitute a nature that can act autonomously to effect change. Instead, they attributed such an act to Allah and, to be more precise, some of them assumed that Allah has by His own obligation accepted the role played out through the nature of things in effecting the cause. Most of these *mutakallimūn* who adopted such views belonged to the Baghdadi group, followers of Abū al-Qāsim al-Kaʿbī. Generally, all these views can be termed "occasionalistic". The philosophical basis for the views of Ashʿaris specifically were drawn in accordance with their proposal of "re-creation". This is one of the basic principles of *daqīq al-kalām* (see Chapter One in this volume), which they had drawn from their understanding of the most fundamental attribute of Allah, that of being the Creator.[12] Likewise, as Allah is active in the universe at all times, and He is described in the Qur'an as being the dominant actor who sustains the universe, the *mutakallimūn* interpreted this attribute of Allah, the Sustainer, through the principle of re-creation. Accordingly, all the implications of this assumption were used to explain the physical world.

The Ashʿaris and almost all of the Muʿtazila agree that Allah is the prime cause for whatever happens in the physical world. Both schools deny that the innate properties (*ṭabʿ*) of things are able to act autonomously to cause a change in the world. For this reason, they denied the effective nature of things. However, they had different views about the details of how the divine effects causes and disagreed over the question of human free will and responsibility for their own actions.

Some Muʿtazila formulated a sophisticated theory of causality that preserved the basic Islamic belief that Allah is omnipotent and can intervene to enforce His will. There are quite a number of works that are very useful in providing a picture of the Muʿtazili views on causality and causal relationships, for example, the book of Qāḍī ʿAbd al-Jabbār (d. 1024), *al-Muhīṭ bi al-taklīf*, and his celebrated encyclopedia *al-Mughnī*. In addition, we find al-Khayyāt's *al-Intisār* quite a useful source, in which we find many quotes from al-Naẓẓām. The work of Abū Rashīd al-Naysābūrī, *Masāʾil al-khilāf*, is a good source for understanding the details of the differences among the Muʿtazila themselves, whereas the book of Ibn Mattawayh, *al-Tathkīyya*, is more concerned with clarifying the concept of adherence (*iʿtimād)* and its implications with respect to causality when discussing the finer arguments in *kalām*.

Analyzing the legacy of the Muʿtazila on causality, I gather that they had identified four types of secondary causal relationships: adherence (*iʿtimād*), conjunction (*iqtirān*), generation (*tawlīd*), and custom (*ʿāda*). These four terms were used to describe different causal relationships in the world.[13] Qāḍī ʿAbd al-Jabbār, who was one of the famous Muʿtazili scholars, rejected nature and natural action and attributed action directly or indirectly to Allah. He accepted that an object may enjoy adherence (*iʿtimād*) only for certain actions, because of, say, its position, in which case it could respond to external effects. As such, this adherence may then play the role of an intermediate cause. ʿAbd al-Jabbār said:

> And when they [the philosophers] mean by "Nature" that which happens from the burning fire, it is what we consider to happen out of the adherences (iʿtimādāt) which generate dissociations. This is as if they call Nature what we call iʿtimād. Similar is what happens to weight on immersing a heavy [body] in water, generating a fall, and similar things. We attribute all these [events] to an actor who is free and able to prevent such generation and response.[14]

Qāḍī ʿAbd al-Jabbār goes further in his explanation to show that the effect of becoming drunk from drinking spirits can be interpreted as a custom (*ʿāda*), which is a concept that was also used by the Ashʿaris and which will be explained later in this section. Here, ʿAbd al-Jabbār is differentiating between two types of causal relationships: one in which Allah is directly interfering as the cause of the event, this is identified as *ʿāda*, and the other is caused by the indirect intervention of Allah, which is identified as both *iʿtimād* and *tawlīd*.

Some prominent Muʿtazili scholars were claimed to have affirmed causality in a way that may appear to agree with the philosophers' conception. Wolfson has spent a great deal of effort proving that Muʿammar and al-Naẓẓām affirmed causality.[15] I find that this claim is not accurate enough. Al-Naẓẓām, for example, although he agreed that objects have some kind of nature that qualifies them to interact with other objects in a systematic (lawful) way, subscribed to the idea that it is in the power of Allah to prevent a causally expected event. Effectively, here, we are dealing with the concept of causal indeterminism. Al-Khayyāṭ quotes al-Naẓẓām, saying that "if it was the quality of water to flow and if it was the property of a heavy stone to fall, then Allah is able to prevent it from doing so".[16] This means that al-Naẓẓām did not agree that action could be caused by an intrinsic nature and, by admitting that it is in the power of Allah to prevent the stone from falling, he was effectively denying causal determinism. On the other hand,

Muʿammar al-Sullamī, who is reported to have accepted the atomic theory of *kalām*, is understood to have suggested that nature follows causally deterministic laws without any intervention by Allah, except for the first creation. He believed that objects have intrinsic natures which have the power to generate accidents (*aʿrāḍ*) without divine intervention.[17] This opinion of Muʿammar was harshly criticized by al-Shahristānī,[18] ʿAbd al-Jabbār,[19] and Ibn Ḥazm.[20]

From the Ashʿari perspective, I present here the views of al-Bāqillānī, the famous Ashʿari theologian who discussed the concept of nature and causality in his work *Tamhīd al-awāʾil wa talkhīṣ al-dalāʾil*. In his discussion, al-Bāqillānī tried to refute three proposals which were known in philosophy:

(1) that the world was produced out of a certain nature that made it necessary to exist once it was available;

(2) that the world is made of the four basic elements: fire, air, earth, and water;

(3) that celestial objects have no effect on Earth, which means that astrology is null and void.

The essence of al-Bāqillānī's argument is based on the requirement that an action by nature would be possible only if nature has a will and ability to choose, for otherwise no action is expected from a blind nature. This argument is found with several Ashʿari theologians and was also adopted by some of the Muʿtazila, such as Qāḍī ʿAbd al-Jabbār mentioned above.

Ibn Ḥazm, the famous theologian, criticized the denial of nature, meaning the existence of the innate properties of things, by the *mutakallimūn* on a linguistic basis, but admitted no intrinsic role for such a nature. Ibn Ḥazm believed in re-creation of the whole world, that in every instance it is being renewed. He said: "and Allah creates in every instance all the world, restarting it without annihilating it".[21] In this statement he was expressing his belief in the doctrine of re-creation, despite having rejected the existence of the non-divisible part proposed by the *mutakallimūn*.

The Ashʿari Theory of Custom (ʿāda)

The Ashʿaris interpreted causal relations and causal determinism in a lenient way, saying that the laws of nature are the sorts of relations that we are accustomed to seeing manifested in natural phenomena. This means that the apparent causal relationships found between causes and their effects are not necessary and it is simply that the world is designed to behave that way. The Ashʿaris saw no meaning in causal relationships, as long as an active role was not assigned to the cause itself, and, since Allah is the direct cause for what happens, therefore causal relationships are no more than a formal expression of the actions behind the phenomena. They accepted that Allah has assigned this kind of enactment to rule the universe. Accordingly, miracles are thought to be an infringement of these customs. There seems to be no known mechanism for the custom to occur, or for how such a custom is brought into existence. This is one of the main arguments that make one wonder about the impact of such an apologetic approach to understanding the world. I would rather say that the concept of custom, although used by Ashʿaris and Muʿtazila, is not a profound concept that can explain anything at all. It would have been better to use the expression "Sunna of Allah" (meaning, the enactments of Allah) instead of *ʿāda*, since it is implied that the laws by which the universe is ruled are the laws of Allah.

It is known that Ibn Ḥazm, who was not Ashʿari, and Abū Rashīd, who was one of the Muʿtazila, criticized the Ashʿaris' use of custom to explain causality. However, it would not be of much value to discuss these criticisms here, but it would be useful to present al-Ghazālī's argument about causality.

Al-Ghazālī on Causality

In the seventeenth discussion of his book *Tahāfut al-falāsifa* (*The Incoherence of the Philosophers*), al-Ghazālī denied that causes are the direct reasons for the happening of events in nature. He denied that causal connections are necessary for events to happen:

> The connection between what is habitually believed to be a cause and what is habitually believed to be an effect is not necessary, according to us. But [with] any two things, where "this" is not "that" and "that" is not "this," and where neither the affirmation of the one entails the affirmation of the other nor the negation of the one entails negation of the other, it is not a necessity of the existence of the one that the other should exist, and it is not a necessity of the nonexistence of the one that the other should not exist—for example, the quenching of thirst and drinking, satiety and eating, burning and contact with fire, light and the appearance of the Sun, death and decapitation, healing and the drinking of medicine, the purging of the bowels and the using of a purgative, and so on to [include] all [that is] observable among connected things in medicine, astronomy, arts, and crafts.[22]

He argued that causal dependence is far from being trivial and that it would need rigorous proof that causes are the necessary and sufficient reasons behind their effects. Al-Ghazālī discussed the example of the burning of cotton and argued that the innate properties of objects cannot be the cause of events, since such properties (such as fire) are inanimate and have no "action":

> As for fire, which is inanimate, it has no action. For what proof is there that it is the agent? They have no proof other than observing the occurrence of the burning at the [juncture of] contact with the fire. Observation, however, [only] shows the occurrence [of burning] at [the time of the contact with the fire], but does not show the occurrence [of burning] by [the fire] and that there is no other cause for it.[23]

Clearly, al-Ghazālī did not consider observation as decisive evidence, since such evidence is no proof of an actual cause but is merely evidence of the conjunction between what is thought to be a cause and what is called an effect. In a similar mode to the arguments given above, concerning the necessary and sufficient conditions for the cause, al-Ghazālī insisted that we claim the sufficiency of evidence as:

> Whence can the opponent safeguard himself against there being among the principles of existence grounds and causes from which these [observable] events emanate when a contact between them takes place [admitting] that [these principles], however, are permanent, never ceasing to exist; that they are not moving bodies that would set; that were they either to cease to exist or to set, we would apprehend the dissociation [between the temporal events] and would understand that there is a cause beyond what we observe? This [conclusion] is inescapable in accordance with the reasoning based on [the philosophers' own] principle.[24]

In addition, al-Ghazālī brought into the analysis the question of the interaction between the object which is considered to be the cause and the affected object. Here he exposes the fact that, for some unknown reason, the cause might not act to produce the expected result. For example, "a person who covers himself with talc and sits in a fiery furnace is not affected by it".[25] Through this example, al-Ghazālī tried to rationalize the possibility of miracles. So, he says that, even if we admit:

> Fire is created in such a way that if two similar pieces of cotton come into contact with it, it would burn both, making no distinction between them if they are similar in all respects. With all this, however, we allow as possible that a prophet may be cast in the fire without being burned, either by changing the quality of the fire or by changing the quality of the prophet.[26]

However, in this respect, al-Ghazālī's argument seems to be weak. He could have used the stronger argument of the *mutakallimūn*, which is the argument

He misunderstood this! Ghazali is showing this through the lens of materialising rationalism.

of re-creation by which it would be legitimate to see a possibility, at least on the theoretical level, of miracles happening. Again, here he resorts to unknown conditions for the occurrence of an effect, by saying that:

> If, then, the principles of dispositions are beyond enumeration, the depth of their nature beyond our ken, there being no way for us to ascertain them, how can we know that it is impossible for a disposition to occur in some bodies that allows their transformation in phase of development in the shortest time so that they become prepared for receiving a form they were never prepared for receiving previously, and that this should not come about as a miracle? The denial of this is only due to our lack of capacity to understand, [our lack of] familiarity with exalted beings, and our unawareness of the secrets of God, praised be He, in creation and nature. Whoever studies inductively the wonders of the sciences will not deem remote from the power of God, in any manner whatsoever, what has been related of the miracles of the prophets.[27]

Al-Ghazālī followed the Ashʿaris in denying causal determinism and attributed the observed causal relations to a custom (*ʿāda*). I consider the above argument on causality to be incomplete. However, the most prominent points in al-Ghazālī's argument are that innate properties are inert and have no actual effect by themselves, and that causes are only known whenever all necessary and sufficient conditions in the relation between the cause and the effect are known. The most important element in his argument, which I call the "minimal principle on causality", is that causal determinism is denied. This basically stems from the Islamic refutation of determinism in nature and is one of the basic principles of Islamic *kalām*.

It is sometimes argued that al-Ghazālī had accepted the existence of intrinsic nature describing the innate properties of things. This is true, and indeed one can find him defining the lightness and weight by saying: "lightness is a natural force by which the body moves away from its position by nature, and the weight is a natural force by which the body moves to its position by nature".[28] He also defined moistness as "a responsive quality by which the body accepts bounding and forming easily without preserving it but retains its shape and status as per motion of its nature".[29] In these definitions, I can guess that al-Ghazālī was following Aristotle. However, in another place he said:

> The basic point regarding all of them is for you to know that nature is totally subject to God Most High: it does not act of itself but is used as an instrument by its Creator. The sun, moon, stars, and the elements are subject to God's command: none of them effects any act by and of itself.[30]

Clearly, then, there is no question about the intentions of al-Ghazālī on using the word "nature" and his understanding of its role in serving the cause.

To summarize the position of the *mutakallimūn* on causality and causal relations, I can identify the following:

(1) They denied the action of any sort by intrinsic nature of things (*tabᶜ*);

(2) They denied causal determinism, assuming that the regularity of causal relationships is only a sort of custom (*ᶜāda*);

(3) They acknowledged the law and order observed in the behavior of the world, but allowed for miracles to happen through the infringement of custom.

Besides the above short explanation, I should remark here that an excellent analysis of al-Ghazālī and his position on causality can be found in Frank Griffel's book *Al-Ghazālī's Philosophical Theology*.[31]

Ibn Rushd's Criticism of the Ashᶜaris' Custom

Ibn Rushd (Averroes) responded in refutation to al-Ghazālī's *Tahāfut al-falāsifa* with a work entitled *Tahāfut al-tahāfut* (*The Incoherence of the Incoherence*). In this text, Ibn Rushd remarked that "to deny the existence of efficient causes which are observable in sensible things is sophistry".[32] He added that the causal properties of an entity are an essential aspect of our understanding of that entity. If we try to strip things of their causal properties to reveal what "real" substance there may remain, we end up with nothing at all. This is because the ways in which we label objects are directly influenced by our grasp of their characteristics vis-à-vis other objects. One who casts doubt on causation damages the quest for knowledge, as causation is intimately connected with our knowledge of the world. To quote Ibn Rushd:

> Logic implies the existence of causes and effects, and knowledge of these effects can only be rendered perfect through knowledge of their causes. Denial of causation implies the denial of knowledge, and denial of knowledge implies that nothing in this world can really be known, and that what is supposed to be known is nothing but opinion, that neither proof nor definition exists, and that the essential attributes which compose definitions are void.[33]

Ibn Rushd further argued that, even though the ultimate cause of every phenomenon is God, He has established a secondary cause for every phenomenon. While God is capable of bringing about satiety without eating, quenching of thirst without drinking, and burning without contact with fire, He does not normally do so and when He does so, it becomes a miracle, which is among the "divine acts and beyond the reach of human intellect".[34]

In several pages, Harry Wolfson[35] presented what he called the "five arguments of Averroes" against the denial by the *mutakallimūn* of nature and causality. Although Wolfson was very keen on referring every sentence made by Ibn Rushd to Aristotle, I could not find a profound argument in his criticism of the denial of the causality that would answer the question of whether "nature" and "natural properties" have the qualities, power, or choice to effect a change autonomously. This is the basic question in respect of causality. To say that God works through secondary causes is not an issue of denying that the innate properties of a thing do effect action in the world to produce results that change the world. On the other hand, a close look through the arguments of *mutakallimūn* shows that they accepted the existence of law and order in the world. The real issue is whether actions in the world can be attributed to those entities (properties, nature) rather than Allah.

Laplace's Determinism

Pierre Simon Laplace (1749–1827) lived in the era of change and innovation. He actively contributed to the development of Newtonian mechanics and paved the way for further works that made the Newtonian picture of the world flourish. Laplace realized that this picture offered a deterministic universe by which we could predict every future once the initial conditions of the system were known:

> We ought to regard the present state of the universe as the effect of its antecedent state and as the cause of the state that is to follow. An intelligence knowing *all* the forces acting in nature at a given instant, as well as the momentary positions of *all* things in the universe, would be able to comprehend in one single formula the motions of the largest bodies as well as the lightest atoms in the world, provided that its intellect were sufficiently powerful to subject *all* data to analysis; to it nothing would be uncertain, the future as well as the past would be present to its eyes. The perfection that the human mind has been able to give to astronomy affords but a feeble outline of such intelligence.[36]

This is perhaps the best description in physics for the deterministic structure of classical mechanics. As one can easily notice, this determinism requires knowing all the forces acting in nature and the momentary positions of all things in the universe, something that cannot be guaranteed. However, taking the possibility of such knowledge as an assumption, one can see that Laplace admittedly pointed to a super being that is "sufficiently powerful to subject *all* data to analysis; to it nothing would be uncertain, the future as well as the past would be present to its eyes". This affirmation underlay a kind of metaphysical speculation over the presence of an omniscient entity. This does not mean, of course, that Laplace either believed in or denied the presence of such an entity, but we can be sure that he denied the intervention of any supernatural power in the ruling of the universe through his answer to Napoleon's remark about the Creator, by saying: "Je n'avais pas besoin de cette hypothèse-là" (I had no need of that hypothesis).[37]

Generally, all laws of physics are deterministic, since they are represented in the form of differential equations. However, this does not mean that these laws will describe with absolute accuracy the laws of nature. As I have shown in Chapter Two, the laws of nature stand for the natural phenomena, whereas the laws of physics are the invention of our minds, formulated within the capacity of our logic. Historically, there was a lot of confusion about this concept, which resulted in thinking that the deterministic laws of physics imply deterministic nature. This is not true; we have the Schrödinger equation, for example, which is deterministic, standing for the most basic equation in quantum mechanics, but we all know that the quantum nature is probabilistic.

Causality in Relativity Theory

In 1905, Albert Einstein proposed the theory of special relativity as a resolution for some fundamental problems in classical physics. He proposed that space and time form an integrated continuum and that the velocity of light in vacuum is a universal constant independent of the state of motion of the observer or the source. With this assumption, Einstein was able to resolve the problem of propagation of light in vacuum without the need to make use of the hypothetical medium called "ether". Space and time became one integrated entity, now called "spacetime". Consequently, a new concept of simultaneity was developed by which the minimum time needed to propagate an effect through space from one point to another is equal to the spatial separation between the two points divided by the velocity of light. No effect can be transmitted within any shorter duration of time, because the fastest signal that can carry the effect is the velocity of light in vacuum, which is about 300,000 km per second. If any effect is thought to be propagated faster than this, it would be considered non-causal. Therefore, a new understanding of physical causality was established by the theory of relativity and this was established by redefining simultaneity and simultaneous events as limited by the finite velocity of light.

Hermann Minkowski described the flat spacetime in terms of causal and non-causal regions. His famous spacetime diagrams considered to be causal those events that fall within only the so-called past and future light cones.

Any point (event) outside these light cones is deemed to be non-causal, since it would need a signal faster than light to deliver it (see Figure 3.1). As seen in the diagram, the whole of spacetime is composed of two main regions: two time-like regions, the past and the future, and two space-like regions. In the time-like regions, all events are connected by signals which travel with the speed of light or slower. This is why they are identified as being causal, where causes and effects obey a chronological order. The space-like regions in the diagram are non-physical, in which events need a signal faster than light to connect them, and thus they are non-causal as causes and effects do not necessarily respect chronological order. In fact, it could be imagined that, in a purely spacial world, time does not exist and we can identify the development of things only through progress over space. This might be an uneasy task to imagine, but perhaps could be comprehended by thinking of the spatial variations as replacing temporal variations. In a space-like world, you are always on the move, transferring from one position to another. With such a continuous change in space, you are proceeding through space and discovering its content.

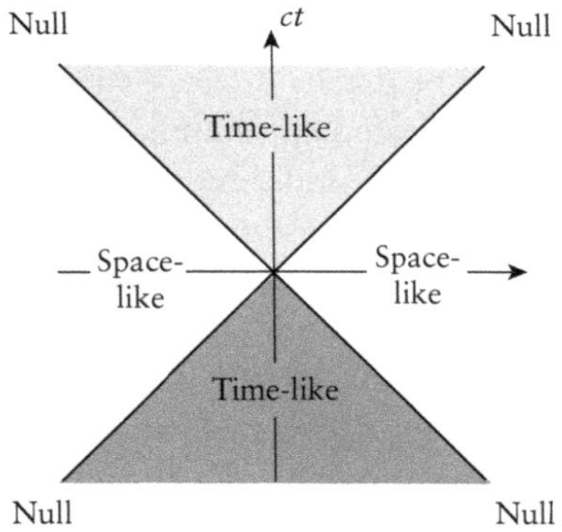

Figure 3.1 Minkowski's Spacetime

Relativity theory has been used in particle physics to explain some non-causal events. This was possible by assuming the existence of particles moving with velocities larger than the velocity of light in vacuum. Such a state is possible only if the particles have an imaginary rest mass. These particles are called tachyons. But the problem is that an imaginary mass cannot be physically measured. For this reason, we cannot consider tachyons to be real particles. However, if we get back to the fact that spacetime is composed of two parts, and assume that these parts are complementary to the extent that the physics of our time-like world might be affected by objects and events taking place in the space-like world, then we might be able to understand many aspects of our world more profoundly and coherently. This includes, for example, the phenomenon of quantum entanglement, which will be explained in the next section and which involves some sort of "spooky action at a distance", as it was described by Albert Einstein. There are many other phenomena that need to be understood through a wider scope in which spacetime is considered with its entire content, so that one might be allowed to see all possible effects and entities; for now, we might see only half the facts of our world. The two aspects of spacetime are complementary and what was considered a "spooky action at a distance" might be explainable within an analysis of the space-like regions of spacetime. There are several such enigmas in our contemporary physics.

The theory of general relativity provided us with a wide arena for considering the integration of space and time on a more profound level. In this theory, spacetime is preserved. Spatial variations are always complemented by temporal variations, and vice versa, so as to keep a specified spacetime interval constant. The physics of compact objects and black holes cannot be understood without the laws of general relativity. The understanding of these objects might be relevant for an appreciation of our future; a huge black hole might be the fate of our universe. Nevertheless, there are some mysteries concerning these objects. For example, we are not sure whether a real singularity exists at the center of black holes or not; it is also not clear what sort of world is to be found inside the event horizon and it is not yet clear if information about objects falling into a black hole is lost forever. The most recent declaration made by Stephen Hawking,[38] in which he says that the event horizon might not be a one-way path, is not much help, since he is still thinking of physics within our time-like universe. Again, in order to understand the full picture, I think it would be necessary to go beyond the time-like universe. This is inevitable, since the region inside the event horizon of a black hole is space-like.

Therefore, we can confidently affirm that the concept of causality in the theory of relativity is not completely clear despite the fact that this theory has established a very well-defined border between the causal and non-causal regions of spacetime.

Causality in Quantum Mechanics

Quantum mechanics is the mechanics of indeterminate nature. It is the best theory known to date that describes matter and energy and their mutual interactions. The quantum nature of matter and energy has exposed that our knowledge about the world is associated with an inherent uncertainty. This is described by the Heisenberg uncertainty principle, which states that the product of the inherent uncertainty in the position of a particle multiplied by the inherent uncertainty in its momentum must be greater than half the value of Planck's constant ($\hbar/2$). This means that we cannot determine the position of a particle and its speed with absolute certainty. This refutes Laplace's determinism; the momentary positions of particles and the forces acting in the universe can no longer be determined accurately enough to verify it. The universe is no longer deterministic; it would be impossible to designate the position of a particle and its momentum simultaneously with infinite accuracy. This discovery shook the very foundations of classical physics. In order to know the exact trajectory of a comet in the sky, for example, we need to know its position and speed at a given time, determined with high accuracy. Without highly accurate initial data, we are uncertain of the possibilities of its trajectory. The consequences of uncertainty become even worse with nonlinear systems where the inaccuracies in the initial conditions might cause highly unpredictable results.

Quantum mechanics has demonstrated that the occurrence of natural phenomena is probabilistic rather than deterministic. Here comes the quantum impact on causality. The availability of the physical conditions (the causes) which are required for the physical phenomena to occur does not guarantee that the phenomena will certainly occur. For example, the emission of nuclear radiation (radioactive decay) is a probabilistic event that cannot be guaranteed to occur once the required nucleus appears with the required properties.

The probabilistic behavior of quantum systems has led to the problem of measurement in quantum mechanics. This problem is reflected in the fact that a measurement outcome is not known for certain unless a measurement is made. This has led to some paradoxes, such as that of Schrödinger's cat[39] and the Einstein–Podolsky–Rosen (EPR) paradox.[40] In the case of the Schrödinger's cat paradox, the principles of quantum mechanics stipulate that the state of a cat inside a closed box together with a radioactive source and a poisoning device that can be initiated by the radioactive source is unknown. In fact, it is a mixed state: the cat might be alive *or* dead, with probabilities depending on whether the radioactive source emits radiation or not. This sort of indeterminism leaves uncertainty over the occurrence of the phenomena, despite all elements being present. From this point of view, causal events no longer have a deterministic nature. However, this does not mean that an event in a quantum world would be non-causal, certainly not, but it is the causal determinism that is abolished here and not causality itself. Nevertheless, there remains the question of whether causes themselves are the reasons by which the events might happen or not. As far as I can see, neither science nor philosophy has given a sensible resolution for this problem.

In the EPR paradox, we have another form of causality breakdown, which is spacetime causality. In this phenomenon, two quantum states separated from one another by a large distance are entangled in such a way that a change in the physical properties of one would cause an immediate change in the corresponding property of the other, irrespective of the distance between them. This is a sort of "spooky action at a distance", since we acknowledge as being causal those events for which effects occur after a time duration that has to be equal or larger than the distance between the cause and its effect, divided by the velocity of light. However, in light of the discussion in the previous section, we may speculate that such an event for which the time duration of transmission is less than the distance divided by the velocity of light occurs through some sort of a space-like channel. Meaning that the signal from one point to another is transmitted through a space-like channel.

The indeterminism of nature, as presented by quantum mechanics, is preserved throughout the time evolution of quantum systems, which is covered by the so-called unitary transformations. However, this indeterminism is not an artifact of the theory, but it is something that is inherent in natural phenomena. Some people do not realize that the laws of quantum mechanics are a kind of empirical law rather than being derivative of a theory. Most of the quantum descriptions of natural phenomena in the microscopic world are the products of observations, whereas theory merely explains what an experiment says. For example, the observation that particles behave like waves is an experimental fact that has been shown through particle diffraction experiments in laboratories. The fact that electrons tunnel through potential barriers that are higher than their energies is a fact that is observed in semiconductor devices, without which our mobile phones and computers would not work. Even the superposition of states and their non-locality, entanglement, and the most bizarre phenomena have all been observed in laboratories.[41] So, it is out of the question that indeterminism could be subjected to invalidation or replacement by a deterministic theory. The hidden variables theory, which was suggested by David Bohm,[42] is not a viable replacement for the indeterministic quantum description. The apparent statistical nature of quantum measurements has led some people to think that one day a new theory might be discovered by which the classical determinism and causality is restored, but such a dream seems to be far-fetched. In John Wheeler's words:

> [A]s the statistical character of quantum theory is so closely linked to the inexactness of all perceptions, one might be led to the presumption that behind the perceived statistical world there still hides a "real" world in which causality holds. But such speculations seem to us, to say it explicitly, fruitless and senseless . . . quantum mechanics establishes the final failure of causality.[43]

It has been already proved by John Bell that non-local hidden variable theories are out of the question and have no real validity.[44] On the other hand, no single prediction is known that can be counted to credit hidden variable theories over the standard formulation of quantum mechanics.

Some of the prominent physicists and philosophers believed in the determinism of the world. Despite being one of the founders of quantum physics, Paul Dirac expressed his belief in a deterministic universe:

> It seems clear that the present quantum mechanics is not in its final form. Some further changes will be needed, just about as drastic as the changes which one made in passing from Bohr's orbits to quantum mechanics. Someday a new relativistic quantum mechanics will be discovered in which we don't have these infinities occurring at all. It might very well be that the new quantum mechanics will have determinism in the way that Einstein wanted. This determinism will be introduced only at the expense of abandoning some other preconceptions which physicists now hold, and which it is not sensible to try to get at now. So under these conditions I think it is very likely, or at any rate quite possible, that in the long run Einstein will turn out to be correct, even though for the time being, physicists have to accept the Bohr probability interpretation—especially if they have examinations in front of them.[45]

It is known that Einstein rejected the quantum probabilistic interpretation with his famous sentence "God does not play dice", a statement which bears a metaphysical assessment. However, it seems to me that the rejection of the probabilistic interpretation of quantum mechanics is caused by an intuition that occupies the minds of physicists who are accustomed to dealing with the macroscopic world on this basis. Otherwise, no strong argument is found against the indeterminism of the quantum world other than the thought experiment suggested by Einstein, by which he expected quantum entanglement of particle pairs, which proved to be true.

In fact, the only major problem now with quantum mechanics is the problem of the interpretation of quantum measurements. The bizarre interpretation proposed by the Copenhagen school is not the end of the story; other interpretations might be found by which the state of indeterminism can be understood by terms better than that of a collapsing wave function, and so on. But, nevertheless, indeterminism remains the correct description of the world. This is the juncture where new developments might be initiated and this is where one can foresee new scope for the extension of the quantum domain.

To finish, I would like to point out that some people might think that the laws of quantum mechanics apply only to systems on microscopic scales. This is not true. Quantum mechanics applies to all systems, even to galaxies and clusters of galaxies, and perhaps to the whole universe, but the fact that the probabilities of macroscopic systems are very high reflects the apparent behavior of a deterministic system. On a highly detailed scale, all systems behave quantum mechanically, it is only that we cannot feel the quantum effects on a large scale.

About the First Cause

It is nearly an inherent assumption in theistic Western philosophy and theology that God is the cause of the universe, because everything is thought to have a cause for its existence. The argument is that, since there cannot be an infinite chain of causes, there must be a first cause for everything. This cause is God. In fact, this assertion implicitly limits the role of a creator to the first moment. And, once we discover that there is no first moment for creation, we would immediately ask whether there is a place for a creator, a question raised by Stephen Hawking on discovering that there is no $t=0$ moment[46] for a quantum universe:

> So long as the universe had a beginning, we would suppose it had a creator. But if the universe is completely self-contained, having no boundary or edge, it would have neither beginning nor end; it would simply be. What place, then, for a creator?[47]

As we can see, there is more than one flaw in this conclusion. The first is the assumption that the existence of God hinges on there being a beginning to the universe. The second is the assumption that the universe is self-contained. I am not sure what Hawking meant by the term "self-contained". Can any event be self-contained at all? What, then, is powering the natural phenomena? Is it the inanimate laws of physics? Certainly not, since these laws have been devised by us to give an approximate, though reasonably accurate, description of the laws of nature.

In another study, the American philosopher Adolf Grünbaum[48] considered the big bang to be a pseudo event since, at $t=0$, there was no time to define the start. Therefore, according to Grünbaum, "the Big Bang does not qualify as a physical point-event of the space-time to which one would assign three spatial coordinates, and one time coordinate".[49] Obviously this is true, but this does not mean that there was no big bang, nor does it imply that the big bang was an uncaused event. Indeed, in a physical world, causal priority entails temporal priority, but this applies to the big bang as well. If we have to admit that all the physics that we know ceased at the moment of creation, then this means that the big bang might have some non-physical (I would not say metaphysical) cause. We have to admit the existence of a supernatural agent. However, the physics that we presently know is not the only physics that humankind will ever discover.

There would be no need for a creator if the universe had popped up spontaneously out of the vacuum, without the intervention of any other physical agent, and there would be no need for a first cause from the point of view of quantum indeterminacy as it is understood now. But surely the universe as I know it from my own research and from the work of others, which are published in the most prestigious peer-reviewed journals, cannot have been created completely out of nothing? Although Paul Davies admits that a highly curved spacetime should exist in order for the vacuum to be converted into energy and matter, it is unfortunate that prominent physicists like Stephen Hawking and Lawrence Krauss, and even Paul Davies himself, seem to overlook this fact, or only touch on it without giving it the importance it deserves. Davies, for example, considers the question of whether spacetime warp is to be regarded as a cause for the particle's appearance as merely being a matter of semantics!

> The fact that the **probability** of particle creation depends on the strength of the spacewarp implies a sort of loose causation. The spacewarp makes the appearance of a particle **more likely**. Whether that is to be regarded as strictly the **cause** of the particle's appearance is a matter of semantics.[50]

By this same argument, can we consider the existence of a high-energy photon as a requirement for the creation of an electron–positron pair a matter of semantics? Surely not. I cannot see why spacetime warp cannot be considered a direct cause for the first creation of matter and energy except for the loose validity of cause in the quantum realm. Nevertheless, beyond spacetime, we do need another cause for creating the strong initial spacetime warp itself. Here we are left with the possibility of a metaphysical question.

Causality: A Modern Islamic Perspective

According to the Qur'an, the whole universe is the grand design of Allah, who has settled everything in the universe according to its vocation, acting under divine orders, and it follows well-defined comprehensible rules that we call the laws of nature. This is the basic belief of a Muslim.

We watch events of the world and comprehend them according to the general rule of cause and effect, and attribute those actions to the apparent agents involved in the events. From an atheistic point of view, the availability of the material ingredients and conditions of an event is sufficient for it to happen. From a theistic point of view, the availability of these requirements is not necessarily enough to produce the event, since those requirements do not have the quality of having to make a choice or intrinsic effect. So, the basic difference between the two viewpoints is that one considers the world to be deterministic and the other considers it to be indeterministic. However, by moving away from classical determinism, we discover that the making of an event or a process takes much more than the required conditions and goes beyond the power of the individual entities that contribute to the event. This motivates one to think of an agent that dominates the whole universe with a plan and to think of a power that makes it possible to have an ordered world ruled according to preset laws that we try to recognize by watching the world's phenomena. We also need to explain how the ingredients of the alleged cause are acting by their own nature in order justify the outcome.

The traditional Islamic understanding of causality has been under frequent attack by philosophers and some scientists. Muslims are repeatedly accused of denying causality and causal relationships. Some authors even think that the basic reason for the backwardness of the Muslim world is due to their denial of causality. In this context, al-Ghazālī usually takes most of the blame since he was the most prominent Muslim scholar to bluntly deny causality and causal relationships, or so it is said.[51] Although there is some error in such blame and accusation,[52] one has to admit that there were a number of occasions in Islamic cultural history when contributions from theologians and philosophers were misused and taken erroneously, resulting in a negative impact on the minds and attitudes of the Muslim masses. Among these, for example, were the concepts of *jihād* and martyrdom; such misconceptions have brought so much disaster to the Muslim world over the last two decades. Therefore, it is the duty of the intellectual to properly reset the course of thought to present religious and philosophical ideas in forms that take into consideration the level of the understanding of the masses as well as the social impact which is expected to result from exposure to such ideas. In this respect, I think it was right for Ibn Rushd to blame al-Ghazālī for spreading philosophical arguments among the masses who might not have appreciated the value of such arguments or their accurate meanings. However, al-Ghazālī had already felt the impact and blamed laymen for misusing the concepts and arguments of *kalām*, and had called to rein them in with his book *Iljām al-ʿawām ʿan ʿilm al-kalām* (*Bridling the Laymen of Kalām*).

Certainly, the concept of causality, and the understanding of causal relationships, is one of the vital subjects that need to be revised and set in a new Islamic perspective. In recent years, a few Muslim scholars have tried to reform the understanding of causality and causal relationships in modern Islamic thought. However, none of them are known to have proposed a self-contained theory of causality that could mitigate the conflict between contemporary scientific facts and the understanding of religious beliefs.

In an article entitled "Quantum Theory, Causality and Islamic Thought", Mehdi Golshani tried to present what he thought to be an Islamic outlook on causality.[53] Golshani discussed the concept in the context of modern physics, more specifically in the context of quantum theory. Admittedly, he agrees that quantum theory has abolished the classical causality and causal determinism, but he is inclined to support the effectiveness of classical causality in nature. For this reason, Golshani has tried to present an Islamic view for causality in an affirmative position, using a few verses of the Qur'an which refer to law and order in nature and to the possibility of some secondary causes, which some verses indirectly point to. Golshani also put forward some prospects for replacing quantum theory with an alternative which might restore causality and causal determinism. This kind of argument is no more than a hope, since every day experiments confirm the predictions of quantum mechanics. Here I cannot say more than what John Wheeler expressed in the sentences quoted above, which Golshani himself has quoted too. New sub-quantum physics might explain indeterminism, but it certainly will not be able to restore determinism, since indeterminism is a profound property of the phenomena in the quantum realm.

In an article entitled "Causality and Divine Action: The Islamic Perspective", Mohammad Hashim Kamali[54] presented a view that goes into the affirmation of causality. Again, this author stressed the claim, without providing enough evidence, that Muslims and the Islamic attitude would support the existence of causality and causal determinism in the world. Nevertheless, Kamali recognized that:

> The Qur'anic evidence on causality and its related themes, free will and determinism is not decisive on any particular position or view that have been taken over these issues. This also means that the Qur'anic evidence on causality is two sided and remains open to interpretation. Numerous passages are found in the Qur'an where God most High identifies Himself as the only cause and originator of things.[55]

In what follows, I will try to propose a reformulation of the concept of causality within the neo-*kalām* approach, which I have outlined in my book *Daqīq al-kalām*. In this approach, I take the truth of Islam as a prime input and consider the facts of science and its methodology for investigating the world as the proper approach to obtaining knowledge about it, which at the same time enable us to verify our understanding of religion. This new reformulation of the concept is deeply rooted in the original Islamic understanding of the world, but this time it is setting our knowledge about the world into its proper context that takes the facts of science into consideration, harmonizing the fundamentals of Islamic creed with the facts of science wherever possible.

Historically, the concept of causality was always under the influence of the basic doctrines of the Islamic belief, which assert that Allah is the only cause of everything that happens in the world. On the other hand, the causal relationship suffered from confusion and much distortion, being perplexed by the influence of observations which assert the action of the laws of nature, their reliability, and their efficiency. At the same time, we have to be faithful to what Allah has clearly stated of the truth of Islam in the Qur'an. It would not be a proper approach in the reconciliation of religion with science to readjust our interpretations of the holy text every now and then, whenever a new scientific discovery is found. This suggestion, which was originally proposed by Ibn Rushd, is certainly nugatory since we now know that some facts of science change continuously and follow the development of the means and techniques used, and, as I have said in the section concerning the phenomenology of a cause, the development of science brings in new concepts which suggest new causes for the phenomena. For example, Einstein's theory of gravity replaced the Newtonian concept of gravitational field with the concept of spacetime curvature. This produced a new vision for understanding the cause of gravity; instead of attributing the cause of gravity to the masses of interacting objects, general relativity attributes the gravitational interaction to the curvature of the spacetime in which those masses exist. On the other hand, the concept of action-at-a-distance, which implies infinite speed for the gravitational interaction, has been demolished by Einstein's relativity and gravitational effect is found to propagate through space at the speed of light. Many other examples can be found in chemistry, biology, and medicine. We all know how many times theories of diseases and diagnosis of causes in the medical profession change. This makes one conclude that our designation of causes is mostly tentative and will never be covered with absolute certainty. Therefore, the development of scientific theories sometimes produces drastic changes in identifying the causes and even the subsequent effects. However, causal relationships are an established fact of the world's phenomena; no phenomena in the world occur without a formal cause that is assigned in association with certain parameters that are related to the innate properties of space, time, and matter.

However, causes cannot be directly attributed to God since we do not know the divine mechanism through which His action is taken to establish the effect. We cannot consider the laws of physics that we identify through studying the phenomena of the world to represent the divine mechanism, since the laws of physics that we formulate are the products of our own minds and not the mind of God.

The assumption of re-creation can play a very fundamental role in formulating the concept of causality. Using this single assumption, it is possible to derive many consequences that agree with, though do not depend upon, the quantum description of the world by which causal determinism was abolished, and at the same time it provides a vivid understanding of the role of the divine in sustaining the world. The re-creation assumption implies some uncertainty exists in a simultaneous measurement of the so-called incompatible observables such as position and momentum, time and energy.[56] Re-creation is effected on the innate properties and consequently any change that takes place due to the interaction between two entities is to be viewed as a new state that resulted from re-creating the respective properties, which duly changes the character of those entities.

In order to see how re-creation can preserve causal relations, we should take into consideration two facts:

(1) change is a basic character of the world; taken on the microscopic scale, the persistence of change is clear and vivid; even the vacuum is known to be a boiling pot of virtual states. Taken on the macroscopic level, change is almost noticeable;

(2) the indeterminism of the world is clearly exhibited within the microscopic world, whereas events of the macroscopic world are *almost* deterministic.

The assumption of re-creation of the innate properties of entities of the world allows for an explanation of indeterministic causal relationships. These relationships are understood to be means through which events in nature are related to each other. Obviously, not all events are related to one another; nevertheless, the re-creation postulate allows for the whole world to be interconnected. This is also part of the holistic entanglement of the universe that is implied by some understandings of quantum physics.

The mechanism of re-creation goes as follows: primarily, we assume that the innate properties of entities of the world allow for interaction capabilities. Since no proof is available for deterministic causality, such interactions should be considered contingent but not necessary, always depending on the efficacy of the innate properties. Under re-creation, the efficacy of the innate properties changes (maybe chaotically). The frequency by which those changes occur is directly proportional to some physical parameters related to the system, namely the energy of the system. High-energy systems acquire high frequencies for re-creation and low-energy systems acquire low frequencies. Every time a physical (observable) property changes due to re-creation, the efficacy related to that property will change assuming a new value and, consequently, the causal event would assume new status. This would result in maintaining indeterministic causal relationships between parts of the world. Note that with this vision the explanation of causality is no longer following an apologetic approach; rather, it is a scientific vision that is based on mathematical description and proof.

The concept of causality being associated with Allah in Islamic *kalām* is fundamentally tied to the principle of re-creation, one of the general principles which were adopted for understanding the world. This principle (or assumption) reproduces the indeterministic character of the world. The affiliation of causality with the agent responsible for re-creation becomes a logical result. This association does not mean that the world is being run miraculously, since it was originally designed to respect certain laws that are firm and mutable. According to these laws, the occurrence of an event happens to be probabilistic and would result in one of the contingent states that are allowed by the law. Indeterminism, then, is reflected objectively in the choice of the outcome, which cannot be accounted for arbitrarily. The observed fact that the evolution of the world is progressing positively into higher and better states is an indication that the choices made from that probabilistic outcome are deliberate and purposeful.

However, causal relations are something else. Whereas the prime cause for every event is Allah, and whereas Allah is the initiator who fuels the laws of nature, causal relationships are deemed to be a part of the original creation by which events and processes are caused to happen through well-defined algorithms and laws exploiting the innate properties of things (which is to be understood as being purposely allocated by the Creator too), expressing the indeterministic causal relationships in the form of laws of nature. The innate properties are real and they exist, but are continuously re-created. Such a continuous re-creation allows for change to take place once any object acts on any other object, influencing it with its properties. That is to say that re-creation allows for the change in the innate properties to take place through the interaction between the objects. Otherwise, if innate properties were mutable, it would be hard to see how it could change at all, even with the influence of one object over the other. This is why Muslims did not accept the concept of causality proposed by philosophers and the role they gave to the nature of things in causal relationships.

Within this view, there is no denial of causality; causal relationships are respected, but at the same time the divine will and choice is fully respected too. This understanding of causality and causal relationships provides us with the necessary explanation that enables us to comprehend the role of the blind laws which are acting in the world efficiently, and it enables us to envisage how the world is progressing at an evolutionary level in the presence of those conflicting blind laws of nature.

CHAPTER FOUR

Divine Action from a Modern Islamic Perspective

The picture of the world given by science suggests revisions in many traditional religious views of the way in which a divine mind is likely to act.

Keith Ward, Pascal's Fire

DIVINE ACTION IS ONE of the hot topics in contemporary science and religion debates. It is thought that this question can be treated within the scientific context so as to establish a link between theology and science. In the era in which we are living, religious beliefs can only be accepted on a large scale when affirmed by rational evidence. Although it is a basic fact that divine action cannot be proved with direct scientific means, modern natural sciences point to a transcendental presence. Modern physics, especially quantum theory and relativity theory, has produced some challenging questions for understanding the mechanism by which the universe is running and, at the same time, has opened up wide prospects for our imagination. These prospects might help us to address those challenges. In one view, we can now question how a world of an indeterministic nature, as presented by quantum mechanics, can be driven spontaneously at all. Indeterminism becomes even more effective in a world of apparently conflicting laws. This suggests that there could be an agent beyond our natural laws that drives nature and coordinates the actions of the laws of nature. The necessity for this assumed agent to be external is based on the argument that, if it were to be an internal agent within the world, then it would have to be a part of it and abide by the same laws; consequently, this would mean that such an agent could not act to coordinate those laws to produce fruitful events. Since world events are indeterminate, coordinating the actions of the laws of nature might be done through selecting the outcome of the indeterministic events so as to produce fruitful results instead of nothing.

Many authors have discussed these challenges and speculated on the prospects revealed by modern theories in the physical sciences. In an excellent piece of academic work, Christoph Lameter presented the views of different authors and discussed them within his argument on the so-called "Quantum Divine Action" (QDA).[1] This argument uses the explanations of quantum systems to provide a mechanism for divine action. There are many views on this proposal, but the main question is centered around the problem of measurement in quantum mechanics. Some authors rejected the proposal of QDA, arguing that it could not be accepted unless a clear resolution to the problem of quantum measurement were to become available.[2] This argument is certainly valid, as the available interpretations of quantum measurement do not address the problem satisfactorily. This leaves the proposed models of QDA at odds with many scientific and theological concepts.

In this chapter, I am first going to address the question of quantum measurement and the interpretation of quantum mechanics. Then I will look for the possible prospects of QDA viewed according to my own interpretation, and I will address some of the criticisms made of QDA by other authors, viewed in the context of this new interpretation.

The basic idea proposed here for resolving the problem of quantum measurement is based on the notion of continual re-creation of the properties of the basic elements composing this world. This notion in its original form is borrowed from Islamic *kalām*. For this reason, one might consider that the views presented here express a rational Islamic understanding of nature. Primarily, the notion of re-creation can provide us with a much more realistic explanation of quantum phenomena that preserves the objectivity of those phenomena. It could be a viable and more acceptable alternative to explaining quantum mechanics, since it can reproduce all those phenomena that are observed naturally. It is as consistent as quantum mechanics itself. The only problem with this notion is that it needs a creator to perform the re-creation process. One might propose that it is the creator who is driving the re-creation process. This might be tolerable once we know that quantum field theory sees the notion of vacuum in a similar way, where a mysterious drive is thought to create and annihilate the virtual particle-antiparticle pairs which are assumed to constitute the physical vacuum. Therefore, this might not pose a dilemma after all, as long as the re-creation notion is taken as a postulate.

The Need for God

In August 1977, I met Stephen Hawking during a coffee break at the Eighth International Conference on General Relativity and Gravitation (GR8) held at Waterloo University (Ontario). I asked him: "Do you think, Professor Hawking, that behind all these equations and mathematical formulations we are presenting on the boards of this conference, there is something that cannot be described with mathematical equations?". Hawking paused for a while, turning his head slowly from left to right, and said: "If there is something I believe, it has to be logical". Then I asked: "But does your intuition tell you anything about this?". He replied: "I can only say that I am searching for the answer".

After getting the result showing that the universe could have existed for an endless imaginary time before its physical existence, Stephen Hawking exclaimed: "What place, then, for a creator?" In this, he is overlooking the fact that imaginary quantities are not directly measurable, despite their role in the mathematical formulations of physics.

Investigating the quantum state of the vacuum, Hawking found that the universe could have been created from nothing by gravity only; accordingly, he claimed in his book *The Grand Design* that there is no need for the creator. Similar claims were made by Lawrence Krauss in his book *A Universe from Nothing*.

Both Hawking and Krauss are ignoring the fact that, if the existence of the quantum vacuum is to be considered trivial, since "nothing" may not need a creator anyway, the existence of gravity, which is needed to produce real particles out of the quantum vacuum, is by no means trivial. The very strong gravity (or spacetime warp) needed to convert nothing into something must have existed in the background and the fluctuations of flat empty spacetime would not have been sufficient to convert the nothing into something.[3]

Confronted with facts that point toward a transcendental existence in a debate with John Polkinghorne, Steven Weinberg declared: "My argument can be falsified if a fiery sword will come from nowhere and hit me for my impiety".[4] In a public lecture, Lawrence Krauss agreed that he might believe in God if one evening he found the stars arranged in the sky to read "I am here". Clearly, both Weinberg and Krauss are implicitly assuming that the existence of God implies that the world is run miraculously, which is not the case.

When Richard Dawkins tried to expand on the hypothesis of a multiverse to refute the pre-setting of a finely tuned universe and put the question to Steven Weinberg during an interview, Weinberg remarked that one should not underestimate the fix that atheists are in, which is that consistent mathematical results cannot be guaranteed to describe a realistic state, since there are many consistent mathematical formulations that do not find real presence in nature.

This implies that both Professor Weinberg and Professor Krauss could see the necessity for God, but only if the universe were to run miraculously. A miraculously run universe is defined by the absence of any order or law that can explain it. Such a universe may not need God altogether, but a mere force to sustain the chaos. This is what one would usually expect out from blind nature.

The problem with the colleagues from the physics community who do not see the need for God is that they would like to see God emerging from one of their equations explaining, say, the masses of elementary particles. Only then would they believe in God. This is perhaps why they call the Higgs boson the "God particle".

The counterargument to a chaotic running of the universe would be to say that an ordered universe, ruled by well-defined laws that do not necessarily lead to fully deterministic results, is what necessitates the existence of God. This is because we need to have an operator for the laws of nature and we need an algorithm by which the actions of these laws are coordinated in order to achieve fruitful results. Otherwise, the actions of the laws of nature cannot be explained. An operator of these laws cannot be something that belongs to the same set, for such an operator would have to abide by the same laws and thus could not be a ruler over them. This understanding of the divine agent rules out the notion of the "God of the gaps", which is a famous accusation against an apologetic argument for the role of divine action in nature.

Let us look at some vital arguments inspired by modern physics that could pose some basic problems for comprehending nature on the theoretical level. Besides the classical problem over the creation of the world, there are a number of problems in front of us that are needed in the investigation. These are:

(1) *The Problem of the Operation.* Classically, it was taken for granted that physical laws, being a set of expressions that describe the relationships between variables of certain phenomena, could operate on their own without the need for an operator. A close look at these laws through quantum theory shows that these laws are expressed as mathematical operators acting on the state of the system that produces the physical observable (called the "eigenvalue"). As such, the physical observable is produced by the action of an operator on the state of the system. Mathematically, the operator is a symbol representing some kind of operation, say an infinitesimal translation. The question concerns

how to realize such an operator in the activity of the real world, and who the real world is being operated by.

(2) *The Problem of Coordination.* Physical laws may effectively be contradictory. This is why pure chance is blind. Without coordinating the actions of these laws (operations), the world would be in a mess. Such coordination is made through the inherent condition of validity of the physical law. Here some determinism may seem to be at work, but this is not the case, since the operation of the physical law within the given condition itself is undetermined.

(3) *The Problem of Belongingness.* A global operator/coordinator cannot be part of the world or belong to the same set of physical laws acting within the world; otherwise, such an operator/coordinator would have to abide by the same status of any other law belonging to the set.

(4) *The Problem of Interaction.* Were the global operator/coordinator to be external to the set of physical laws that are at work in the world, the question arises over its form and its means of interaction with the world.

A set of several coordinated operations constitute what I would call an algorithm. This is a set of steps that are needed to carry out a given process and establish the causal joint between the individual steps of that process. The algorithm is predestined, but the outcome may not be so. The interplay between contingency and necessity is what would lead to fruitfulness. Contingency is the primary setup for every item in nature; it is the possibilities, the innate properties acquired by the object, or, as we call it in reductionist terminology, the "number of the degrees of freedom", and necessity is what would make the choice. That is why necessity implies destiny.

A choice made would mean that a *will* would have to be at work. The world does not have a will of its own, but does have freedom. This freedom is expressed through the contingency of events and algorithms. That is why we are in need of a global operator/coordinator that will take care of all operations, which must, as I have pointed out, be inherently predestined.

Divine Action in the Traditional Islamic Worldview

Divine action and causality in traditional Islamic thought were interlocked. Causality was always realized with reference to God the Creator, the Omniscient and Omnipotent. The traditional theological view adopted by the juristic schools of *fiqh* asserts that God alone is the real cause of everything and His Will is not subjected to causality or a purpose, because the Will of God is independent of a cause-and-effect relationship.[5] At the philosophical level, this question was dealt with by two groups of Muslim thinkers: the *mutakallimūn*, who represented scholastic theology, and the philosophers, who tried to reconcile Greek philosophical views with the Islamic creed. Both the schools of jurists (*fiqh*) and of *kalām* agreed on the assessment that God is the Creator and Sustainer of the world.[6] However, they disagreed on how such sustainment is carried out.

It is not my intention to review the historical development of the problem of divine action in Islamic thought or Islamic *kalām* in this chapter; rather, my target here is to develop a basis for a modern Islamic worldview of divine action by utilizing the doctrines that were adopted by the *mutakallimūn*, especially the notion of re-creation, in an endeavor to restructure the problem and to set it on a basis that conforms with the stipulations of the Qur'an and the original foundation of the Islamic creed. Those wanting to study the subject of causality and divine action in its historical context may consult the available standard references.[7] However, in order to present the traditional Islamic view from its original sources, we need to consult the prime source: the Qur'an. We will not deal with any other source, since these would take us beyond the aims of this chapter.

Divine Action in the Qur'an

The *fuqahā'* (the practitioners of Islamic jurisprudence, *fiqh*) did not provide a detailed mechanism for the relationship between God and the world, nor how He would sustain creation, except by claiming that it is the Will of God which is the basic requirement for any event to happen; the rest is just "Say 'be' and it is" (*kun fa yakūn*). This understanding is obtained from some verses of the Qur'an, for example:

> The Originator of the heavens and the Earth. When He decrees a matter, He only says to it: "Be!" – and it is. (2:117)

In respect of the birth of Jesus Christ, the Qur'an describes this event as being done through the order of God in a direct intervention beyond the known laws of nature. This is a sheer miraculous event and an example of how God can convey His word into a direct action:

> She said (Mary): "O my Lord! How shall I have a son when no man has touched me". He said: "So (it will be) for God creates what He wills. When He has decreed something, He says to it only: 'Be!' and it is". (3:47)

In another verse, the Qur'an stresses the ability of God to intervene and achieve His will:

> Verily! Our Word unto a thing when We intend it, is only that We say unto it: "Be!" and it is. (16:40)

Again, here it is the word which has been effected into action.

At face value, the Qur'an seems to attribute every action in nature to God, including those acts which are thought to be attributed to man. We read the following verses. On reminding the Sons of Israel of His care and providence, God tells them:

> We shaded you with clouds and sent down on you Al-Manna. (2:57)

As for natural processes such as the growth of plants, the Qur'an states:

> Verily! It is God Who causes the seed-grain and the fruit-stone (like date-stone, etc.) to split and sprout. He brings forth the living from the dead, and it is He Who brings forth the dead from the living. (6:95)

And:

> It is He Who sends down water (rain) from the sky, and with it We bring forth vegetation of all kinds, and out of it We bring forth green stalks, from which We bring forth thick clustered grain. (6:99)

Perhaps the most prominent place in the Qur'an where we see God telling us frankly of His action in the world is Sūrat al-Wāqiʿa, where we read the following verses:

> Tell Me! The seed that you sow in the ground. Is it you that make it grow, or are We the Grower? (56:63–4)
>
> Tell Me! The water that you drink. Is it you who cause it from the rainclouds to come down, or are We the Cause of it to come down? (56:68–9)
>
> Tell Me! The fire which you kindle, Is it you who made the tree thereof to grow, or are We the Grower? (56:71–2)

Looking through the above verses of the Qur'an, one may get the impression that events in the world are taking place as a result of the direct intervention of God in the world, as He is the only cause of events. The only thing we have to note is the sequence Divine Will → Order → Divine Word. This understanding of the jurists (*fuqahāʾ*) allows for miracles to happen at any time and, according to this, it would seem that the whole world is run miraculously. Sufis have philosophized the divine order (Be) and have given it a transcendental, spiritual meaning.[8]

However, looking through other verses of the Qur'an, one can easily notice that this is not necessarily the case. In other verses, the Qur'an attributes events to secondary causes. For example, elaborating on the second verse above (3:47) concerning how the will of God affected Mary, the Qur'an states that:

> She placed a screen (to screen herself) from them; then We sent her our angel, and he appeared before her as a man in all respects. She said: "I seek refuge from thee to (Allah) Most Gracious: (come not near) if thou dost fear Allah". He said: "Nay, I am only a messenger from thy Lord, (to announce) to thee the gift of a holy son". She said: "How shall I have a son, seeing that no man has touched me, and I am not unchaste?" He said: "So (it will be), your Lord said: 'That is easy for Me (Allah): And (We wish) to appoint him as a sign to mankind and a mercy from Us (Allah), and it is a matter (already) decreed, by Allah'". (19:17–21)

Here we see that God delegated to the Angel Gabriel, presented in the form of a man, of whose intentions Mary was suspicious, but soon she knew that it was the word of God delivered to her through a messenger. This is even better elaborated by this verse:

> Christ Jesus the son of Mary was (no more than) a messenger of Allah, and His Word, which He bestowed on Mary, and a spirit proceeding from Him: so believe in Allah and His messengers. (4:171)

The example given above clearly indicates that God puts His orders into effect in the world by delegating through secondary means. But, why should God need to delegate something to achieve His order? This question has been thoroughly discussed in Islamic theology, but no fully satisfactory explanation has been given; perhaps the best account came from al-Ghazālī in the third discussion of *Tahāfut al-falāsifa* (*The Incoherence of the Philosophers*).[9] The Qur'an explicitly mentions that God is the Sustainer of the world:

> Allah! La ilaha illa Huwa (none has the right to be worshipped but He), the Ever Living, the One Who sustains and protects all that exists. (2:255)

A similar phrase is repeated in suras 3:2 and 20:111. This is the pivotal point in describing divine action according to the Islamic creed, and I will come back to it when presenting the views of *kalām*. However, the Qur'an does not elaborate on any mechanism for the divine action or the teachings of the Prophet Muhammad (peace be upon him). This matter is left for man to contemplate and deduce. The Qur'an instead suggests to mankind that they should investigate how creation came about:

> Say: "Travel through the earth and see how Allah did originate creation; so will Allah produce a later creation: for Allah has power over all things". (29:20)

In this verse, God is urging mankind to investigate how the first creation took place. The aim is to achieve an understanding of divine action in the creation and a realization of how He is capable of producing the next creation, which is the resurrection of people. But, how can one understand divine action through investigating the world, since no logical sequence is available to understand divine will and the mechanism of His order? Can one pick out any hint from the Qur'an on this matter? In fact, yes, the Qur'an has elaborated on this matter by more explicitly stating that God created the Earth and the firmament "with truth". In several verses, we read this affirmation:

> Do you not see that Allah has created the heavens and the earth with truth? If He will, He can remove you and bring (in your place) a new creation! (14:19)

And:

> He has created the heavens and the earth with truth. High be He Exalted above all they associate as partners with Him. (16:03)

Also we read:

> He has created the heavens and the earth with truth. He makes the night to go in the day and makes the day to go in the night. And He has subjected the sun and the moon. Each running (on a fixed course) for an appointed term. Verily, He is the All-Mighty, the Oft-Forgiving. (39:5)

In these verses, the word *ḥaqq* might be understood to mean "truth", "justice", or "reason", but a more suitable meaning here might be that God created things to follow certain laws. Truth and justice follow a reasonable course and justifications that are accepted on a rational basis, though not necessarily independent of God or the belief in God. It is noticeable that the emphasis on the concept that God has made His creation with *ḥaq* always comes in the context of procedural events that follow what we know as the laws of nature, such as the motion of celestial bodies. This is a further indication of the intention to realize the logical (procedural) basis of the creation.

Clearly, a proper understanding of these and similar verses enlightens our comprehension of the act of creation as being brought about according to certain pre-set laws of conformity. These are the laws of nature but not necessarily the laws of physics.[10] The laws of nature as a prescribed set of laws that are devised by God are fundamental to Islamic belief.

This makes one conclude that God is the prime cause of everything. This is a very basic rule in Islamic theology. This understanding, which we obtain directly from verses of the Qur'an, is one of the most controversial topics among Muslim theologians, *mutakallimūn*, and philosophers. In this, we encounter the questions of causality and human free will. I will concentrate on the nature of divine action in a scientific context, specifically through the possibilities offered by quantum mechanics.

Divine Action in Kalām

The *mutakallimūn* considered divine action within a comprehensive theory of nature and established their views in a series of dialogues and debates that formed a whole structure of thoughts called *ʿilm al-kalām* (the science of *kalām*).[11] The *mutakallimūn* based their understanding of divine action on the power of God to do everything and explained the action of God in nature and His sustainment of the universe through the process of continued re-creation. This is the pivot on which the understanding of divine action in Islamic *kalām* rests. This was asserted by both the Muʿtazila and the Ashʿaris in several of the original *kalām* texts.[12] However, both schools of *kalām* differed on the existence of innate properties associated with matter and the existence of a certain set of rules by which the divine abides. This exposed their controversy over the laws of nature and consequently their positions on causality and human free will.

As mentioned in the introduction to this book, the *mutakallimūn* devised a theory of creation by which all the world's entities were atomized (see also Chapter One). The Islamic atom is composed of a unique entity called the *jawhar* (substance or substrate), and the *ʿaraḍ*. Unlike the Greek atomization, the concept of *jawhar* alone stands for an abstract entity, not a material substance. The *jawhar* cannot exist alone, but has to be complemented by the *ʿaraḍ*; only then it can be realized ontologically. The *aʿrāḍ* (plural of *ʿaraḍ*) are the possible attributes which stand for the innate properties that the *jawhar* may acquire. It is the composition of both the *jawhar* and its *ʿaraḍ* that constitute the smallest part of matter. This Islamic atomism has been discussed at length by prominent Western scholars,[13] and I do not need to go into such detail here. The important thesis of the *mutakallimūn* was their suggestion that any *ʿaraḍ* does not endure two instants of time. Al-Ashʿarī (d. 950), who was the leader of the Ashʿari school of *kalām*, said that "some [of the *mutakallimūn*] say that all *aʿrāḍ* do not endure for two instances".[14] Al-Bāqillānī defined *aʿrāḍ* as "those [attributes] that do not endure and which are in association with the *jawāhir* [plural of *jawhar*] and bodies, but diminish in the next instance of existence".[15] The smallest non-divisible unit of time in the scheme of *kalām* atomism is called an *āna*. Consequently, and since *jawāhir* cannot exist without being associated with *aʿrāḍ*, the renewal of *aʿrāḍ* inevitably leads to a continued re-creation of things. This re-creation, which is assumed to take place by God, ensures the sustainment of the world. This concept was well established among the followers of both schools of *kalām*.[16]

For reasons associated with the way the *mutakallimūn* advanced their approaches to formulate Islamic scholastic theology, *kalām* was banned, as it was evidently not well received by the public, and was accused of being a route to heresy. Whereas the schools of *fiqh* have continued to have followers to this day, the schools of *kalām* lost support and became nearly extinct. This is why *kalām* did not continue to deliver its message coherently and it became especially muddled with philosophical concepts and methodologies from the eleventh century.

My claim here is that Islamic *kalām* can provide the basis for a better understanding of divine action taken not in its theological context, but through a more down-to-earth understanding within the available scientific views. As was concluded by Lameter,[17] the main problem that hinders the development of a model for, or sound understanding of, QDA is the fact that quantum mechanics suffers from a problem of interpretation, mainly a measurement problem. Therefore, in order to be able to develop an understanding of divine action in the context of quantum physics, we need to resolve the interpretation problem in quantum physics. I will try to propose a resolution to this problem first and then use this for a realization of divine action.

Divine Action in Modern Perspectives

The worldview which is based on classical mechanics implies a causal block universe. That worldview has been challenged by the development of quantum mechanics.[18] One of the founders of quantum mechanics, Werner Heisenberg, considered the classical concept of causality to be questionable in the light of the uncertainty principle, one of the fundamental principles of quantum mechanics. Therefore, a theory of divine action compatible with contemporary physics is a fundamental requirement for a credible consideration of how God could act in the framework of our contemporary scientific worldview. That is, at the least, what we would rationally adopt.

In modern Western thought, reductionists view the world as a collection of mechanisms described by scientific laws.[19] However, it should be understood that what is meant by scientific laws are those formal descriptions that are devised by the human mind to describe natural phenomena, which do not necessarily correspond to the actual laws governing the natural phenomena (see Chapter Two). Both conservative and liberal theologians have struggled and continue to struggle with this concept. Liberal theologians believe that God does not violate natural processes, as He is actually acting through such processes. On the other hand, conservative theologians assert that religious language is factual, which means that God can intervene and violate the laws that govern the universe.[20]

The Problem of Measurement in Quantum Mechanics

The discovery of the wave properties of particles and the particle properties of waves, through several famous experiments that were carried out during the last decade of the nineteenth century and the first few decades of the twentieth century, has established the need for a new description of the entities of the microscopic world. At the beginning of the twentieth century, many basic problems in atomic physics were addressed, leading to the establishment of quantum mechanics as a paradigm to explain the observed properties of the atomic realm. The most fundamental notions of early quantum mechanics were based on the assumption that particles behave like waves. The main difficulty in realizing a wave-like description for the particles lay in the fact that particles are localized, whereas waves are extended. This problem was overcome by Louis de Broglie's suggestion that a particle can be represented as a plane-wave, which has a wavelength inversely proportional to its momentum. This notion was soon utilized to obtain a description of particles in terms of a de Broglie wave-packet, with the wavelength being that of a group of superimposed waves representing the particle. This description opened the way to reformulate classic localized (point) particle mechanics in terms of wave mechanics. Accordingly, a wave equation was formulated by Erwin Schrödinger in 1926 to describe the time development of atomic particles under the influence of a field of force.[21] The need to consider particles moving with high speed required introducing the special relativistic formulation of the problem and led to the well-known Dirac equation of the electron, which was discovered a few years later.[22]

In essence, the wave-like description of atomic particles benefited from all the properties of wave phenomena, and it was soon realized that the microscopic world (the world of atoms and molecules) enjoys some basic properties that make it different from the macroscopic world (the sensible world of everyday life). Particles, such as atoms and electrons, are now being identified as "quantum states" symbolized by an abstract entity called the "wave function": $\psi(x, y, z, t)$. This is a mathematical expression summarizing the physical content of a physical system in terms of spacetime coordinates and other parameters of the system such as energy and momentum. The mathematical nature of the wave function had already been recognized in the early days of the formulation of the Schrödinger equation, and it was realized that the wave function has no direct physical meaning in itself. Richard Feynman pointed out that the wave function describes some possible states of quantum systems and, therefore, should not be understood as a regular description of classic realities. It is true that the wave function develops in a deterministic fashion, but the wave function does not describe a scenario in the terms of a classic physical concept.[23] Max Born[24] identified $|\psi^*(x)\psi(x)| = |\psi(x)|^2$ as representing the probability density[25] of finding a particle in a position x.

The wave-mechanical description of particles set out by Schrödinger was best realized by saying that a particle is a wave-packet that is composed by superposing many basic (plane) waves. This allows the wave function to represent many different states of a system, as many states as are available.

Shortly before Schrödinger had formulated his wave equation, during the early summer of 1925, Werner Heisenberg[26] conceived the idea of representing physical quantities with sets of complex numbers. This was soon elaborated on by Born, Jordan, and Heisenberg[27] himself into what has become known as "matrix mechanics", the earliest consistent theory of quantum phenomena.

Both views, the wave mechanics of Schrödinger and the matrix mechanics of Heisenberg, are said to be equivalent despite differences in some basic concepts and in formulation. A few years later, John von Neumann[28] showed that quantum mechanics can be formulated as a calculus of Hermitian operators in Hilbert space. The physical system was represented by a complex vector in an infinite-dimensional space covered by basis vectors. According to the formalism set by von Neumann, a physical system is completely described by a state function symbolized by $|\psi>$, which is to be taken as a vector in an infinite-dimensional Hilbert space. A measurement of any observable a belonging to the system is the result of the action of a mathematical operator $\hat{A}$ corresponding to that observable on the state vector representing the system. The result of such an operation is to produce a value (a number called the "eigenvalue") that stands for the observable at the moment of measurement. By this new comprehension, natural objects objectively identified as ontologically existing things became known as new epistemological entities that are represented by abstract mathematical forms. It should be emphasized that this is a very important turning point in the history of scientific thought. The fact that $|\psi>$, which represents the physical system, is a mathematical expression that has no direct physical meaning, as noted earlier, and the fact that physical observables are obtained as a result of operating by certain mathematical operators on $|\psi>$ is surely a clear indication of the fundamental turn that was implied by quantum mechanics.

According to the basic principles of quantum mechanics, any physical quantity a (the observable) can have many possible values; what we measure at any moment could be one of these possible values. However, theoretically we can obtain the average of all those values and this is what we theoretically expect to get out of the measurement. This is then called the "expectation value" of the physical quantity.

The Heisenberg Uncertainty Principle

Much to the curiosity of physicists, some aspects of the wave-like description of particles led to some uncertainties in simultaneously measuring pairs of observables such as position and momentum, energy and time, and others. This was expressed by the Heisenberg uncertainty principle, which, in one of its forms, states that the position of a particle and its momentum can never be determined simultaneously with infinite accuracy, which means 100 percent certainty. This principle contributed to the indeterminacy of the quantum world and has attracted much attention and interest from physicists. The Heisenberg uncertainty principle is deeply rooted in the wave-mechanical description of particles; once we represent a particle as a wave, it is inevitable that we should allow for some kind of distribution of position and momentum. The price we pay for the wave description of a particle is non-locality.

The Fourier analysis of such a description shows that the wave description requires some inevitable non-locality of position, which leads to the inherent uncertainty in these variables. A similar situation applies to the measurement of energy, where it would lead to mutual uncertainty in time intervals and the corresponding energies. It is important to note that indeterminacy of position and momentum caused a tremendous shock to physicists, who used to deal with nature on a classical basis. The classical equation of the motion of a particle requires knowing both its initial position and its initial momentum. Having been denied such knowledge, physicists were puzzled by the solutions to the equation of motion. This caused the downfall of classical mechanics, at least in the microscopic world. The glory of classical mechanics, especially in its most sophisticated form devised mainly by Lagrange and Hamilton, still provokes some physicists to reestablish the reign of classical physics.

One major problem with the new mechanics of indeterminate nature has been to understand the meaning of the wave function. As this function is representing the physical system, which is now thought to be in different possible states, the question has arisen over why instruments in a laboratory always show a definite value and not a set of possibilities, as suggested by the wave function. This is the essence of the problem with quantum measurement.

One other facet of the problem with quantum measurement is the behavior of particles passing through two adjacent slits, the so-called "double slit experiment", whereby we experience the wave-like behavior of a particle causing the appearance of interference in dark and bright fringes. In the early days, this behavior was accepted as being part of the bizarre properties of the microscopic ensemble of particles. But, as experimental technologies advanced further, it became possible to perform the double slit experiment using one single quantum state, say, a photon. Alain Aspect and his collaborators have done several experiments which have shown that projecting single photons onto a double slit device produces the same interference pattern as that produced by a beam of light.[29] The results of such experiments imply that the single photon passes through the two slits simultaneously. On the other hand, if a detector is placed along the path of the photon, then it becomes quite clear that the photon is passing through one of the slits, and not both slits simultaneously. This is something that cannot be accepted logically if the photon is to make any ontological existence, or perhaps a new interpretation in quantum states is needed.

Discreteness and Continuity

The quantum indeterminacy problem is deeply rooted in the long-lasting question of discreteness and continuity. This is an issue which has been under persistent debate since the early days of the Greeks, throughout the Islamic period which witnessed fierce debates between the philosophers and the *mutakallimūn*,[30] up until today.

The problem of quantum measurement today, more than three-quarters of a century after the advent of the theory, is still an issue of unprecedented dissension. In fact, it is by far the most controversial problem in current research into the foundations of physics, dividing the communities of physicists and philosophers of science into numerous opposing schools of thought.

The main issues in this division seem to be centered around two things: quantum jumps and measurement indeterminacy. A quantum jump is an indication of the discrete nature of the atomic world. If this is to be a fundamental characteristic of the microscopic world, then continuity of the macroscopic world would seem to be only fictitious. Schrödinger reportedly once said "if all this damned quantum jumping were really to stay I shall be sorry I ever got involved with quantum theory".[31] The Schrödinger equation is a deterministic equation that adopts the principle of continuity and the concept of infinite divisibility. However, it is a differential equation which has helped provide an approximate picture of the quantum world. The discrete features of the quantum world are now being presented as products of the wave-mechanical nature that allows for the superposition of waves producing interference pattern. Consequently, one can avoid thinking of the abrupt quantum jumps in favor of some more lenient thinking in terms of the probability distribution, such that some kind of continuity between discrete states is maintained. Therefore, instead of having the macroscopic continuity becoming an apparent feature that hides the underlying discreteness, we now have discreteness appearing as an emergent product of some phenomena of the continuum. Beyond this, it is important to note that precise analysis of the quantum phenomena of two-slit interference shows a fundamental characteristic departure from the standard wave-interference phenomena.[32] In these experiments, a particle remains non-divisible. However, such a departure awaits an explanation which can precisely identify in both phenomena those features that make them different.

The Applicability of Quantum Mechanics

In this context appears the question of whether quantum mechanics is a theory that can be applied to a single particle or whether it is a theory of ensembles. Physicists have different opinions on this issue. Some of them, such as Bohr and Heisenberg, believe that quantum mechanics is suitable for describing single particles as well as many-particle systems. This is generally the view held by the Copenhagen school. Others physicists, such as Einstein and Born, believe that quantum mechanics is only applicable to ensembles rather than to individual particles, and accordingly it can only be interpreted statistically. Others, such as Everett and Wheeler, believe that quantum mechanics is essentially an interaction theory that can be realized only through the interaction between the observer and the system. In one way or another, this will allow for a subjective interference in determining quantum states. In fact, the basic formulation of the equation of motion in quantum mechanics, Schrödinger's equation, suggests that it can be applied to single particles; on the other hand, having the values of observables coming out only as an average may suggest that we are talking about an ensemble of particles in which each particle holds a different value for that observable. The general behavior of the system of these particles then is represented by the behavior of the average. However, this restriction becomes unnecessary if we interpret the existence of an average as coming as a result of many measurements being performed on the same particle. In this case, the implicit fact will be that the value of the observable assigned to the system (the single particle in this case) is not fixed but is ever changing. But then, the question arises of whether this change in the value of the observable is due to the changing state of the system or to the process of the measurement itself. Here we find the different pictures of quantum mechanics. We have the Schrödinger picture, in which the states carry the time-dependence of the system and the operators are fixed in time, and we have the Heisenberg picture, in which the states are time-independent and it is the operators which store the time development of the system.

If we assume that it is due to the changing state of the system, then the process of measurement can be taken to be completely passive. On the other hand, if it were to be considered a result of the measurement itself, then we are assuming primarily that the measurement itself has a disturbing effect on the system. This assumes the existence of an interaction between the system and the measuring device. With microscopic systems being so small and delicate, no one can deny that such possible interactions may cause subsequent disturbances. Therefore, such interactions will decohere the quantum system. The disturbances caused by the measuring devices are generally non-systematic and so complicated that they are unpredictable. On the other hand, one might expect that in some cases the disturbances caused by the macroscopic measuring device can be so great that they overwhelm the basic value of the observable under measurement. The third point to make here is that such disturbances, if known, can be accounted for in the equation of motion through the potential term. Accordingly, the case will always be that of an interacting system for which the equation of motion may be solved exactly or through numerical techniques. Virtually anything environmental can be included in the potential of the system, which controls the behavior of the system through the equation of motion. Taking these notes into consideration, it would be odd to assume that quantum indeterminacy is the sheer result of the incision of measurement.

Interpretations of Quantum Measurements

In a given individual experiment, the result of the measurement is one of several alternatives. A repetition of the experiment under identical initial conditions may lead to one or another of these possible alternatives. This is incompatible with the unitary evolution of Schrödinger: in a unitary evolution of a state, the probabilities are preserved. Since the different states of a system have different probabilities, how then can the same value be preserved as the experiment is showing us? Several solutions have been proposed for this apparent inconsistency. The main ones are as follows.

The von Neumann Interpretation: Wave Function Collapse

To explain the process of measurement, von Neumann suggested that the state function changes according to two different ways:

> *Process* 1. A discontinuous change brought about by the observation by which the quantity with eigenstate $|\psi\rangle$ is projected onto the state $|\phi\rangle = \hat{A}|\psi\rangle$

instantly with probability $|<\psi|\phi>|^2$. This determines the overlap between the state $|\psi>$ and the state $|\phi> = \hat{A}|\psi>$.

Process 2. A change in the course of time development according to the deterministic Schrödinger equation.

The description in Process 1 refers to the "wave function collapse", which means that the state $|\psi>$, after measuring the observable A, will be converted into the state $|\phi> = \hat{A}|\psi>$.

In this formulation by von Neumann, a fundamental problem was recognized long ago. The problem is the apparent inconsistency between the indeterministic nature of Process 1 and the deterministic nature of Process 2. This inconsistency has been presented in different forms and it is in fact deeply rooted in the formulation of quantum mechanics from its very beginning. Josef Jauch[33] presented the problem as follows: the problem of measurement in quantum mechanics concerns the question of whether the laws of quantum mechanics are consistent with the acquisition of data concerning the properties of quantum systems. This consistency problem arises because the system to be measured and the apparatus used for the measurement are themselves systems which are presumed to obey the laws of quantum mechanics. Therefore, the evolution of the state of such systems is governed by the Schrödinger equation. However, the measuring process exhibits features which are apparently inconsistent with Schrödinger-type evolutions. The typical process ends with the establishment of a permanent and irreversible record. This contradicts the time-reversible Schrödinger equation. So, despite the fact that von Neumann's interpretation of quantum measurement was adopted by the Copenhagen school, nevertheless it suffers from some fundamental problems.

The Statistical Interpretation

For this, we have two views:

Viewpoint 1. Quantum mechanics is understood to apply to ensembles and not to single particles. Albert Einstein was an advocate of this interpretation. Einstein said: "The function ψ does not in any way describe a condition which could be that of a single system: it relates rather to many systems, to 'an ensemble of systems' in the sense of statistical mechanics".[34] Einstein hoped that a future, more complete, theory might describe quantum mechanics as an approximation of a more general one.

Viewpoint 2. Proposed by Born and supported by Bohr, the wave function ψ was understood to be symbolic of a representation of the system and that $|\psi(x)|^2 = |\psi^*(x)\psi(x)|$ is taken to describe the probability density for the system to be in the position x. But, probability can only have meaning through a population. In this case, the population is that of the many repeated measurements. This can be asserted by the fact that Born was of the opinion that his suggestion had the same content as Einstein's and that "the difference [in their views] is not essential, but merely a matter of language".[35]

One can say that the Einstein interpretation is covered by the fact that, in any measurement on a quantum system, we measure macroscopic quantities, a fact that was originally emphasized by Bohr. If, however, we come to measure a microscopic quantity, then the Einstein interpretation would not be valid. On the other hand, by requiring that many measurements are to be made of the same system, Born's interpretation implicitly assumes that the system will remain in the same state for the duration of all those measurements. Obviously, this cannot generally be guaranteed.

The Hidden Variables Interpretation

This interpretation was championed by David Bohm,[36] who assumed that quantum mechanics is incomplete and that there are some hidden variables that should complement the physical description in order to get the full picture of the physical world, which, in Bohm's view, is assumed to be deterministic. There are several kinds of hidden variable theories, some are local and some are non-local. Belinfante[37] gave a very detailed account of these theories, of both their scientific content and their historical development. By Bell's theorem,[38] the local hidden variable theories were shown to be inconsistent with quantum mechanics. None of the existing non-local theories has concluded any prediction that is new to the standard formulation of quantum mechanics.

The Multi-world Interpretation

The multi-world interpretation was originally proposed by Hugh Everett[39] in 1957. Everett reformulated the process of measurement, abandoning the concept of wave function collapse of the von Neumann formalism set out in Process 1, while keeping the assumption of the deterministic evolution of the system under Schrödinger's equation. Everett criticized the von Neumann scheme's requirement for external observers to obtain measurements, and went on to consider the system as being composed of two main subsystems: the object and the measuring device (or observer). This formulation established the concept of "relative states". The treatment led Everett to conclude that:

> throughout all of a sequence of observation processes there is only one physical system representing the observer, yet there is no single unique state of the

> observer (which follows from the representations of interacting systems). Nevertheless, there is a representation in terms of a superposition, each element of which contains a definite observer state and a corresponding system state. Thus, with each succeeding observation (or interaction), the observer state branches into a number of different states. Each branch represents a different outcome of the measurement and the corresponding eigenstate for the object-system state. All branches exist simultaneously in the superposition after any given sequence of observations.[40]

Everett went further to suggest that:

> the trajectory of the memory configuration of an observer performing a sequence of measurements is thus not a linear sequence of memory configurations, but a branching tree, with all possible outcomes existing simultaneously in a final superposition with various coefficients in the mathematical model. In any familiar memory device the branching does not continue indefinitely, but must stop at a point limited by the capacity of the memory.[41]

John Wheeler supported the Everett theory, emphasizing its self-consistency.[42] An elaboration of the Everett interpretation was also the subject of a study by Neill Graham[43] working under the supervision of Bryce DeWitt. It was assumed that the eigenvalues associated with the observer's subsystem form a continuous spectrum, whereas the eigenvalues associated with the object form a discrete set; and, in order to reconcile the assumption that the superposition never collapses with ordinary experience, which ascribes to the object system after the measurement only one definite value of the observable, it was proposed that the world will be splitting into many-worlds existing simultaneously where in each separate world a measurement yields only one result, though this result differs in general from one world to another.

Re-creation: A Possible Interpretation of Indeterminism

The notion of re-creation might give a more realistic interpretation of the quantum phenomena. What are the consequences of re-creation? Here comes the physics. I have studied *kalām*'s principle of re-creation in an attempt to find a resolution for the measurement problem and indeterminacy in quantum mechanics.[44] This interpretation is a whole package that is self-consistent and offers a deeper understanding of related matters, such as the uncertainty principle, the eigenvalue spectrum, non-locality, quantum entanglement, the double slit interference with single particles, quantum coherence, and the range of applicability of quantum mechanics. The interpretation also provides us with some predictions about quantum states and enforces some conditions on observing delicate phenomena such as the quantum Zeno effect. This interpretation is based on two postulates:

Postulate P (1). All physical properties of microscopic systems are subject to continued re-creation.

Postulate P (2). The frequency of re-creation is proportional to the total energy of the system.

It will be shown below that the re-created observable assumes a new value every time it is re-created. This causes the observable to have a distribution of values across a certain range (width) that is always controlled by the re-creation frequency. The higher the total energy of the system, the narrower the range of values across which the dispersion is expected, and vice versa. For this reason, macroscopic systems are expected to behave classically, whereas microscopic systems mostly exhibit quantum behavior. Clearly, the narrower the dispersion of values, the more determinable the value of the observable and vice versa.

Re-creation and the Uncertainty Principle

Once created (determined as existing), an observable assumes a given basic value defined by the state of the system at that moment. According to the re-creation postulate, the physical parameters of any system are in a natural process of continued re-creation irrespective of the measurement operation. However, values of those parameters can only be known at the time of measurement. Re-creation is a process of change. Once a given parameter has been re-created, other related parameters of the system will be affected, thus changing their values in accordance with the laws of nature concerned. All the parameters of the system are tied to their generators. For example, on re-creating the position x, we are generating a new x. This means that, in general, we are generating a change in x. This is best understood in terms of generating an infinitesimal translation in space. The generator of this infinitesimal translation is $\partial/\partial x$ and this is just proportional to the momentum operator. This will duly cause the system to change every time it is re-created, thus presenting a distribution of values for x instead of it acquiring one single value. Conversely, if the momentum p is re-created, then the whole system will change by $\partial/\partial p$, but this will cause an infinitesimal shift in the value of p and, consequently, a shift in the value of the position parameter x. Therefore, every time an x is re-created, a change in the momentum of the system will occur and, conversely, every time the momentum is re-created, a change in the value of the position will occur. This means that re-creating the position will result in creating momentum and vice versa. If the system itself is to stay invariant under the process of re-creation (conserved), then we must have:

$$\left(\frac{\partial}{\partial x}x - x\frac{\partial}{\partial x}\right)|\psi>=|\psi>$$

Using the operator formulation for the position and momentum this would imply:

$$\hat{p}\hat{x} - \hat{x}\hat{p} = [\hat{p}, \hat{x}] = -i\hbar$$

In other words, the effect of change is logically being seen as a commutation of the parameter and its generator (which were also called complementary observables). This is the well-known commutation relation that led to the Heisenberg uncertainty relations. In this scheme, however, measurements could be passive action that does not necessarily affect the system itself. That is to say, there is no role for the observer and physics remains purely objective.

Physical Implications of Re-creation

There are several implications of the proposed re-creation scheme described above. Some of these may be used to test the theory. However, because of the mostly technical nature of these implications, I will only provide an overview of some of those that might be of interest to people working on issues in science and religion debates.

Applicability of Quantum Mechanics

This proposal of re-creation maintains the statistical nature of the quantum system. It resolves the question of whether quantum mechanics is applicable to a single particle or whether it is applicable to an ensemble of particles. Here we see that the single-particle state is undergoing continued re-creation, thus forming an ensemble of values of its own, if a memory is available to keep record of all the values assumed under re-creation. Nevertheless, a measurement of an observable taken over a duration of time exceeding the re-creation period will always yield an average of the values assumed by the system during the period of measurement. Since the re-creation frequency is very high (for an electron it is about 10^{21} Hz), the re-creation period is very short (10^{-21} s); so, when we measure any event practically, we measure average values every time we perform a measurement. Unless we perform measurements on this temporal scale, we cannot observe the instant values prescribed by the eigenvalue spectrum of the system. This explains how probabilistic behavior arises in the case of a single-particle quantum system. According to the above scheme, we always measure average values with very low dispersion for macroscopic objects; the re-creation frequency is very high and, consequently, the time measurement cannot cope with the re-creation period. This is what gives the macroscopic world its classical, apparently deterministic, character and this is why the measured values of the observables of a macroscopic system are always very close, even identical to the theoretical expectation values of the observables. On the other hand, in microscopic systems the re-creation frequency is relatively low and, therefore, we would expect the dispersion of values to be high enough to expose the indeterministic character of the world. For very small masses, the re-creation rate is much lower than for massive particles; for this reason, particles with extremely small masses such as the neutrino exhibit their alternative states on measurements in the form of oscillations. Here, the alternative quantum states are revealed through measurements over a low re-creation frequency.

This proposal also provides us with a better understanding of the origin of the uncertainty relations. Here we see that the appearance of uncertainty in the values of complementary observables is a direct result of re-creation and the entanglement of such observables. This implies that indeterminism is a direct consequence of continued re-creation.

Quantum Entanglement

This is a very interesting phenomenon by which pairs of particles are known to exhibit non-causal relationships whereby, if a property belonging to one particle is changed, then the other of the pair will feel the change and consequently will react by changing the corresponding property. This confirms that parts of the universe in one way or another are entangled. The important point here is that we do not yet have a full explanation of this phenomenon; we have only a good description of it as offered by standard quantum mechanics. However, the re-creation mechanism might explain this phenomenon by the fact that particles created from the same initial state ought to have their re-creation frequencies interconnected, such a connection would seem to be established through the phase of re-creation. A single state being split into two states will generate two states with frequencies that are re-created in phase, even though the two frequencies might be different. This phase connection allows for a non-causal signal to connect the two states.

Quantum entanglement operating through some sort of non-causal channel allows us to think of non-causal links that might be at work between the constituents of the world. This also might provide scope for thinking about the intervention of God in the world by choosing probabilities through controlling the phases. This is an important argument for the existence of a divine action in the world. However, this needs more detailed analysis that goes beyond the scope of this chapter.

Quantum Coherence

In simple terms, coherence is an expression describing the collective behavior exhibited by components of a system in full harmony. This is one basic feature that is realized in quantum systems, and it is customarily known that coherent systems are quantum systems. Such systems always feature high efficiency, for example, lasers. The availability of a macroscopic quantum state may make it plausible to expect the occurrence of macroscopic coherent states too, thus opening the way to understand some very obscure phenomena such as gamma-ray bursts, which are known to occur at the far rim of the universe. Apart from this, the re-creation postulate allows for a new definition of coherence by which two systems can be considered coherent if their re-creation frequency is identical and their re-creation occurs in the same phase.

Miracles

What is a miracle? There are several definitions of this term; some are vague, such as the one attributed to Hume, who said that a miracle is the "violation of the laws of nature", something which can be seriously criticized. Other definitions are better suited to describing a miracle. I find the definition given in the *Oxford English Dictionary* to be the closest to a suitable description. It says that a miracle is "an event not ascribable to human power or the laws of nature and consequently attributed to a supernatural, especially divine, agency".[45] But, does it need to break the laws of nature to be a miracle? Suppose that a ball is thrown at a brick wall and suddenly we find it going through the wall without making a hole or demolishing it. Can we consider this event to be a miracle? In the language of physics, we say that the potential energy of the wall is much greater than the kinetic energy of the ball and that therefore the ball cannot go through the wall. But, according to quantum mechanics, an electron with less energy than the potential energy of a semiconductor barrier can cross this potential in a phenomenon called "quantum tunneling". This is happening all the time inside the electronic circuits of your mobile phone sets. If this is possible, why are we not able to see a ball go through a brick wall? The answer is related to the difference between the two systems. Whereas the electron–barrier system is a simple microscopic system, the ball–wall system is a composite macroscopic system. Basically, on a macroscopic scale, quantum tunneling should be possible theoretically, however with much less probability of occurrence. The ball–wall system is composed of many particles which are in a non-coherent state and cannot be treated with a simple linear Schrödinger equation, whereas the electron–barrier system is a simple system that can easily be described by a single Schrödinger equation. Therefore, practically, the chance of the ball tunneling through the wall is zero. This is why we can confidently say that we are accustomed to nature preventing the ball from tunneling through the wall, while we are also accustomed to light tunneling through glass. Therefore, one way or another, the law of nature that we recognize is the one that is customary.

Part of the problem with divine action is this possibility of miracles taking place. The philosophical question that emerges here is what would prevent God from choosing to play with the probabilities of odd results? Why should God abide by the deterministic laws of physics? The answer is that God is not abiding by the laws of physics but is enforcing His will through the laws of nature, and these laws are generally indeterministic (see Chapter Two). As such, we have a consistent realization of miracles being low-probability events. In quantum mechanics, there are no miracles but only very low-probability contingent events (see Chapter Three, where the arguments for causality and re-creation are presented). According to this view, re-creation is considered the basic act of God through which He is expressing His action in the world and this explains the divine freedom to choose between contingent events within a prescribed set of laws that the Creator Himself has devised as part of His creation. This means that God does not act miraculously, despite the fact that re-creation is a miraculous act per se. God does not play dice, despite what we may think at first glance.

Divine Action in Modern Western Thought

Current approaches in science and religion debates in the West seem to follow trends similar to those of the Greek philosophers, reconciling some Christian theological doctrines with scientific theories by rationalizing theology in a scientific context. Such an approach has its positive side, as it follows a paradigm of free rational inquiry, but it would, unfortunately, lead to redesigning God, His attributes, and His actions to fit in with the contemporary logic of science. This has already resulted in notions such as the "God of the gaps" and the more subtle notion of intelligent design. Genuine scholars of science and religion are aware of this danger, but only to a limited extent. The reason why such a compromising approach may lead to distortions in a theological sense is the embedded eagerness to have a complete theory that would harmonize science and religion and explain everything, a mistake that the old *mutakallimūn* could not avoid, resulting in an inconsistent theology. A safer approach would assume certain theologically based doctrines, which may or may not find an immediate realization within the framework of science, and then to seek a better and deeper understanding of nature and human action through that approach. As Polkinghorne puts it: "Both theology and science have to speak of entities which are not directly observable. In consequence, both must be prepared to make use of model and metaphor".[46] Such a use of model and metaphor can be realized through the paradigm of *kalām* rather than through the paradigm of science alone, or through that of philosophy. This is a more fruitful approach, since in this way religion can give feedback on science and vice versa. The outcome will be a framework within which religion and science can, hopefully, both develop genuinely into convergence.

In order to evaluate the view we propose, we have to compare it with other views to see what kinds of solutions it might offer. Our view proposed here for divine action is in agreement with that of Pollard, which is expressed in his book *Chance and Providence: God's Action in a World Governed by Scientific Law*.[47] Pollard argued that the world is characterized by chance. This he concluded from the fact that quantum mechanics demonstrates that the fundamental behavior of matter is probability-based and therefore indeterminate. Pollard understood the causal structure of the world to be open and providing innumerable alternatives from which God can select a desired outcome.[48] Pollard's key thesis was that divine action is possible through God's providential action in the probability-based processes of nature. Since this implies that God's action does not take the form of a natural force, he suggested that the proposal for divine action cannot be pursued as a natural theology. Pollard reasoned that one cannot argue *from* nature to theology and that belief in divine action is based on theological grounds, but that it is affirmed in a scientific context.[49] Indeed, the conclusion that the belief in divine action cannot be pursued from nature to theology conforms with the approach followed by the *mutakallimūn* in which they pursued divine action on theological grounds and affirmed it in a scientific context.

The difference between our view here and that of Pollard's is in the assumption that the laws of nature, including those of quantum mechanics, are not independent according to our views; the divine action of re-creation provides the driver for these laws. Therefore, in our model, God is not a spectator but is a fully active driver who re-creates, prescribes laws that He respects, and then selects the outcome.

Human Freedom

Human freedom is different from natural freedom because human freedom implies that man has his own intrinsic will; he can make his own choices without the need for some external body to dictate him. However, all his physical acts are in need of an operator/coordinator, no matter whether we assume the top-down or the bottom-up causation model. Human free will is superior to that of the rest of the world for one good reason: humans are intelligent beings that are curious and able to discover, analyze, and construct. A human's will is validated by the practical realization of his or her actions. If these actions are not realized in practice, human will would have no practical value. Since the validation of human will goes through natural effects and actions, therefore it is reasonable to assume that human will is bound by the destiny of the world.

Perhaps the idea that I find most plausible in contemporary debates about divine action is that of John Polkinghorne: that God interacts with the world through information input, not energy input. God created Jesus through information. According to the Qur'an, Jesus was the word of God revealed to Mary. God is described to be knowledgeable and experienced, the one who knows all that is hidden; this idea is indeed quite generic and can explain many things. However, we do not have to stick to the notion of a personal God, since the notion of a personal God would imply that He may be a localized body.

Freedom of the World

Sir John Polkinghorne believes that "God has given freedom to the whole world",[50] and it is beautiful to see how he justifies his claim. According to Polkinghorne, we have love and faithfulness, attributes of God, reflected as freedom and reliability in the act of the world, which result in chance and necessity. However, as he points out, this will make some people say that "the role of chance subverts the religious claim that there is a purpose at work in the world".[51] But then, if we insist that chance (or the so-called "happenstance") is "operating within a context of lawful regularity", then the intent of chance would be lost. This is why it would be better to talk about contingency instead of chance. We would say that the fruitfulness of the world is an interplay between contingency and necessity, and this is what the old *mutakallimūn* were saying. Contingency is a type of freedom that is given to the world to be as it is and to allow for the different possibilities or facets that it might show.

However, if we claim that God has allocated certain intrinsic properties to nature that would allow things to choose their own courses of action, then this would imply that nature has some sort of decision to make for every action that takes place, and that nature does have a mind of its own. The question arises over how nature would work under the auspices of divine action. Here again we face a "God of the gaps" being hidden under the notions of chance and necessity. Although Polkinghorne would find that the "fruitful interplay between chance and necessity is a reflection of the twin gifts of freedom and reliability which God has given to the world, gifts which are the reflections of his combined Nature of love and faithfulness",[52] unfortunately such mystic reflections on this serious ontological matter do not help to resolve the problem of the conflict between God's choice and nature's choice. Unless we mean to say that nature's will may win over the divine will in order to explain the existence of a natural evil such as cancer, I find no reason why the divine will should be superseded by nature's will. But then if we were to accept this kind of conflict between nature and God, we would implicitly assume the existence of more than one player, or more than one god. It is wise to admit that this problem is one of the most serious that has arisen in connection with the required reconciliation between science and religion. The importance of and challenge presented by this problem come from the fact that we see nature behaving according to practically reliable laws. Nature can adapt itself and change an environment to achieve a balance in favor of certain goals, this is what led to the Gaia hypothesis. An example of this is in the adapting of Earth's atmosphere that took place a long time ago in order to achieve the proper percentages of oxygen and nitrogen in the air to make life possible.

The better alternative, I find, is to assume that nature has no freedom and that it would be correct to say that it is in full submittal to God. In this context, a sort of "divine democracy" would be at work instead of a divine tyranny. This submittal comes through obeying God's orders, being the operator and the coordinator of the laws that nature abides by. Nature has been given the right to expose itself through its allocated properties and qualities, but God operates it and makes the final decisions. So God, the lawgiver, has designed the world in such a way that things are associated with certain properties that characterize what we call the "*nature* of things". But then, such a nature acts under the auspices of the divine will through the need for operation and coordination. Here is the necessity for the world to be created anew in every moment by the divine action taking place through operating the given law. Through this we can realize the true meaning of divine providence.

But the question remains of how a merciful and compassionate God could order an evil act of nature to take place. It seems to me that God did not create this world to entertain humans; otherwise, He would not have created the qualities and laws that enable natural evil to happen in the first place. Rather, it seems that the challenge put forward for humans in this world is to behave within our given freedoms and capabilities, in order to fulfill the goals that we are tasked to achieve. This goal is the actual destiny behind the whole game of creation and the development of mankind and the universe. Theories of cosmology tell us that there could be many worlds out there, empty of any developed life, and that our universe is very accurately fine-tuned to make our existence possible. Therefore, surely a human is destined to do something of great value that justifies his or her existence in a world that is so delicate and complex. This is the so-called "anthropic principle", which, I admit, has different interpretations, though we cannot escape the unique fact of being in a very low-probability universe with a special allocation of qualities that makes us capable of asking questions and searching for the answers. This, by itself, is a kind of destiny marking out a goal for us both individually and collectively.

One final point is due here and that is to say that the laws of physics are, in fact, our realizations of how the world would act; in no way are these laws necessarily expressing true and actual divine algorithms.[53] These laws are *our* algorithms for the world. Therefore, I would say that we are far from conceiving of how the "mind of God"[54] works, and we are far from being able to "catch God at work".[55]

Nancy Murphy suggested there is an "under-determination" by which God seems to cooperate with the innate properties of his creation. This suggestion implies that matter has its own consent which makes it an independent authority to rival God. This is missing the point that such properties cannot be validated without the consent of the divine, for God is the one who would power such entities no matter what degree of independence they enjoyed:

> This principle of God's respecting the integrity of the entities he has created is an important one . . . I further suggest, on the strength of a similar analogy with the human realm, that we speak of all created entities as having "natural rights," which God respects in his governance. This is the sense in which his governance is cooperation, not domination.[56]

However, this certainly implies that the world is sharing the divine action and this would require that the world enjoys a kind of consciousness, a mind, and a free will of its own, which is by no means self-evident. The case is different when it comes to the human act; here we have some freedom furnished by the consciousness and will that humans enjoy. But, one might say that other creatures might have consciousness and will too. We are not aware yet of the level of consciousness that other creatures enjoy, which would enable us to decide on their level of contribution to the running of the world. In any case, one might rule out the contributions of lower creatures with the argument that they do not enjoy an independent rational agency of their own. The divine cooperation is best restricted to humans, as they are known to have a mind and a manifested free will. Accordingly, the cooperation can be realized by saying that God has created the world and has allowed us to make our choices within this world according to our own free will; nonetheless, bringing those choices about is subject to God's will, which either endorses or denies them. If God endorses what we wish for then it comes into effect, but, if not, then something else might happen to prevent us from achieving our wishes. This introduces cooperation into a well-defined process by which God's will plays the prime part and, at the same time, allows for the contribution of man's free will to play a role in selecting an outcome. By such a mechanism, God's sovereignty and supremacy is preserved and, at the same time, human free will is maintained even though a human's choice might not be realized, as God's will might supersede. Our responsibility for what happens is ascribed by the choices we make. Sometimes a good choice is effected and we are happy; other times our bad choices are effected, which we may regret.

This suggestion for effecting the divine action and the interaction between God and nature allows for the marginal role of supplications and prayer made by a human to be taken in consideration by the divine. Clearly, there is no sharing of command here in ruling the events of the world, as it always remains the divine choice whether to accept or reject our supplications.

Discussion

The re-creation proposal might be considered metaphysical. This is because what we call divine action in nature cannot be understood without reference to a transcendental agency that drives the action. However, no full explanation can be given to nature without metaphysical assumptions one way or another. If nature were understood without such reference, then there would be no need for the divine. Much of our work in quantum mechanics and other fields embodies metaphysical assumptions. Neils Bohr and Werner Heisenberg were accused of bringing their metaphysical preconceptions into quantum theory in favor of indeterminism.[57] Einstein's famous response to Bohr's claim by saying that "God does not play dice" revealed a certain metaphysical inclination in Einstein's thinking about quantum mechanics. In a letter to Max Born, Einstein clearly displays this inclination:

> Quantum mechanics is certainly imposing. But an inner voice tells me that it is not yet the real thing. The theory says a lot, but does not really bring us any closer to the secret of the "old one". I, at any rate, am convinced that He is not playing at dice.[58]

Indeed, according to the interpretation provided by the re-creation postulate the "old one" is not playing dice, but the outcome of His actions causes the dice play. David Bohm was also engaged in metaphysical speculations. Bohm's research into hidden variables, sub-quantum regularities and realities in quantum mechanics carries over into a generalized concept of order, which he then relates to spirituality, human society, and the evolution of the world.[59] In his article *The Metaphysics of Divine Action*,[60] John Polkinghorne noted that any discussion of agency requires the adoption of a metaphysical view of the nature of reality. He claims that there is no way of going from epistemology to ontology, but for him the strategy of critical realism is to maximize the connection between epistemology and ontology:

> One could define the program of critical realism as the strategy of seeking the maximum correlation between epistemology and ontology, subject to careful acknowledgement that we view reality from a perspective and subject to pushing the search for knowledge to any natural limits it may possess. Its motto is "epistemology models ontology"; the totality of what we can know is a reliable guide to what is the case.[61]

Indeed, this is why most physicists interpret the Heisenberg uncertainty principle as implying actual indeterminacy in the physical world, rather than an ignorance of its detailed workings. Polkinghorne thinks that no proposal is available that would take the concept of divine action beyond a crude starting point and hopes that progress in the area of quantum chaology will provide opportunities for further development of divine action concepts. Polkinghorne has also suggested that "bold metaphysical speculations, which takes science into account but relatively uninhibited in pressing on to grander designs" will be a necessary step in developing new approaches.[62]

I believe that my proposal of re-creation presented here is the one that might achieve Polkinghorne's wish, since it is a bold assumption that is unhindered by further ambitions. However, we still need to understand how re-creation order and probability selection are achieved. This might be pursued through utilizing Polkinghorne's suggestion that epistemology models ontology. This idea is not well established yet and will need more elaboration and, consequently, a convincing mechanism will have to be set.

It should be noted that the re-creation proposal, as an interpretation of quantum indeterminacy, preserves the basic symmetry contained in quantum mechanics, since the position and momentum are kept interchangeable; one remains the generator of the other. Bohm's theory was criticized by Wolfgang Pauli and Werner Heisenberg for violating this symmetry.[63]

We need to understand the true implications of modern, twentieth-century science as much as we need to understand the original doctrines of religion. Conceptions proposed by quantum theory and the mathematical structures of quantum mechanics are still in need of deeper understanding. The meaning of an "operator" in quantum mechanics is as obscure as the meaning of the unpredictability of measurements. The role played by the imaginary quantities in physics, although they are directly unmeasurable entities, is something worth studying too at the conceptual level in order to understand much of its practical naturalistic meaning.[64] In theoretical physics, most of us play the game of generating equations that sometimes do not have clear explanations. An example of this is string theory. In the general theory of relativity and curved spacetime physics, we are not yet ready to understand the full meaning and implications of a space-like universe. For this reason, many of the black hole physicists were taken by surprise by the declaration of Stephen Hawking that information is not completely lost when a particle falls into a black hole.[65] In cosmology, despite the eminence of the big bang theory, we are still far from deciding whether the universe did have a start in time or whether it has an infinite extension into the past; the point singularity that contains all matter and energy that exists in our universe stands not only as an epistemological challenge but as an ontological dilemma too. Indeed, science is firm and strong on the practical side of the story, but is far from reaching a climax on the theoretical side. That is why we should not speculate too much. Instead, we should have some fixed basic principles and doctrines, and some sort of an epistemic paradigm, while finding our way through science and religion.

Re-creation is concerned with the basic constituents that compose a quantum event. A body is a collection of interacting constituents (atoms and molecules). Each of these is being re-created at high frequency. Since a body is not composed of all coherent states, therefore the body is not necessarily getting re-created at any rate. By coherence I mean that it has the same re-creation frequency and that it is in phase. Any decoherence will be reflected in expressing classical behavior for the system. Practically, only microscopic systems will exhibit quantum behavior on re-creation, because large bodies which are composed of many particle systems, even if made of identical particles, will have high energy content and consequently are re-created with much higher frequencies. Accordingly, the possible values for the states of the system form a very narrow Gaussian distribution which reflects a classical behavior. A large body which is composed of coherent constituents forms a macroscopic quantum system and exhibits quantum behavior. This is what we normally see in a Bose–Einstein condensate, lasers, and in superconductivity.

Within the scope of re-creation, the Schrödinger cat puzzle has no place, as it would be a wrong question to ask whether the cat is alive or dead inside the box. The cat is a macroscopic system and can by no means be represented as being in one or the other of two quantum states. In fact, the cat could be alive or dead as the contingent classical possibilities and this would depend on many factors, such as whether the poison was liberated from the bottle or not, whether the falling hammer had hit the bottle or not, whether the mechanism of the falling hammer had worked or not, and whether the electrical connections had worked or not, and so on. All these fall within classical conditions and possibilities. The state of the cat at any time is a classical state, as long as its body does not form a coherent state.

If divine action is visualized as being the choice of the divine that is the outcome of quantum fluctuation, then it would be difficult to understand how divine action can be realized macroscopically. Quantum events do not happen in macroscopic systems unless a coherent state is ready, and this makes the possibility of observing divine action in macroscopic systems very rare indeed. This is why miracles are very rare. Otherwise, if we assume that God is enforcing some kind of miraculous state of coherence in order to effect his action on a macroscopic level, it would be a much rarer event to happen, so rare indeed that it might need to be investigated in quantum chaology, as Polkinghorne once suggested.

Here, it seems to me that the re-creation proposal does not offer an immediate model for divine action apart from being divine action itself, but, as I have shown, this proposal offers a resolution to the problem of quantum measurement. This, according to the conjecture of Polkinghorne, might be a step forward in modeling divine action. Much work is needed before we can probe the intervention of the divine at a macroscopic level.

CHAPTER FIVE

Space, Time, and *Kalām*

The time is originated and created, and before it there was no time at all.

al-Ghazālī

IN THEIR VIEWS ON space and time, Muslim philosophers such as al-Fārābī, Ibn Sīnā, and Ibn Rushd almost followed the Greek philosophers, mainly Plato, Aristotle, and Plotinus. The *mutakallimūn* followed another approach; they constructed their views mainly from the Qur'an, the prime source of Islam. The *kalām* views were different from those of the philosophers in some fundamental aspects. The *mutakallimūn* presented their views about space and time when discussing a number of fundamental issues in religion and natural philosophy, most important of which was the problem of creation. They encountered the concepts of space and time when discussing this problem, and the problem of motion. Most of the *mutakallimūn* considered time to be discrete, composed of non-divisible units called (*ān*), meaning an "instant". In conformity with their atomic theory, the *mutakallimūn* viewed the motion of a particle as composed of finite (discrete) transitions over a trajectory separated by stationary points. This concept was fundamentally different from the conventional Aristotelian concept in which motion was described as the transition from one place to another during a given duration of time.

The interesting point to note is that the *mutakallimūn* described space and time as being an integrated entity that is manifested in the occurrence of the event; moreover, they considered both space and time to be described on relative scales, as they are always to be addressed in comparison with other references, refusing the notion of absolute space and absolute time.

In this chapter, besides describing the views of the *mutakallimūn* about space and time, and, inevitably, motion, I will consider the views of two of the great traditional scholars of Islam, who did not formally subscribe to the schools of *kalām*, but who nonetheless frequently espoused some of the doctrines of *kalām* in their arguments, despite having different views about certain other matters. They are Ibn Ḥazm al-Ẓāhirī and Abū Ḥāmid al-Ghazālī. I have chosen these two thinkers because they represent perhaps the highest level of traditional Muslim intelligentsia and they had expressed *kalām* theories in a theological context as well as theological concepts within the framework of *kalām*.

Ibn Ḥazm (d. 1064), who was born and lived in Córdoba (Spain), expressed most of his philosophical views in his famous book *Kitāb al-fiṣal fī al-milal wa al-ahwāʾ wa al-niḥal*, in which he discussed the philosophical thoughts and views of many religious groups and factions. Primarily, he stressed the importance of sense perception, asserting that human reason can be flawed. This might be contrary to the doctrine of al-Ghazālī. While recognizing the importance of reason, and acknowledging that the Qur'an encourages rational reflection, he believed that this reflection is concerned mainly with revelation and sense data. So, it is a form of sensory reminder to admire the glory of God. Accordingly, he concluded that reason is not to be taken necessarily as a faculty for independent research or discovery, but that sense perception should be used in its place, an idea that sounds like a forerunner for empiricism. Although Ibn Ḥazm did not subscribe to any of the *kalām* schools, despite his critique of the Muʿtazila and Ashʿaris, it is not difficult to see that he used some of their thoughts in his arguments. This obviously stems from having a common base with those arguments, which were, of course, based on Islam.

On the other hand, Al-Ghazālī (d. 1111), the most famous Muslim intellectual and thinker, lived and taught in Baghdad at the Niẓāmiyya School during the last two decades of the eleventh century. Al-Ghazālī, too, did not officially subscribe to any of the two main schools of *kalām*, but he certainly used their arguments in his book *Tahāfut al-falāsifa* (*The Incoherence of the Philosophers*). In his arguments, he used the concepts of *kalām* extensively and added much elaboration and ingenuity to those concepts, which were then used in *kalām*. Al-Ghazālī shared some of his views with Ibn Ḥazm and sometimes used the same arguments for the problem under discussion.

In this chapter, I will present the views of both scholars, revealing their most important ideas in an attempt to demonstrate an important part of the Islamic view of space and time. I do not intend to set the discussion in a historical context, nor will I present a history of thought on the concepts of space and time, but I will rather concentrate on presenting the ideas and views of these two Muslim thinkers in the context of *kalām*. However, whenever necessary, I will also discuss the thoughts of other theologians or philosophers in order to briefly cover the basic thinking. In order to provide a full coverage of the concepts and thoughts to date, I will also present the views of the two main theories of the twentieth century, namely Einstein's relativity and quantum mechanics. These are presented as references for comparison and to assess the richness of traditional Muslim scholarship, which I leave the reader to appreciate.

Earlier Views

The earliest of the theological views on time in the West was presented by St. Augustine (d. 430), who was born and lived in what is now Algeria. He expressed his views about time in two works: *The City of God* and *The Confessions*. In these, he presented his arguments about time and eternity and discussed the question of the presence of time before the creation of the universe.

It is very elegant how St. Augustine described the experience we all have about the passage of time, through which he presented his views about eternity. He pointed to the fact that there is a difference between eternity and the presence of time as measures for the rate of passing events. Whereas the extension of time from past to present and the future is something that we appreciate consciously through the occurrence of events, eternity is a fixed moment that contains all the past, the present, and the future:

> Who shall hold it and fix it so that it may come to rest for a little; and then, by degrees, glimpse the glory of that eternity which abides forever; and then, comparing eternity with the temporal process in which nothing abides, they may see that they are incommensurable? They would see that a long time does not become long, except from the many separate events that occur in its passage, which cannot be simultaneous. In the Eternal, on the other hand, nothing passes away, but the whole is simultaneously present. But no temporal process is wholly simultaneous. Therefore, let it see that all time past is forced to move on by the incoming future; that all the future follows from the past; and that all, past and future, is created and issues out of that which is forever present.[1]

By this argument, Augustine has set out the divine presence as being what we call in our modern terminology a space-like state. This is something that I find fascinating indeed. After this, Augustine answered the question: what was God doing before he created the earth and the heavens? His answer was that before creating them there was no time:

> For thou madest that very time itself, and periods could not pass by before thou madest the whole temporal procession. But if there was no time *before* heaven and earth, how, then, can it be asked, "What wast thou doing then?" For there was no "then" when there was no time.[2]

Again, that there was no *real* time[3] before the creation of the universe is indeed the answer that we get from theories in modern cosmology. Augustine then argued:

> Yet I say with confidence that I know that if nothing passed away, there would be no past time; and if nothing were still coming, there would be no future time; and if there were nothing at all, there would be no present time. But, then, how is it that there are the two times, past and future, when even the past is now no longer and the future is now not yet? But if the present were always present, and did not pass into past time, it obviously would not be time but eternity.[4]

Here again, in the last sentence of the above paragraph, Augustine tells us that eternity is a *still* moment that never moves. Eternity is not an infinite extension of time. Eternity is the complete absence of time. We will see later how al-Ghazālī continued this discussion with his elegant style of argumentation. Using the analogy of space and time and the interplay between the *before* and the *after* in analogy with the *above* and the *below*, exchanging space and time dimensions, he successfully challenged the presence of time before creation.

Space and Time According to Aristotle

Aristotle rejected the existence of the void and could not accept the visualization of empty space as an extension without any material content. He identified space as being the envelope which surrounds a body. Without bodies there could be no space. A simple void (vacuum) does not exist. All places are somehow filled, if with nothing other than a hypothetical medium called ether. The celestial spheres in which the Sun, Moon, and the planets are supposed to reside are composed of this hypothetical element. It should be noted here that Aristotle's concept of space is highly local, which is very much associated with the existence of bodies. In this view, the existence of bodies is essential to the existence of space.

John Philoponus (d. 570) criticized Aristotle's concept of space by arguing that, if the place of the stone is to be the adjacent boundary, then a stone held in a current of water would change its place continuously, since the water which envelops it is changing, a result which is self-contradictory. Consequently, Philoponus considered the stone's place to be the inner surface of the first immobile body, in this case the riverbed. That is to say, Philoponus considered the riverbed as a frame of reference for defining the position of the stone.

Aristotle's concept of time is different from his concept of motion, since motion is many and varied, whereas time is always one; nevertheless, time is inseparably connected with motion. He wrote: "It is evident, then, that time is neither movement nor independent of movement".[5] The motion of a body in Aristotle's philosophy is considered to be continuous in accordance with his view of the infinite divisibility of bodies.

The concepts of *before* and *after* are related primarily to place, but these concepts can also be applied to motion. Thus, since time is intimately connected to motion, the concepts of *before* and *after* also apply to time. This led to Aristotle's definition of time as a "number of motion in respect of before and after".[6] To put it differently, time is a sort of counter of motion. Although motion is a continuous process, because magnitudes are continuous one can still distinguish a series of phases in the process, which one can identify as a series of "nows". ("Now" is the moment that links the past with the future.) Since motion is continuous, the division of motion into a series of nows represents the arbitrary division of an infinitely divisible process. Time is that by which change is measured, and there can be no measure without the enumeration of the units of the process of change. Time is also the measure of rest, because what is at rest can be moved. Aristotle points out that, in one sense, there is not a series of nows, but one "now" that is associated with different events and that produces the experience of before and after: it is as if the nows were a substratum that takes on different properties as it becomes associated with different events in the process of motion. He said:

> Hence in these also the "now" as substratum remains the same (for it is what is before and after in movement), but what is predicated of it is different; for it is in so far as the "before and after" is numerable that we get the "now".[7]

It is clear that time is secondary to change or motion and presupposes the occurrence of change; there can be no time without change. He describes the present as the extremity of past and future, the indivisible, shared limit of both.

Many Muslim philosophers and scientists of the Islamic era shared the views of Aristotle about space, time, and motion. Most famous of those were Ibn Sīnā and Ibn Rushd.

Space and Time in Physics

In this section, I will present the concepts of space and time in theories of classical and modern physics, specifically the Newtonian and the Einsteinian concepts. I find this presentation relevant for what will follow later, where I will consider the concepts of space and time according to the *mutakallimūn*, as expressed by Ibn Ḥazm and al-Ghazālī. Of course, we will find that some of the views share common concepts or presentations.

Space and Time in Newtonian Physics

Newton considered space as an extension that is available to contain objects, and accordingly he understood it as an absolute space that is available everywhere in an infinitely extended universe. In the *Principia* we read:

> Absolute space in its own nature, without relation to anything external, remains always similar and immovable. Relative space is some movable dimension or measure of the absolute space; which is commonly taken for immovable space; such is the dimension of a subterraneous, an aerial or celestial space, determined by its position in respect to the earth. Absolute and relative spaces are the same in figure and magnitude; but they do not remain always numerically the same. For if the earth, for instance, moves, a space of our air, which relatively and in respect of the earth remains always the same, will at one time be one part of the absolute space into which the air passes; at another time it will be another part of the same, and so, absolutely understood, it will be continually changed.[8]

This new concept of space replaced the Aristotelian concept associated with the boundaries of bodies. In the Newtonian concept, space exists without the need for bodies, thus is absolute in character, not by being infinitely extended, but by being independent of anything else. No doubt that the works and ideas of Galileo Galilei and René Descartes influenced Newton in one way or another. Newton identified relative spaces by the bodies that are present in the absolute space. But, contrary to the Cartesian concepts of infinite extension, Newton used the concept of "mass-point" to allocate the body. This concept, which is used in present-day textbooks, marks the gap that separates Newton's concept of mass from Descartes' concept of spatial extension.

Absolute space is an epistemological (logical) and ontological necessity to Newton; it is a necessary prerequisite for the first law of motion. Rectilinear uniform motion has to be measured with reference to a fixed coordinate system; the state of rest also presupposes such an absolute space. In his *Principia*, Newton made it clear that absolute motion is a translation from one absolute place into another, and relative motion is the translation from one relative place into another.

Max Jammer noted that Newton, being motivated by his mathematical realism, endowed his concept of absolute space with an independent ontological existence:

> For Newton the introduction of the concept of absolute space into his system of physics did not result from methodological necessity only. Newton was led by his mathematical realism to endow this concept, as yet merely a mathematical structure, with independent ontological existence.[9]

This is an important point in considering the question of mathematical realism, where we sometimes see arguments that respect mathematical structures as having realistic existence. This is what happens nowadays with string theory, a point I briefly discussed in previous chapters.

Newton also introduced the concept of absolute time. In the *Principia*, we read:

> Absolute, true and mathematical time, of itself, and from its own nature flows equably without regard to anything external, and by another name is called duration: relative, apparent and common time, is some sensible and external (whether accurate or unequable) measure of duration by the means of motion, which is commonly used instead of true time.[10]

Clearly Newton considered time to be absolute, that is, independent of the existence of bodies or motion. Rather, time is an entity by which we measure durations or intervals with respect to which we measure motion. This was a practical and concise understanding which enabled Newton and all physicists that followed him to shape the laws of physics and the time development of physical systems in measurable quantitative forms.

This understanding of time is very practical, but it does not delve into the deeper meaning of time; therefore, it has little philosophical yield.

Space and Time in the Theory of Relativity

The theory of special relativity, which was proposed by Albert Einstein in 1905, suggested that space and time should be considered as one complex entity by which we can define an event. Instead of dealing with three-dimensional space, or viewing events as occuring in places defined by three coordinates, Einstein added a fourth coordinate to represent time. In order to harmonize this new coordinate with the three-space coordinate, Einstein assumed that the velocity of light in vacuum is a universal constant independent of the state of motion of the observer or the source. Accordingly, spacetime was viewed as being defined by four dimensions, three for space coordinates and one for time. The theory defined the "spacetime interval" as the distance between any two points in this four-dimensional spacetime. This distance was found to be invariant with respect to all inertial observers (coordinate systems). In this visualization, physical quantities should be articulated in terms of four components belonging to more general entities expressed in the four-dimensional spacetime. Consequently, the laws of physics should be expressed in a form that is invariant with respect to all inertial observers. This would preserve the unity of physics at every point in the four-dimensional spacetime.

The theory of special relativity abandoned the notion of absolute space and absolute time and considered all inertial observers to be equivalent. Measurements of spatial separations and temporal intervals became observer-dependent quantities, but always preserved the overall spacetime interval invariant. Consequently, a temporal interval with respect to a given observer might be longer than that measured by another observer, but then the spatial interval as measured by the observer has to be shorter so that the sum of the spatial and temporal intervals is constant and invariant with respect to all inertial observers. This implied the relativity of space and time and resulted in a new definition of simultaneity in the universe. Events which occur simultaneously with respect to one observer might be non-simultaneous with respect to another observer. This was expected to have an impact on the conception of causality, and indeed it did.[11]

Apart from explaining many experiments and phenomena, this new vision of the space and time provided us with a new physics in a relativistic framework. Relativity theory made serious predictions which have had a great impact on our lives, most important of which, perhaps, was the discovery of the equivalence of mass and energy. In short, mass was found to be a sort of compressed energy, therefore mass can be converted into energy, and this is what we now enjoy as electricity produced from nuclear plants.

In the theory of general relativity, the concept of spacetime preserves its original character of being relative, but in this case takes on the new character of being curved. The curvature of spacetime exhibits itself in the force of gravity; masses of bodies create curved spacetime according to which masses move. As John Wheeler put it, "mass tells spacetime how to curve and spacetime tells mass how to move".[12] The curvature of time is manifested by a time dilation so that, when light passes through a medium in which time is dilated, its wavelength gets longer and we say that light is "redshifted". This is the gravitational redshift that takes place near very massive compact celestial objects, such as white dwarfs and neutron stars.

As for the question of the finiteness of the universe and the existence of a space or time beyond the universe, the theory of general relativity stipulates that there can be no space or time beyond the universe, since the universe occupies all space and time. Using the language of mathematics, we say that the spacetime manifold is itself the whole universe. The observed universe is described by the theory of general relativity as a three-dimensional surface embodied in a four-dimensional spacetime. The three-dimensional surface is the three-dimensional space that we are living in. It is called a "surface", rather than a volume, because it is envisioned geometrically as a cross-section of the four-dimensional spacetime. At any moment, this cross-section constitutes a three-dimensional surface (hypersurface). The universe, therefore, has no center; any point on this hypersurface can be considered a center.

The spacetime in the theory of relativity is bound by the light barrier, which constitutes the physical boundaries of our time-like world in which events are deemed to be causally connected. Beyond this region of spacetime, we have a space-like region in which events are non-causally connected. This has been shown by the Minkowski diagram, which was discussed in some detail in Chapter Three.

Despite not giving details about the nature of time itself, the theory of relativity, through its description of space and time as an interwoven entity and with the speed of light being the "signature" of spacetime, has partly uncovered the nature of time. As it passes, space light follows curved lines called "spacetime geodesics". These geodesics mark the topology (the shape) of the spacetime. When light rays curve spatially, this indicates that the spacetime is curved spatially and, once light is redshifted, it means that time is becoming warped. This is the beautiful connection between space, time, and light. At the event horizon of a black hole, light is bent so drastically that it is forced to have a circular orbit around the singularity which is at the center of the black hole. The space curves so much that it becomes a spherical top. Time becomes so warped at the event horizon that light is frozen. Since the passage of time defines the past and the future through a moving moment—the "now"—frozen time stands as a still moment, at which point all pasts and all futures are in congruence. This is what I would call the "divine moment", which St. Augustine tried to express in his definition of eternity. It is something beyond our time-like comprehension. It is the same moment through which, while writing these words, I believe that I have deeply shared in the inner feelings of St. Augustine as he wrote his words describing eternity. This is a great moment for human consciousness indeed, by which we can appreciate the value of this consciousness that goes beyond spacetime and light to ride on the inner light of our souls and surf through eternity.

It is this perspective which gives us the imagination to envisage a pathway to our destiny. A giant black hole is the most expected destiny of a closed universe, and a closed universe is the destiny for our universe according to the Qur'an.

> The Day when We shall roll up the heavens as a recorder rolleth up a written scroll. As We began the first creation, We shall repeat it. (It is) a promise (binding) upon Us. Lo! We are to perform it. (21:104)

Therefore, it might be sound to think, as a Muslim, that the day after the "rolling up" of the heavens might be understood in terms of the world passing through the inner region of a black hole. Incidentally, all black holes that exist in our present universe are connected through their identical singularities. All our souls in the form of projected holographic presentation will rotate one day around a black hole and finally return to the giant black hole. This will take our souls with all the information contained therein, including all of our past time-like curves, to live the "divine moment", meeting Allah:

> And guard yourselves against a day in which ye will be brought back to Allah. Then every soul will be paid in full that which it hath earned, and they will not be wronged. (2:281)

What I say above might sound like unscientific speculations, but surely they are simply reflections of what the holy scriptures of all the monotheistic religions stipulate, but put into a scientific context? Nobody can claim with any certainty what will happen, but, given the well-organized structure and delicate formation of this universe we are living in, it would be reasonable to talk about a purpose and destiny for such a highly talented creature as the human being. It just cannot be true to say that this universe is purposeless. For that would mean that all space, all time, and therefore all of our science and whatever we know about the universe, are nothing but meaningless illusions. Would such a tragic result be acceptable to Steve Weinberg and Richard Dawkins, and to those who share in their views?

Space and Time in Quantum Mechanics

Quantum theory was originally developed as a theory of matter and energy. Space and time had nothing to do with matter, and energy content was taken as it is in the Newtonian sense. However, as quantum mechanics was further developed, it was inevitable to consider space and time. Physical systems such as particles and so forth, represented now as mathematical functions of space and time, would need a well-defined space and a well-defined time coordinate system to be an arena in which these functions could play out. The Newtonian concept of space and time remains suitable for such a role, but soon it was found that the position of a particle in space is closely connected with its momentum and that time is closely connected with its energy through the different representations of the wave function in different spaces. Moreover, it was found that such relations are bound by a minimum uncertainty imposed on the product of complementary variables, such as momentum and position, time and energy. The concepts of space and time became more complicated once quantum mechanics was presented with the more accurate form of "operators". Energy and momentum are represented as mathematical differential operators, while space and time have preserved their status as parameters that are necessary to describe the physical system in the form of wave functions or the more abstract form of "state vectors".

In quantum mechanics, space and time have a different role from the one they play in classical mechanics. The basic difference between the two is that, whereas in classical mechanics space and time provide the background for the physical arena in which events are taking place and absolute physical values are being measured, in quantum mechanics the wave functions describe the states of the particles and space and time take a more modest role. Alternative spaces such as the "phase space" are good replacements for the formal space. It should also be remembered that space and time are independent of each other in non-relativistic quantum mechanics.

In relativistic quantum mechanics, space and time are diffused according to the requirements of the theory of special relativity. However, no fully general relativistic quantum formulation is available till now. Once it becomes available, this could provide us with a theory of quantum gravity. This theory would seem to require quantization of space and time, a requirement which is far from being tenable within the present formulations. Some physicists talk about "spacetime foam" near the Planck scale, which is a very minute scale of space and time by which the unit of distance is 10^{-33} cm and a unit of time is 10^{-44} seconds, but most agree that intervals or durations cannot be infinitely subdivided. At this level, spacetime becomes a parameter defining an entity which characterizes the behavior of other parameters in the universe in such a way as to share their effect instead of only being occupied by it.

In more speculative theories such as string and superstring theories, we encounter other dimensions beyond the four known spacetime dimensions. These presentations are mostly mathematical and are hard to be realized on a common-sense level, as such extra dimensions are said to be compact. However, no one can deny that many formulations which were at first thought to be mathematical in nature gained their physical realization later through actual applications and interpretation of natural phenomena. Likewise, we might become accustomed to dealing with some of the mathematical presentations of string and superstring theories one day, as they become more familiar concepts.

Space and Time According to Islamic *Kalām*

Perhaps the best definition of space according to Islamic *kalām* is the one given by al-Jurjānī: "the conceived empty place which is occupied by the body and in which its dimensions are extended".[13] This implies that space is an envisaged place that does not get its ontology except by being occupied with a body. This is a subtle concept indeed, since it might be understood to mean that space cannot exist unless a body is occupying it. To clarify this position, we need to explain another term which is directly related to the concept of space: "occupancy" (*taḥayyuz*). This means, according to al-Juwaynī, one of the fathers of the late Ashʿari school, "the place for an envisaged *jawhar* [the indivisible part: the atom]".[14] In this respect, we should remember that, according to most of the *mutakallimūn*, the *jawhar* (see Chapter One) has no size or area. However, as for the other concept of empty space (*khalāʾ*) the *mutakallimūn* considered it to mean "the space which is left behind when the occupying body is removed".[15] So, empty space should exist; without it no motion could be achieved. Ibn Mattawayh, a famous Muʿtazili, presented an argument in favor of the existence of *khalāʾ*.[16] These concepts were commonly understood by Ashʿaris and Muʿtazila, although they had different views on some of the finer details.

The concepts of space and time in Islamic *kalām* are very much connected with the principle of discreteness (atomism) and the principle of re-creation, which was developed by the *mutakallimūn* to apply to all discrete properties.

Space, as well as time, was conceived as being discrete. Al-Jurjānī defines time as "a known renewable by which an envisaged unknown is estimated".[17] Clearly, in this definition, we can spot two features given to time: the first is intrinsic, being renewable, and the second is functional, by which we connect two events. Perhaps one might say that the second feature makes this definition of time include simultaneity, since the adjunction of two events requires defining two times, thus involving simultaneity.

The discreteness of space is another subtle concept, which might not be as clear as in the case of time. However, this discreteness might be clarified first by pointing to the way in which the *mutakallimūn* added two or more *jawhar*s together. In this case, they denied that two *jawhar*s might be diffused into one another, but insisted that they can only touch each other (*tamās*). When two *jawhar*s are attached to each other, a line is formed; to make a two-dimensional surface we would need four *jawhar*s, and to make a three-dimensional volume we would need eight. This describes the fundamental construction of an extension in space according to *kalām*. This exposes an abstract understanding of the basic elements that constitute matter, for example. In this respect, Max Jammer raised the question of whether it was sheer coincidence for Leibniz to suggest monadology, in which he sketched the metaphysics of simple substances, or "monads". Jammer presents an argument pointing to the possibility that Leibniz may have adopted the atomic theory of *kalām*. On the other hand, he says that "consequential thought led the *kalām* to the conclusion that space as well as matter (and time), is of atomistic structure".[18]

Related to the concepts of space and time, we naturally come to the concept of motion. Since space and time were taken to be discrete according to *kalām*, motion becomes a discontinuous process. Motion is viewed as a series or a sequence of momentary leaps; the *jawhar*s occupy different individual places in succession, thus physical motion has to be discontinuous.

Jammer presented a beautiful argument affirming the discreteness of space according to *kalām*, which goes as follows:

> The discrete structure of space according to the theory of kalām, can be inferred from the two premises (1) of the discreteness of time (the third fundamental proposition of kalām, according to the enumeration of Maimonides); (2) of the Aristotelian inference from the continuity of space to that of motion, and from the continuity of motion to that of time. Since the consequent, according to the first premise, is denied, the formal application of the *modus tollens* leads to the conclusion that space is not continuous.[19]

However, the *kalām* theory of motion leads to many complications. First, it would suggest a new concept of velocity by which the faster body is not that which covers larger distances during equal time intervals, but it is that trajectory on which there are fewer moments of rest (*sukūn*). This means that there is one universal speed, but a different number of still points for different trajectories of motion. In a modern description of such a concept, I would say that the *kalām* description of motion resembles the motion as depicted by a digital stream of sequential frames viewed on a cine projector at one speed; a fast object is seen on only a few frames, whereas a slow object would appear on many frames. This *kalām* conception of motion was challenged with the question of the revolving millstone, an example which was put forward by opponents of discreteness. In the words of Maimonides:

> Have you observed a complete revolution of a millstone? Each point in the extreme circumference of the stone describes a large circle in the same time in which a point near the center describes a small circle; the velocity of the outer circle is therefore greater than that of the inner circle. You cannot say that the motion of the latter is interrupted by more moments of rest; for the whole moving body, i.e., the millstone is one coherent body. They [*mutakallimūn*] reply: during the circular motion, the parts of the stone separate from each other, and the moments of rests interrupting the motion of the portions nearer to the center are more than those which interrupt the outer portions.[20]

Maimonides commented further by saying:

> [W]e ask again; how is it that the millstone, which we perceive as one body and which cannot be easily broken even with a hammer, resolves into its atoms when it moves, and becomes once again one coherent body, returning to its previous state as soon as it comes to rest, while no one is able to notice the breaking up of the stone?[21]

We now know that the above argument used by Maimonides was not valid, since, in theory, we can dismantle the millstone into individual parts and consider the motion of each part separately, as we always do in analytical mechanics. As it is clear from the *kalām* description of motion, the speed of the body is trajectory dependent. The more important question is how we can justify the motion of two particles of the same mass on the same trajectory with different speeds. How can a slower particle be at more stationary points than a faster one? Thus, one would think, it is not the trajectory that defines the speed but something else, a problem that is left for further research.[22] Incidentally, as was noted by Landau and Lifshitz,[23] the concept of instant velocity in quantum mechanics is quite obscure. This is because instant velocity is obtained as the first derivative of the distance with respect to time, and this implies the assumption that the duration of time Δt goes to zero. But, according to Heisenberg's uncertainty principle, the energy of the system will then be completely undetermined, a situation which makes the concept of instant velocity in quantum mechanics obscure.

Jammer claims that Galileo's discussion of the problem of discrete motion in his *Discorsi e Dimostrazioni Matematiche Intorno a Due Nuove Scienze* (*Discourses and Mathematical Demonstrations Relating to Two New Sciences*), and his treatment of the "infinite and the indivisible", is "reminiscent of the ancient teachings of the *kalām*".[24] Apart from this, very little is known about the influence of the *kalām* conception of space and time on scholastic thought in medieval Europe. But, since it is well established that the works of al-Ghazālī and Maimonides, with their references to the atomistic space theories of *kalām*, were widely read by scholars, Jammer seriously questions the possibility that this atomistic theory of space could have escaped their attention.[25] This is a very important question indeed, taking into consideration the influence of discreteness on Leibniz, which was mentioned above, and the influence on Galileo, also mentioned above. But, to resolve this question, we would need to invest a great deal of impartial effort into analyzing this scholastic legacy. Perhaps this is part of the homework that modern Muslim scholars specializing in the history of science could do.

Space and time are two entities that are essential for our understanding of our physical world. Space seems to be more real than time, as it is objectively present; it is part of what we see around us. Time is not so tangible to our senses, as it seems to be less objectively present. Events need to occur for us to feel the presence of time and our world cannot endure two instances without something changing. It was thought that time exists like a river running independent of any concern for those at its banks; it can only be affected by the topography of the land through which it passes, running quickly as the land slopes and slowly as it climbs a hill. Similarly, time is affected by the topography of space through the mutual play that keeps the path of light intact.

Time seems to have only one direction, regardless of the many mathematical formulae that allow for time reversal. Nature, through the requirements imposed by thermodynamics, prevents time reversal and that is why we have a time arrow. Translation in space can take forward or backward directions; we can retrace back our path as we move, but can never retrace our past time; time reversal is a fiction.

Space and Time According to Ibn Ḥazm

Ibn Ḥazm was born to a rich and influential Córdoban family; he received a distinguished education in religious sciences, literature, and poetry. Profoundly disappointed by his political experiences and offended by the conduct of his contemporaries, Ibn Ḥazm subsequently left public life and devoted his last thirty years to literary activities and produced a reported 400 works, of which only forty still survive. He covered a range of topics, which included Islamic jurisprudence, history, ethics, comparative religion, and theology, as well as producing his famous work, *The Ring of the Dove*, on the art of love. Ibn Ḥazm was a leading proponent and codifier of the Ẓahirī school in Islamic thought. The *Encyclopaedia of Islam* refers to him as having been one of the leading thinkers of the Muslim world and he is widely acknowledged as the father of comparative religious studies.[26]

In his treatise *Kitāb al-fiṣal fī al-milal wa al-ahwāʾ wa al-niḥal* (*al-Fiṣal*) on Islamic science, philosophy, and theology, Ibn Ḥazm stressed the importance of sense perception. While he recognized the importance of reason, since the Qur'an itself invites reflection, he argued that this reflection mainly refers to revelation and sense data, because the principles of reason are themselves derived entirely from sense experience. He concludes that reason is not a faculty for independent inquiry, research, or discovery, but that sense perception should be used in its place, an idea that forms the basis of empiricism.[27] In this argument, perhaps Ibn Ḥazm was criticizing the Greeks, who were known to have stressed the value of reason and mindful works without much need for experimentation. In what follows, I will present Ibn Ḥazm's views on space and time as he has presented them, mainly in *al-Fiṣal*. First of all, we should know that Ibn Ḥazm refused to acknowledge the existence of any physical infinite, including space and time. He tried to refute the infinite extension of time by simple logical arguments. He said: "Everything that exists in reality is confined by number, countable by its own nature, and by [the term] nature we mean the force in the thing by which its properties are run". Then he said: "Everything that is confined by number would be countable by its own nature, therefore it is finite, consequently the world is finite".[28] Accordingly, he refused to accept the existence of anything which has infinite extension:

> An infinite would in no way exist in reality, and whatever might exist but only after an infinite regress could not exist at all, because being "after" necessitates finiteness, and an infinite has no "after". Consequently, nothing can exist after another in infinite regress and, since things do exist one after the other, therefore all things are finite.[29]

So, this is how Ibn Ḥazm thought of the impossibility of infinity. It is this argument by Ibn Ḥazm which makes me think that in fact he was adopting the doctrine of the finite divisibility of things, despite his denial of *kalām* atomism, which was based on his theological argument that Allah is able to divide things infinitely. Otherwise, and as I have found previously, Ibn Ḥazm agreed that a non-divisible part may exist in reality but not in theory.[30]

Ibn Ḥazm defined time as "the duration through which an object stays at rest or in motion, and if the object is to be deprived of this [rest or motion] then that object will cease to exist and time will cease to exist too. Since the object and the time both do exist, therefore they both co-exist".[31]

Clearly, in this definition, Ibn Ḥazm associated the existence of time with the existence of the body, which pointed to the connection between space and time, and then he argued that the time of the world has a finite duration as well as a beginning:

> Any object in the world and every accident associated with an object and every time are all finite and have a beginning. We see this sensibly and objectively because the finiteness of an object is obvious through its size and through the time of its existence.[32]

Therefore objects of the world are finite and in these sentences it is clear that Ibn Ḥazm denied the existence of anything infinite of any sort. But, in the case of time, he went even further to consider time as being composed of finite instances, moments that pass one after the other:

> The finiteness of time happens though what comes after that which has passed, and the exhaustion of every time [period] after its existence, as "now" is the limit of it, and it is this [now] which separates the two times: the past and the future, and it is as such that one time ends and another would start. And every period of time is composed of finite times that have beginnings.[33]

This makes it clear that Ibn Ḥazm considered time to be discrete on the ontological level, despite his general denial of the "indivisible parts". Ibn Ḥazm used these concepts to argue that God existed in neither space nor time:

> Because God is not occupied with time and has no duration or end, because the time is the motion of whatever is timed, its motion from one place to another, or its duration when at rest in one place, and God is neither in motion nor is at rest and [there is] no doubt that He is not timed and has no duration or end, and He is originally not confined to one place.[34]

Consistently, on the same issue in another place, he wrote:

> God is not [confined] to a time and has no duration, because time is the motion of any timely object and its transition from one place to another or the duration of its stay at rest in one place and God neither is movable nor is at rest.[35]

It should be noted from the above quotations that Ibn Ḥazm understood time to run sequentially. He thought that the passage of time occurs in sequential moments, one after the other; as the moment passes, it becomes past. Subsequently, a new moment replaces the old one, and so time passes.

Although Ibn Ḥazm did not seem to accept the principle of discreteness envisaged by the *mutakallimūn*, his sentences above express that time is divided into finite instances, a notion very similar to time discreteness. Indeed, for Ibn Ḥazm to have been consistent in his views about space, time, and the creation of the world, he should certainly have adopted the discreteness and finiteness of parts. Those who claim the contrary should read all the available descriptions and analyze all of his arguments, not only in their expressions but in their consistency, to see that he could not but have adopted discreteness, despite his refusal to accept the notion of a non- divisible part on a theological basis.

Concerning space, it seems that Ibn Ḥazm adopted the Aristotelian view to define space and argue for the absence of voids. In *al-Fiṣal*, he defined space in a similar way to Aristotle: "Because the space that we know is the place surrounding the body localized within".[36] It is also noted that Ibn Ḥazm tried to refute the existence of absolute space (in the Newtonian sense, despite preceding Newton). He referred to a group of people with whom he was engaged in a discussion about space and time, finding them to claim the existence of absolute space and absolute time:

> They say that absolute space and absolute time is not what we have defined previously, because they are changing, and it would suffice to refute their argument of defining an unaccustomed concept of space and an unaccustomed concept of time without having evidence for it.[37]

This absolute space he described as being the void that exists independent of objects or bodies. In order to refute this claim, Ibn Ḥazm used lengthy dialectical arguments, which are not very convincing. A similar discussion was considered by al-Ghazālī, but with more sophisticated arguments.

Space and Time According to al-Ghazālī

Al-Ghazālī was a prominent thinker who produced such a colorful range of thoughts that it is a puzzling task to associate him definitively with any one school of thought, other than to say that he belonged to a special school of his own. He might be considered an Ashʿari theologian, a philosopher, or a Sufi monk. He expressed a multitude of thoughts in his writings and was experienced in all the possible methodologies of his time.

Al-Ghazālī viewed space and time as being two entities that should be treated on the same footing. His best presentation on this subject can be found in his treatise *Tahāfut al-falāsifa*, where he tried to refute the philosophers' claim about the eternity of the world. Al-Ghazālī presented similar arguments about time to those of St. Augustine, some of which I have mentioned above. However, one can confidently say that, in presenting these arguments, al-Ghazālī was also speaking as a representative of the *mutakallimūn*, since he was using their dialectical method and their concepts about space and time. It would also be fair to say that al-Ghazālī presented these arguments with much originality and thought, for which he deserves the credit. He used an analogy between space and time, the *above* and the *below* versus the *before* and *after*, in order to proclaim an equivalence between spatial and temporal extensions.

Al-Ghazālī considered that time was created alongside the world, and not before it:

> Time is originated and created, and before it there was no time at all. We mean by our statement that God is prior to the world and time, that He was and there was no world and that then He was and with Him was the world.[38]

In response to the question about the time that had passed before the creation of the world, al-Ghazālī replied by presenting an analogy of space, where we are not accustomed to accepting that there is nothing above our heads. But, he said, when we talk about the world as a whole, we should realize that there is nothing beyond the surface of the world:

> Similarly, it will be said that just as spatial extension[39] is a concomitant of body; temporal extension[40] is a concomitant of motion. And just as the proof for the finitude of the dimensions of the body prohibits affirming a spatial dimension

> beyond it, the proof for the finitude of motion at both ends prohibits affirming a temporal extension before it, even though the estimation clings to its imagining it and its supposing it, not desisting from [this]. There is no difference between temporal extension that in relation [to us] divides verbally into (before) and (after) and spatial extension that in relation [to us] divides into (above) and (below). If, then, it is legitimate to affirm an "above" that has no above, it is legitimate to affirm a (before) that has no real before, except an estimative imaginary [one] as with the (above).[41]

The most important piece of information in the above quotation is the reference made by al-Ghazālī to the term "temporal extension" alongside the term "spatial extension". This was something new for the intellectual era in which al-Ghazālī lived and indeed it does reflect a deep understanding of the meaning of space and time in our real world, and the reason for their absence before the creation of the world.

Al-Ghazālī continued arguing on the relativity of the "before" and the "after", responding to criticism that may be directed against his analogy of time with space, where it could be said that space and time cannot be treated on an equal footing:

> This comparison is contorted because the world has neither an "above" nor a "below," being, rather, spherical, and the sphere has neither an "above" nor a "below". Rather, if a direction is called "above" this is inasmuch as it is beyond your head; the other [direction is called] "below" insofar as it extends beyond your foot.[42]

But then al-Ghazālī retaliated by saying:

> This makes no difference. There is no [particular] object in assigning the utterance "above" and "below," but we will shift to the expressions "beyond" and "outside" and say, "The world has an inside and an outside: is there, then, outside the world something which is either filled or empty space?" [The philosophers] will then say, "Beyond the world there is neither a void nor filled space. If by 'outside' you mean its outermost surface, then it would have an outside; but if you mean something else, then it has no outside." Similarly, if we are asked, "Does the world have a 'before'?" we answer, "If by this is meant, 'Does the world's existence have a beginning, that is, a limit in which it began?' then the world has a 'before' in this sense, just as the world has an outside on the interpretation that this is its exposed limit and surface end. If you mean by it anything else, then the world has no 'before,' just as when one means by 'outside the world' [something] other than its surface, then one would say, 'There is no exterior to the world.'" Should you say that a beginning of an existence that has no "before" is incomprehensible, it would then be said, "A finite bodily

existence that has no outside is incomprehensible: If you say that its 'outside' is its surface with which it terminates, [and] nothing more, we will say that its 'before' is the beginning of its existence which is its limit, [and] nothing more."[43]

Al-Ghazālī continued his discussion on this issue, presenting and defending persistently his concepts of space and time. The discussion led him to question the size of the universe and whether it could have been created larger or smaller than its known size. This is a challenge that I will discuss in the next chapter.

Therefore, I may conclude that al-Ghazālī, adopting the basic views of *kalām*, considered space and time to be on an equal footing and was able to envisage the relationship between them in a way that perceived their relativity in the sense of how it is accounted for by the observer (obviously, not in the Einsteinian sense). Accordingly, he was able to present the reason for there not being an arrow of time before the creation of the world.

Concluding Remarks

Space and time are entities that our consciousness encounters on two levels: one is through direct sensation, which gives us the feeling of being in a place surrounded by things such as walls, furniture, and the environment, including the changes around us. The other level includes the mental comprehensions by which we try to translate the first level into a more meaningful one, by philosophizing to go beyond the trivial sense. The purpose of this, then, is to be able to understand all phenomena which are related to changes in space and time. At this point, we start doing physics. For this reason, our view of space is a fundamental milestone in understanding the world. The history of knowledge has persistently proved this throughout the different ages of philosophical thinking.

The description of motion in *kalām* resembles the motion depicted by a digital stream of sequential frames, viewed on a cine projector at one speed: a fast object is seen in only a few frames, whereas a slow object would appear in many frames. If our world is predestined, then we have no choice but to believe in the analogy of the film reel, that our life is nothing but a film. On a film reel, events come in discrete frames and time is defined by the number of frames. Our world, if predestined, should be described as "space-like". I would not say that it is purely spatial, since, when tracing sequential frames, time is also passing, which is to say that the time dimension is realized through moving from one frame into the next. This may provide us with a clearer understanding of eternity, in confirmation of the accurate description given by St. Augustine. Now, if God knows the future of everything, and if we assume that He enjoys the capabilities that Pierre Laplace assumed a supernatural being to have, then the world would surely be deterministic in the eyes of God. Accordingly, it would be true to say that "God does not play dice", but our consciousness does play dice; it is the way the world appears to us rather than how it really is.

As for our present age, we seem to be on the verge of a new era in our vision of space and time; this vision goes beyond the standard picture provided by relativity theory and the standard theory of quantum mechanics. The new vision will challenge our consciousness as well as our mental capabilities and, in order for such a vision to be fruitful, it has to be realized in actual practice through new discoveries. As such, the new understanding could provide us with explanations for many phenomena that might have been considered until now as being so obscure that they do not belong to our physical world. This new vision comes as a compilation of both the old and modern ideas about space and time, and it will elevate our thinking to a new level through our journey to understand this world.

CHAPTER SIX

Cases from Old Debates: The Size of the Universe and the Fate of the Sun

Al-Ghazālī is an outstanding thinker by any stretch of the imagination.

Oliver Leaman

In the history of Islamic philosophical thought, the arguments which were presented by al-Ghazālī and Ibn Rushd on issues of natural philosophy stand as a remarkable monument that reflects the high intellectual level and standard of discourse that existed in their times. Such a splendid debate is a good original resource for identifying the intellectual themes at the time that al-Ghazālī wrote his book *Tahāfut al-falāsifa* (*The Incoherence of the Philosophers*), in which he tried to refute the philosophical approach to comprehending the relation between God and the world and to present an alternative from the Islamic perspective. He thought that following the philosophical approach would corrupt religion:

> [A] group who, believing themselves in possession of a distinctiveness from companion and peer by virtue of a superior quick wit and intelligence, have rejected the Islamic duties regarding acts of worship, disdained religious rites pertaining to the offices of prayer and the avoidance of prohibited things, belittled the devotions and ordinances prescribed by the divine Law, not halting in the face of its prohibitions and restrictions.[1]

Al-Ghazālī also wrote that:

> the source of their unbelief is their hearing high-sounding names such as "Socrates," "Hippocrates," "Plato," "Aristotle," and their likes, and the exaggeration and mis-guidedness of groups of their followers in describing their minds, the excellence of their principles, the exactitude of their geometrical, logical, natural, and metaphysical sciences, and in [describing these as] being alone

> by reason of excessive intelligence and acumen—[capable] of extracting these hidden things; [also hearing] what [these followers] say about [their masters, namely] that concurrent with the sobriety of their intellect and the abundance of their merit is their denial of revealed laws and religious confessions and their rejection of the details of religious and sectarian [teaching], believing them to be man-made laws and embellished tricks.[2]

Al-Ghazālī claimed to have written his book:

> in refutation of the ancient philosophers, to show the incoherence of their belief and the contradiction of their word in matters relating to metaphysics; to uncover the dangers of their doctrine and its shortcomings, which in truth ascertainable are objects of laughter for the rational and a lesson for the intelligent—I mean the kinds of diverse beliefs and opinions they particularly hold that set them aside from the populace and the common run of men.[3]

In his treatise, al-Ghazālī mostly adopted the views and the approach of *kalām*. It was his intention to expose the failure of the philosophical argument in proposing a truly reconciliatory view of God and the world to which Muslims could subscribe without infringing their beliefs. He brought the conflict between Islamic *kalām* and philosophy to a head by undertaking a refutation of twenty philosophical doctrines, out of which seventeen were condemned as being heretical innovations and three as being totally opposed to Islamic belief. In part, al-Ghazālī targeted two prominent Muslim philosophers, al-Fārābī and Ibn Sīnā, for their views about the emanation of the world and the resurrection of bodies. The philosophers he condemned were not atheists and in fact their philosophies rested upon the affirmation of God and the recognition that all in existence emanate as the necessary consequences of the divine essence. Nevertheless, al-Ghazālī saw this as meaning that God has produced the world by necessity, in the same way that an inanimate object like the Sun was said to produce light by its very nature. For him, the views presented by the philosophers meant the denial of the divine attributes of life, will, power, and knowledge. Al-Ghazālī maintained that, denied these attributes, the god of the philosophers was not the god of the Qur'an.

Despite the fact that his *Tahāfut al-falāsifa* had brought the conflict between philosophy and more traditional Islamic beliefs to the fore, al-Ghazālī had in fact largely contributed this treatise to explain some important philosophical arguments. Owing to its intellectual caliber, his book marks a high point in the history of medieval Islamic thought. Although its motivation was religious, as shown above by his own words, it made its case through closely argued criticisms that were, ultimately, philosophical. It is important to note that al-Ghazālī based his critiques of the philosophical arguments related to natural philosophy on a consistent body of thought which embedded what I call the "principles of *daqīq al-kalām*" in a most efficient manner. This, as we will see below, is not an isolated argument, but is rather a full range of arguments which encompasses detailed comprehension of fundamental concepts such as space, time, causality, the laws of nature, and several others. And, to a large extent, one can say without any equivocation that al-Ghazālī affirmed Ashʿari causal theory. For him, divine power is pervasive and is the direct cause of each and every created existent and each and every temporal event. The basic principle he adopted is that inanimate things have no causal power, a view which he also asserted in other works, such as *al-Iqtiṣād fi al-iʿtiqād*.

Ibn Rushd, the philosopher of Islamic Spain, adopted the views of Aristotle and provided a great service to Greek philosophy by explaining Aristotle's legacy. He found the work of al-Ghazālī to be a sort of forgery of philosophy; accordingly, he devoted his work *Tahāfut al-tahāfut* (*The Incoherence of the Incoherence*) to refuting al-Ghazālī's presentation, following him paragraph by paragraph, mostly reinstating the position of Aristotle on those questions.

In this chapter, I will present two problems which were originally discussed by al-Ghazālī in the context of his critique of the philosophers: the size of the universe and the degeneration of the Sun. The first problem appeared in the context of discussing the presence of time before the creation of the universe, where al-Ghazālī tried to show that time is not eternal and only existed once the universe existed, alongside space. He treated time on an equal footing with space and accordingly he tried to draw an analogy by which the temporal moments *before* and *after* are similar to the spatial allocations *above* and *below*, designations which can only be defined with respect to a given reference point. Consequently, time has no absolute reference except with respect to the moment of creation. In order to establish this analogy, al-Ghazālī went on to question the theoretical possibility that the universe could have been created larger or smaller than it is. If such a possibility is allowed, then the question arises over whether the universe has an exterior into which it can be extended. This was a challenging question for the philosophers, who denied such a possibility, always asserting the finiteness of the universe within a fixed size and shape. Hence, they had no alternative but to admit that beyond the universe there could be neither a body nor a void. This would mean that the volume of the universe is all which can be recognized to exist. Accordingly, and since time is associated with space and matter, no recognition of time would be possible unless the universe existed. Hence, the question of a time existing before the creation of the universe is deemed to be meaningless. Al-Ghazālī's genius was presented in this argument, which makes one admire the consistency of his argument and the boldness of his suggestion that time should be treated on equal footing with space. It might be said that the visualization of time existing alongside the creation of the universe had already been mentioned by St. Augustine (see Chapter Five on spacetime). This is true and it might be that al-Ghazālī adopted this visualization; however, it is important to note that he extended the argument of the analogy of space and time into a realm well beyond that of St. Augustine, by recognizing that the universe has no exterior and that the temporal extension is a dimension that has to be treated on an equal footing with spatial dimensions, a concept that we acknowledged in our modern age only after Albert Einstein's discovery of the theory of relativity.

The second problem, the question of the corruption of the Sun, was presented in the *Tahāfut al-falāsifa* in the context of discussing the post-eternity of the world, time, and motion. In this respect, al-Ghazālī did not deny the possibility of the post-eternity of the world on a rational basis, but he suggested that this could only be denied on a religious basis:

> No one maintains that the world should necessarily have an end except Abu al-Hudhayl al-'Allaf. For he said: "Just as an infinite number of past [heavenly] rotations is impossible, the same is true of the future." But this is false because the future does not enter at all into existence, either successively or concomitantly, whereas all of the past has entered into existence successively, even though not concomitantly. And if it has become evident that we do not deem it rationally remote for the world's duration to be everlasting, but regard either its rendering it eternal in the future or annihilating it as [both] possible, then which of the two possibilities becomes fact is only known through the revealed law. Hence the examination of this [question] is not connected with what is rationally apprehended.[4]

This is a good point to recognize indeed within the general view that al-Ghazālī held regarding the fate of the world. It does reflect that his religious belief motivated some of his positions on issues of the old metaphysics. And this is indeed what *kalām* was all about. It would affirm the *kalām* approach which I have outlined in Chapter One of this book, which starts with revelation and, according to which, it goes on to build a worldview.

Al-Ghazālī based his argument for rejecting the post-eternity of the Sun by refuting the argument which had been made to affirm its eternity. That argument took the observational fact that the Sun has continued to look the same, without withering, for a very long period of time as evidence for its eternity. Al-Ghazālī showed that this argument was flawed, since it was based on poor observations that were inadequate for recognizing small mass loss from the body of the Sun that might be taking place at a very slow rate.

Both problems were reconsidered by Ibn Rushd in his defense of the philosophers' arguments. Ibn Rushd had fully adopted Aristotelian cosmology and, accordingly, he tried to show that the universe could not be larger or smaller than its given size, because such a possibility, according to him, would change the universal order. He also tried to affirm Galen's position concerning the eternity of the Sun. In his refutation, Ibn Rushd was mostly apologetic and did not provide enough evidence, other than those which were available within Aristotle's metaphysics. However, at certain points through the discussion, one cannot deny that Ibn Rushd made certain notes and hints that reflected his own genius.

The presentation of these two problems here is intended to provide important historical examples of how the views of *kalām* and those of the philosophers constituted two rival theories in respect of natural events.

In concluding this chapter, I will try to assess the views that al-Ghazālī and Ibn Rushd presented on these two problems from the scientific standpoint which is currently held and based on the discoveries of modern astrophysics and cosmology.

Greek Sciences in Islam

The subjects of the creation of the firmament, including all the celestial objects, and of the design and development of the cosmos are some of the main considerations of many verses of the Qur'an. The main goal in presenting this issue, it seems, is to turn people's attention to the signs that demonstrate the glory of the Creator who designed the cosmos, and to appreciate the need for such a creator and designer. These signs mentioned in the Qur'an encouraged Muslims to contemplate the cosmos and try to understand God's action in the world through pure reason according to the philosophical trend. On the other hand, the transmission of Greek astronomy contributed positively to the scientific movement in the Islamic world to the extent that Muslim astronomers were able to develop their own new techniques for astronomical observations and to criticize Ptolemy's geocentric system, as well as develop an alternative astronomical system to replace that of Ptolemy.[5]

Most Muslim scientists and philosophers were overwhelmed by the Greek sciences and philosophy to the extent that they could not circumvent the main propositions of the Greeks with respect to their views of the cosmos. This applied to philosophical trends as much as to some other scientific trends in Islam. Greek philosophers such as Plato and Aristotle—"men of wisdom", as they were called in the Islamic media—were highly respected by most of the Muslim philosophers and especially by al-Fārābī, Ibn Sīnā, and Ibn Rushd. Some Muslim philosophers admired Plato and Aristotle to the extent that they considered them to be gifted wise men comparable to prophets, a status which would make it nearly impossible to breach their doctrines. For this reason, it would not be surprising to know that genuine contributions by Muslim philosophers to the philosophical achievements were quite modest and that most of their works echoed the original Greek views, despite their endeavor toward reconciling Islamic belief with philosophy.

On the other hand, Muslim rational theologians, who were rehearsing an independent style of thought based on the Qur'an, were less affected by the philosophical thoughts of the Greeks. This strongly applied to the pioneering practitioners of *kalām*, the *mutakallimūn*, who were active during the eighth and ninth centuries. This is why we see that *kalām* was able to reflect the true value and originality of Islamic creed.

Apart from some minute details, the picture that Muslims had about the firmament was almost the same as the one that was adopted and developed by the Greeks, in which the five planets, the Sun, the Moon, and the fixed stars were thought to be associated with concentric celestial spheres at the center of which Earth resides. This is the so-called "geocentric model" of the planetary system. In its most sophisticated form, this model, as mentioned above, was devised by Ptolemy and was adopted to calculate the positions of the celestial objects for more than 1,200 years. The fact that the calculations did not accurately fit with the observations required many readjustments of the model through the well-known epicycle assumption, by which astronomers had to suggest new values for the parameters every time they found their calculations did not fit the actual observations.

The Firmament in the Qur'an

The terms heaven (singular) and heavens (plural) are mentioned in the Qur'an 310 times. In so many verses, these terms come in the context of descriptions of divine providence and God's care of mankind. The Qur'an stresses that Allah has created the firmament and that He is developing it. However, the concept of the firmament does not have a definitive meaning in the Qur'an. It could mean the clouds, the atmosphere, the open sky, the solar system, the branch of the galaxy to which we belong, the galaxy, the whole universe, or even other universes that are beyond our comprehension. The meaning of the firmament is so widely presented that one cannot but treat every mention within its given context.[6] What is of interest at this point is the way that the Qur'an has presented the development of the firmament:

> Have not those who disbelieve known that the heavens and the earth were joined together as one united piece, then We parted them? And We have made from water every living thing. Will they not then believe? (21:30)

Despite some contextual similarities, this description for the creation of the firmament is somewhat different from what is given in the Old Testament. Here we understand that the heavens and the earth were one entity and that they were separated. The heavens were not born out on the surface of the water, as is stated in the Old Testament. Nevertheless, creation originated from water in the sense that water is the basic composition of living creatures. This provides a more detailed and accurate picture of the event of creation. Moreover, it seems that this event of creating the firmament is running continuously: "We constructed the firmament with our hands, and we will continue to extend it" (Qur'an 51:47).

This clear statement shows the development of the firmament after its creation to be one of continuous expansion. Such an expansion might entail the continuous creation of space, but it is not clear whether such a creation is accompanied by the creation of matter and energy, or whether it is space only which is expanding. Yet, the Qur'an does not specify where the expansion is taking place, whether within a larger volume of space or whether expanding from within. The word "extending" is different from the word "expanding", which has been used by some translators of the Qur'an. To expand may mean to increase the space between the constituents of a structure, say a city, without adding any new buildings. But to extend a city implies the adding of new buildings and an area to it. In the above verse, the sentence in the Qur'an indicates that the firmament constitutes a block that is being extended by the addition of new structures and spaces. So, one may say that space is being expanded possibly with the addition of new matter.

However, such expansion will not go forever, according to the Qur'an. It has to stop one day and will start to contract, taking the universe back to where it started:

> And (remember) the Day when We shall roll up the heavens like a scroll rolled up for letters, as We began the first creation, We shall repeat it, (it is) a promise binding upon Us. Truly, We shall do it. (21:104)

This clearly indicates that the firmament is going to contract and revert to the state of its first creation. In modern cosmology, this is called the "big crunch". The rolling up of the scroll is an interesting image which indicates a flat universe. Arguably, late discoveries of the accelerating universe may indicate that the universe will go on expanding forever. Nevertheless, this fate might be challenged by introducing other factors affecting the status of the universe, such as the so-called "cosmological constant", and some studies allow for the possibility of a collapsing flat universe.

Al-Ikhwān al-Ṣafā' (the Brothers of Purity) was a secret group of the Ismaili sect, which adopted the Aristotelian model of the heavens and tried to integrate it with Islamic belief through interpretations of the relevant verses of the Qur'an. They imagined seven ethereal spheres holding seven celestial bodies as being the seven heavens and the seven earths that the Qur'an has mentioned. So, for them, the world is no more than these objects surrounded by the sphere of the fixed stars and encircled by the Atlas orbit, which they interpreted to be the throne of God.

However, they did not tackle the question of the expanding or extending world mentioned in Sūrat al-Dhāriyāt. For this reason, we can say that their Aristotelian view was not of much help in covering the stipulations of the Qur'an concerning the development and the fate of the universe.

On this point, al-Ghazālī did not use the religious argument for asserting the possibility of an expanding universe; however, he may have been motivated by the stipulations of the Qur'an concerning such a possibility. Contrary to the mainstream philosophical thinking at that time, which considered the universe to be static and eternal, al-Ghazālī believed that the world was temporal, being created out of nothing, ex nihilo, and that its creation marked the beginning of both space and time. This understanding was actually borrowed from the *mutakallimūn*, who earlier in the Islamic history of thought had devised a theory of creation by which the universe came into being by the sheer will of Allah. In our present time, William Craig has made some serious efforts in elaborating on the Kalām Cosmological Argument, which stipulated that the universe must have a cause for its existence since it has a beginning.[7]

The Size of the Universe

In the first discussion of his *Tahāfut al-falāsifa*, al-Ghazālī discussed the problem of the temporality and the eternity of the world. His strategy was based on defying what he considered to be the strongest arguments of the philosophers in claiming that the world should be eternal, raising some challenging questions for the philosophers, discussing their views and showing that their arguments were inconsistent. In this context, al-Ghazālī presented a very deep and thoughtful discussion of space and time, defending the necessity to recognize the fact that space and time allocations should not be taken as absolute, but should always be considered in reference to a given point in space or time. This was indeed a very advanced comprehension of a topic that might well be considered a problem for the modern science of the twentieth century. Al-Ghazālī used the terms "spatial dimension" and "time dimension".[8] He refused the notion of a space that goes beyond the world and refused the existence of time before the creation of the world.[9] And it was through this comparison between space and time that he introduced the question about the size of the world, allowing for the possibility that the world could have been created larger or smaller than it is. With his sophisticated concept of space and time, and his realization of the analogy between space and time, al-Ghazālī refuted the philosophical claim that an infinite extension of time should have existed before the creation of the world. The most important argument which was placed in this context was the notion that both space and time existed only after the creation of the world, a concept that was established only by the modern theory of cosmology.

One of the arguments of al-Ghazālī concerned the size of the universe, where he posed the question of whether the universe could be larger or smaller than it is. This he posed in order to challenge the philosophers, trying to force them to admit one thing or another in their views concerning the existence of time before the creation of the universe. The philosophers used to argue that, if the universe were not eternal but had been created in time with a well-defined beginning, then why did the Creator wait so long before creating it? Obviously, this question implicitly assumes that the Creator lives in time.

Al-Ghazālī first questioned the philosophers over whether the world could have been created by God larger than its known size: "Did it lie within God's power to create the highest heaven greater in thickness by one cubit than the one He had created?".[10] Then he commented: "If they say, 'No,' this would be [the attribution to Him of] impotence. If they say, 'Yes,' then [it follows that God could have created it] greater by two cubits, three cubits, and so on, ascending ad infinitum".[11]

Consequently, al-Ghazālī concluded that, if the answer was "yes", then this would imply the affirmation of a space beyond the world that has a measure and quantity, since that which is greater by two cubits does not occupy the equivalent space as the one greater by one cubit. Accordingly, he said:

> Then, beyond the world there is quantity, requiring thus that which is quantified—namely, either body or the void. Hence, beyond the world there is either void or filled space.[12]

By setting this argument, al-Ghazālī posited a fundamental paradox that the philosophers were required to solve. The paradox had two faces: they could have said that beyond the world there is a void into which the world could be expanded. But the existence of such a void went against the doctrines of the philosophers, who refused the existence of voids anywhere in the world. Alternatively, they could have said that beyond the world there is a matter-filled space. In this case, there would be no reason why such a filled space should not be part of the world itself, since it would then be no more than an extension of the world itself.

Similarly, al-Ghazālī posed the other question of whether God is able to create the world's sphere smaller by one cubit, then by two? Accordingly, if one could accept that the measure of the world is reducible in size then, according to al-Ghazālī, this would imply that the void which is left when we reduce the size of the world is measurable, while being nothing. The other side of the paradox was to challenge the philosopher about the limit of God's authority with respect to creating and sustaining the world, a challenge that Muslim philosophers certainly would not have been able to stand.

In fact, the aim behind posing these questions concerning the size of the world was tactical rather than strategic. Al-Ghazālī had no intention of showing that the universe could be expanded or contracted, he intended to show only that we must consider the temporal designations in respect of the *before* and the *after* on an equal footing with the spatial assignments of the *above* and the *below*. That is to say, the temporal assignments of events should be done with respect to a given reference rather than being absolute. Therefore, here al-Ghazālī's argument served a dual purpose: one by which he intended to show that there is no basic natural objection to having a universe larger or smaller than the existing one, and the other that such a possibility would certainly reassure the conceptual integrity of space and time. Consequently, he made an effort to use these results to refute the claim that a temporal world necessitates the existence of a time duration *before* creation had taken place. For this reason, it could be said that al-Ghazālī would be quite happy with the contemporary argument put forward by Adolf Grünbaum,[13] which says that the moment of creation does not qualify as a physical event, since there was no physical moment *before* the initial moment of the big bang. Indeed, according to al-Ghazālī, the creation of the world did not happen *in* time but happened *with* time, as he put it. For this reason, it is legitimate to argue that there is no well-defined moment of creation, since real time only started *with* that moment. This would indeed be quite consistent with an earlier argument of al-Ghazālī:

> Similarly, if we are asked: does the world have a "before"? we answer: If by this is meant does the world's existence have a beginning, that is, a limit in which it began, then the world has a "before" in this sense, just as the world has an outside on the interpretation that this is its exposed limit and surface end. If you mean by it anything else, then the world has no "before," just as when one means by "outside the world" [something] other than its surface, then one would say: there is no exterior to the world. Should you say that a beginning of an existence that has no "before" is incomprehensible, it would then be said: a

> finite bodily existence that has no outside is incomprehensible: If you say that its "outside" is its surface with which it terminates, [and] nothing more, we will say that its "before" is the beginning of its existence which is its limit, [and] nothing more.[14]

So it is here that the moment of creation is considered unique, in that it has no similarity to any other subsequent moment. To confirm this, al-Ghazālī further emphasized the premise that God is timeless and, therefore, the question of what God was doing before the creation of the universe becomes meaningless, a position similar to that put forward by St. Augustine.

Ibn Rushd Responding

In *Tahāfut al-tahāfut*, Ibn Rushd tried to refute the claims of al-Ghazālī by criticizing his arguments and presenting counterarguments. As far as the question of the size of the universe is concerned, Ibn Rushd at first denied that the philosophers had said that God could not change the size of the universe, and rejected the accusation that their position on this matter implied that God is impotent:

> This is the answer to the objection of the Ash'arites that to admit that God could not have made the world bigger or smaller is to charge Him with impotence, but they have thereby compromised themselves, for impotence is not inability to do the impossible, but inability to do what can be done.[15]

Clearly, to say that impotence is not the inability to do the impossible but the inability to do what can be done is true with respect to human acts, but not to divine acts, for we are not sure whether anything is impossible for God. Ibn Rushd confirmed this attitude by saying:

> This consequence is true against the theory which regards an infinite increase in the size of the world as possible, for it follows from this theory that a finite thing proceeds from God which is preceded by infinite quantitative possibilities. And if this is [an] allowed for possibility in space, it must also be allowed in regard to the possibility in time, and we should have a time limited in both directions, although it would be preceded by infinite temporal possibilities.[16]

He then concluded:

> The answer is, however, that to imagine the world to be bigger or smaller does not conform to truth but is impossible. But the impossibility of this does not imply that to imagine the possibility of a world before this world is to imagine an impossibility, except in case the nature of the possible were already realized and there existed before the existence of the world only two natures, the nature of the

necessary and the nature of the impossible? But it is evident that the judgment of reason concerning the being of these three natures is eternal, like its judgment concerning the necessary and the impossible.[17]

This means that it is not contingent at all for the size of the universe to be smaller or larger than it is, but is something which falls between being either necessary or impossible. With this digression, Ibn Rushd shifted the argument from the arena of metaphysics to the arena of physics. By such a designation, Ibn Rushd thought he could refute al-Ghazālī's conclusions and win the argument. From his point of view, it is impossible for the universe to be larger or smaller than its natural size, since the specified size of the universe is a necessity. Accordingly, a larger or a smaller universe would be rather impossible. As for the designation of the necessity and the impossibility, it is clear that Ibn Rushd was adopting the naturalistic dogma which assumes that whatever happens in the world has to be effected through purely natural causes and that it should take place in accordance with the laws of nature. However, this can be validated only if we have full knowledge of the laws of nature; but, since we now know that our knowledge of the laws of nature is incomplete (see Chapter Two), it would be rather more humble to allow for the possibility of the event happening rather than to deny it. This is, in fact, the contemporary approach adopted by the modern science that we have developed through the ages, and according to which new discoveries are made.

Ibn Rushd further embraced his denial of a possibility for the universe to be larger or smaller than its known size, trying to substantiate his views with more arguments which stemmed, perhaps, from his inability to visualize time on an equal footing with space. Thus, he was unable to accept the notion of spacetime integrity and the absence of absolute space and absolute time, such points which were very essential to the argument used by al-Ghazālī. In fact, Ibn Rushd suggested that, if the universe were allowed to expand, then there is no reason why it should not do so forever:

> Therefore, he who believes in the temporal creation of the world and affirms that all body is in space, is bound to admit that before the creation of the world there was [a] space, either occupied by body, in which the production of the world could occur, or empty, for it is necessary that space should precede what is produced.[18]

Again, it is clear that Ibn Rushd had missed the point made by al-Ghazālī that space itself was non-existent before the creation of the world. This is because he thought of space and time as two independent entities. From the point of view of al-Ghazālī, the existence of an empty space into which the universe could be extended would be unnecessary, as space was born along with the creation of the universe. The same argument applies to time, since space and time are integrated and should be treated on an equal footing, at least on the conceptual level.[19]

Clearly, al-Ghazālī had allowed for two possibilities for the universe to be larger or smaller than it is. He could foresee no rational reason to prevent such a possibility. It might be true that his argument stemmed from his submission to the belief in the unlimited power of Allah to do whatever was contingent. On the other hand, Ibn Rushd had based his argument on the Aristotelian proposition that the size of the universe is fixed and no other possibility is allowed. His argument that, once the universe is "allowed" to be bigger, there would be nothing to stop it from expanding further was unacceptable, since this would lead to an infinite universe once we assume that it had no beginning, a result which would be in contradiction with the Aristotelian doctrine of a finite universe. Aristotle argued that the universe is spherical and finite. Spherical, because that is the most perfect shape; finite, because it has a center, namely, the center of the earth, and a body with a center cannot be infinite. Therefore, based on the arguments presented by al-Ghazālī which implied that the universe could have been created larger or smaller than its known size, we conclude now that the philosophers should either have abandoned their assumption of the eternity of the world or their doctrine of a geocentric universe. It would be fascinating to see how this conclusion echoes in the modern understanding of the cosmos, a question which I leave for further research.

Scientific Assessment

By the beginning of the twentieth century, some astronomers had started a program of observations aimed at studying the motion of nearby galaxies. It was found that most of these galaxies, which are called "the local group", are descending away from us. Through patient observations that were made during the first two decades of the last century, it was established by the works of Vesto Slipher and Edwin Hubble that the universe is in fact expanding. Hubble deduced that the further away a galaxy is from us, the faster it is descending.[20] Using this discovery, George Gamow and collaborators suggested a scenario to explain the natural abundance of elements, that is the average percentage of each of the ninety-two natural elements found in the universe. This scenario was later called the "big bang theory". A continuously expanding universe was already an option suggested by the theory of general relativity. This theory was proposed by Albert Einstein in 1915 and, having been confirmed by many observations, it was adopted to be the standard theory of space, time, and gravity. The theory replaced Newton's law of gravity, which had served the astronomical calculation of the solar system for about 300 years. Almost all models of modern cosmology are based on this theory, according to which the universe is being driven to expansion by its own internal energy. Indeed, modern cosmology allows for an infinite universe as a possible solution to the Einstein field equations, although the universal model which was proposed by Einstein himself was static, finite, but unbound. The Einstein static model was a sort of artifact that was designed by Einstein after modifying his field equations. Einstein was driven by the prevailing belief that the universe is finite and static, a belief that might be a relic of Aristotle's universe. The Einstein universe cannot expand nor can it collapse, for once it starts to expand it will do so forever and once it shrinks it will go on shrinking to a point. This critical behavior makes Einstein's universe extremely unstable, like a pencil standing on its tip. It is interesting to note that Ibn Rushd's conjecture concerning the ever-expanding universe echoes in Einstein's model. However, since the discoveries made by Hubble and others have confirmed an expanding universe, the Einstein static universe became redundant. Other dynamic models were alternatively proposed, which were deduced by solutions of the original (unmodified) Einstein field equations. These provided us with three options: a universe which expands forever at an ever-accelerating rate, and this was called the "open universe"; a universe which expands forever but with less acceleration, to reach an ultimate terminal speed at later times, and this was called the "flat universe"; and the third model is a universe that expands until reaching a maximum size within a finite duration of time and then starts a collapse, at the end of which phase it returns to its original state, and this was called the "closed universe". It is this third model here that may correspond with what the Qur'an points to in verse 21:104.

However, if the universe is expanding now, then this means that in the immediate past it must have been smaller in size. Therefore, one might ask where the universe is expanding to. Is it that beyond the universe there is a void into which the universe is expanding? Modern cosmology, which is based on the theory of general relativity, assumes that the universe is four-dimensional, three dimensions are for space and the fourth dimension is time, into which the universe is expanding. Accordingly, the universe has no outside and if we have to talk about the universal volume in space then we have to accept the fact that we can only see the surface of the universe from within. This is realized in the cosmological model for the universe set forth by the theory of general relativity, by saying that the volume of three-dimensional space that we see is actually a three-dimensional surface embodied in a four-dimensional spacetime, hence time is the axis along which space is expanding. For this reason, cosmological expansion is understood as being the growth of space in between large cosmological structures. This allows us to view the situation in analogy with the expansion of a two-dimensional balloon surface, where we see dots separated by larger and larger distances as the balloon is inflated.

It might be astonishing to know that al-Ghazālī had realized the fact that the universe has no outside. He expressed his understanding by saying:

> If you mean by it anything else, then the world has no "before," just as when one means by "outside the world" [something] other than its surface, then one would say, there is no exterior to the world.[21]

This sentence came in the context of describing that the world has a beginning but no moment before that beginning, stressing the notion that space and time existed with the creation of the world but not before. Furthermore, al-Ghazālī treated space and time on an equal footing:

> It is thus established that beyond the world there is neither void nor filled space, even though the estimation does not acquiesce to accepting [this]. Similarly, it will be said that just as spatial extension is a concomitant of body, temporal extension is a concomitant of motion . . . There is no difference between temporal extension that in relation [to us] divides verbally into "before" and "after" and spatial extension that in relation [to us] divides into "above" and "below". If, then, it is legitimate to affirm an "above" that has no above, it is legitimate to affirm a "before" that has no real before, except an estimative imaginary [one] as with the "above".[22]

This is surely an advanced conceptual understanding that is in agreement with the current understanding of modern cosmology and the theory of general relativity.

The Degeneration of the Sun

The Sun, which is the brightest object in the sky with all its influence on terrestrial life on Earth, has attracted the attention of man since the very early times of his existence. Some nations worshiped the Sun and on many occasions the Sun was taken to symbolize power and life.

According to al-Ghazālī, the Greek philosopher Galen proposed that the Sun is an eternal heavenly body that should not corrupt or diminish. The fact that heavenly bodies were believed to be non-corruptible is one basic doctrine of the philosophy of Aristotle and his followers.[23] The Sun, the planets, and all the stars were believed to be formed of a fifth element called "ether". It was the sub-lunar world only, the air and the Earth, which was believed to be corruptible.

In the second discussion of the *Tahāfut al-falāsifa*, al-Ghazālī tried to refute the proposition put forward by the Greek philosophers that the world, space, and time are eternal. Post-eternity of the world was the main issue in this discussion and for this reason he considered the example of the fate of the Sun and he first discussed whether the corruption of the Sun could only take place through withering. The argument put forward by the philosophers (which al-Ghazālī attributes to Galen) said that, should the Sun diminish, it would suffer from withering, something which has not been seen despite the long time of observing the Sun. Al-Ghazālī tried to refute this implicit pre-condition on the corruption of the Sun by suggesting that such a pre-condition is unnecessary: "But we do not concede that a thing is corrupted only by way of withering. Rather, withering is but one way of [a thing's] corruption".[24]

Then al-Ghazālī argued that, even if the argument of withering is conceded for, how then would one know about withering except through astronomical observations? But, since astronomical observations are not so reliable, we cannot detect a small diminishing in the size of the Sun. Al-Ghazālī stated that, as the Sun is a very large object, a loss of a small part of it might go unnoticed:

> Should the Sun, which is said to be a hundred and seventy times larger than the Earth, or close to this, be diminished by the size of mountains, for example, this would not be apparent to the senses . . . The senses, however, would have been unable to apprehend this because estimating [such an amount] is known in the science of optics only by approximation.[25]

He then made an analogy of the assimilation of a ruby, where it loses a very small amount of its mass over a long period of time:

> This is similar to the case of rubies and gold that, according to [the philosophers], are composed of elements and are subject to corruption. If then a ruby is placed [somewhere] for a hundred years, what diminished of it would be imperceptible. Perhaps the ratio of what diminishes from the sun during the period of the history of astronomical observations is the same as what diminishes of the ruby in a hundred years, this being something imperceptible.[26]

So, as we see here, al-Ghazālī not only believed in a corruptible Sun, but had conjectured that the Sun might actually be diminishing at a very slow rate that would go unnoticed by the optical techniques available at his time, even by observations extending over a large period of time. This is what our current knowledge would certainly endorse.

Ibn Rushd Defending Galen's View

Ibn Rushd tried to defend Galen's view, claiming that "Galen's statement is only of dialectical value".[27] Then he argued that if the heavens were to suffer such a major change as celestial objects becoming corrupt, then such a corruption would produce a sixth element:

> Should heaven, however, lose its form and receive another, there would exist a sixth element opposed to all the others, being neither heaven, nor earth, nor water, nor air, nor fire. And all this is impossible.[28]

This he said because the fifth, heavenly, element (ether) is supposed to be non-corruptible according to Greek philosophy, so, if it were to suffer corruption, then the element of which it is composed would have to change. As no such element had been identified in the composition of the world, thus for him such an element did not exist. Ibn Rushd then questioned further the possibility of the decay of the Sun by wondering about the secondary effects produced by the decay, which, he thought, would affect the sub-lunar world:

> If the Sun had decayed and the parts of it which had disintegrated during the period of its observation were imperceptible because of the size of its body, still the effect of its decay on bodies in the sublunary world would be perceptible in a definite degree.[29]

This was a reasonable expectation, since a decaying object would certainly produce some output that could be traced in the world through their secondary effects. The reason why such secondary effects are expected to happen is because:

> For everything that decays does so only through the corruption and disintegration of its parts, and those parts which disconnect themselves from the decaying mass must necessarily remain in the world in their totality or change into other parts, and in either case an appreciable change must occur in the world, either in the number or in the character of its parts.[30]

In this statement, Ibn Rushd is expressing the law of conservation of matter,[31] a notion which is so clear and bold here that it does make one admire his genius. However, for him such an effect had not been observed and this therefore supported the proposition that the Sun does not corrupt. Furthermore, Ibn Rushd concluded his response to al-Ghazālī by resorting to a metaphysical argument:

> To imagine, therefore, a dissipation of the heavenly bodies is to admit disarrangement in the divine order which, according to the philosopher, prevails in this world.[32]

This was not much of an argument, since we cannot see how the divine order would become disarranged unless we believe that the metaphysical order requires the heavens to be immune to corruption or change. This was what Ibn Rushd believed, that literally any change could cause such a disarrangement and may cause a change to the divine order.

Scientific Assessment

Modern astrophysics has shown that the Sun, and indeed all other stars in the universe, generates a tremendous amount of energy through the process of nuclear fusion. This happens when four protons (hydrogen nuclei) fuse at a high temperature and pressure, producing one helium nuclei. Consequently, a large amount of energy is released from the core of the Sun in the form of heat, light, and other radiation. According to the law of mass–energy equivalence, which was discovered by Albert Einstein, the amount of energy radiated by the Sun in every second, in the form of heat, light, and other radiations, is equivalent to 4.2 million tons of mass. But this amount of radiation is only a small portion of the Sun's immense mass. At this rate, the Sun loses only about 0.001% of its mass every 150 million years. The Sun is believed to have a sufficient amount of hydrogen to sustain its energy production for the next five billion years or so, by which time the useful percentage of the hydrogen will have been exhausted and the Sun will then undergo a series of changes that will develop by fusing helium nuclei into carbon and oxygen, meanwhile releasing a huge amount of energy during this explosive fusion and causing the Sun to expand tremendously, increasing its size by one hundred and changing it into a "red giant". This late phase constitutes only a relatively short part of the Sun's life and the Sun will end up collapsing into its final fate as a little "white dwarf" that can hardly be seen from Earth. This happens as the red giant cools and the generation of heat and pressure ceases. Consequently, the Sun cannot sustain itself against the gravitational pull of its parts, causing it to collapse in a colossal event to become a white dwarf with a size smaller than that of Earth and to glow with only a faint light. All stars that have approximately the same mass as the Sun will undergo a similar fate. Other stars that are more massive than the Sun will develop into neutron stars, objects mainly composed of a neutron core and with a size of only about 10 km. Stars that are more than 3.4 solar masses will continue the course of their collapse and become black holes, objects with such a strong gravity that even light cannot escape it.

Accordingly, it is reasonable to conclude that the view of al-Ghazālī was more realistic than the one expressed by Ibn Rushd, despite the very interesting objections that the latter had raised against al-Ghazālī's arguments.

Al-Ghazālī's Position on Science and Religion

On many occasions, we read that al-Ghazālī was against science and scientific thinking and recently two well-known physicists[33] claimed that al-Ghazālī was one of the main reasons for the decline in science and scientific thinking in the Islamic world. Here, I will present excerpts from his introduction to *Tahāfut al-falāsifa*, which show that al-Ghazālī actually stood by the exact sciences and proper scientific thinking while opposing philosophers and the atheistic view of the world. There are several other places where al-Ghazālī expressed his respect for the exact sciences, but these can be reported on another occasion.

Al-Ghazālī introduced his book *Tahāfut al-falāsifa* with a prologue in three parts. In the first part, he wrote about the main addressees of his book, who were mainly Aristotle and Plato:

> Let us then restrict ourselves to showing the contradictions in the views of their leader, who is the philosopher par excellence and "the first teacher." For he has, as they claim, organized and refined their sciences, removed the redundant in their views and selected what is closest to the principles of their capricious beliefs, namely, Aristotle.[34]

In the second part, al-Ghazālī differentiated between those subjects of philosophy that he was targeting and those he was not:

> One into the refutation of which we shall not plunge, since this would serve no purpose. Whoever thinks that to engage in a disputation for refuting such a theory is a religious duty harms religion and weakens it. For these matters rest on demonstrations, geometrical and arithmetical, that leave no room for doubt.[35]

At this point, al-Ghazālī went even further to discuss some of the dogmatic suspicions among Muslims about scientific achievements and the possible claims that they might be in contradiction with the stipulations of the Qur'an and the teachings of the Prophet:

> When one studies these demonstrations and ascertains their proofs, deriving thereby information about the time of the two eclipses [and] their extent and duration, is told that this is contrary to religion, [such an individual] will not suspect this [science], only religion. The harm inflicted on religion by those who defend it not by its proper way is greater than [the harm caused by] those who attack it in the way proper to it.[36]

Al-Ghazālī dwells further on this topic, refuting claims of conflicting views on this matter from religious teachings and proposing that the proper understanding of those teachings did not to contradict scientific methodologies and results:

> If it is said that God's messenger (God's prayers and peace be upon him) said, "The sun and moon are two of God's signs that are eclipsed neither for the death nor the life of anyone; should you witness such [events], then hasten to the remembrance of God and prayer." How, then, does this agree with what [the philosophers] state? We say: there is nothing in this that contradicts what they have stated since there is nothing in it except the denial of the occurrence of the eclipse for the death or life of anyone and the command to pray when it occurs. Why should it be so remote for the religious law that commands prayer at noon and sunset to command as recommendable prayer at the occurrence of an eclipse?[37]

Clearly, the above examples, which we have presented here at length, reflect al-Ghazālī's positive impression of exact scientific methods and calculations that are not and should never be in conflict with the proper understanding of religious teachings. I hope this will partly refute the infamous claims spread in the West that al-Ghazālī was against science and that he was one important reason for the decline of scientific pursuit in the Islamic world.

Summary Conclusions

In this chapter, I have highlighted the opinions of al-Ghazālī and Ibn Rushd on two problems of the physical sciences: one was the question of the size of the universe and whether it was possible to have been created larger or smaller than it is; the other was the question of whether the Sun might become corrupted over long periods of time. Al-Ghazālī presented arguments which may be summarized by saying that there is no reason why it should not be possible for the universe to have been created smaller or larger in size. It is true that al-Ghazālī brought this question under the auspices of God's ability; however, his main intention was not to question God's ability, but to question the status of the space beyond the world, if any. He actually intended to confuse the philosophers on this question, as they claimed that their approach satisfied the omnipotence of God. For this reason, we find that Ibn Rushd confirmed the philosophers' belief, from the perspective of God's ability to do whatever he wishes within the canonical framework of creation. Al-Ghazālī, it seemed, was aware of such an attitude and for this reason he took the question further to puzzle the philosophers on the question of the designations of the *after* and the *before*. Obviously, al-Ghazālī had no knowledge about the expansion of the universe, nor had he conjectured such an expansion, and for this reason the question that followed in connection with this argument was related to the recognition of a temporal succession of events marking a beginning for time, a point with which al-Ghazālī wanted to refute the eternity of the world claimed by the philosophers. As far as I know, this problem and the argumentation presented by al-Ghazālī have not yet been studied, and, as is shown in the related arguments and the concluded views here, it does have a sound value in modern cosmology even though al-Ghazālī might not have intended to claim such a target.

The second problem was the question concerning the post-eternity of the world, for which al-Ghazālī took the example of the post-eternity of the Sun. He posed the question of whether the Sun suffers any corruption over time, a point which was pivotal in Greek philosophy. This question was directly related to the classification of the world into corruptible and non-corruptible parts, since it was known that Aristotle had classified the heavenly bodies as being non-corruptible, therefore raising this point was of high importance for al-Ghazālī in order to demolish that classification. In fact, some Muslim theologians and well-known *mutakallimūn* have always suggested that the heavenly bodies are of a different composition from Earth.

Al-Bāqillānī, one of the prominent Ashʿaris and the grand mentor of al-Ghazālī, clearly rejected the notion of ethereal celestial bodies:

> As for those saying that celestial bodies are of a fifth nature, not fire nor earth, air nor water, [I would say that] this is flawed and has no proof.[38]

Moreover, we see that al-Bāqillānī, who rejected the notion of the four basic elements and their intrinsic natures, also rejected astrology on a rational basis and denied any effect of the celestial bodies on Earth and its constituents. We find him in his *Kitāb al-tamhīd al-awāʾil* saying:

> If someone were to say, "why do you deny that the maker of this world and His performer, ruler [. . .] could have been the seven spheres that are the Sun, Moon, Saturn, Mars, Jupiter, Venus and Mercury?", we would say: "we deny that because we know that these stars are created and they are following the course of other objects in the world since it has similar constraints of limits, finiteness, composition, motion, rest and change from one state into another which applies to all other bodies of the world. Thus if it were to be eternal all other objects should be eternal too".[39]

In other places in his discussion of the effects of celestial bodies, al-Bāqillānī tried to refute any claim for astrological effects emerging as a generative effect on the basis that all celestial bodies are of the same quality:

> If it would be acceptable for these effects to be generated then the Sun should generate the same effects as those generated by the Moon and solid rocks should generate the same effects as generated by those celestial spheres, since they are all of the same quality.[40]

Here, again, we find that *mutakallimūn* have presented an advanced view of the world, making the point that the world is one and the same in respect of the basic constituents and in respect of the laws that are in action. The reason why the *mutakallimūn* refused to attribute actions to inanimate matter is the requirement that such actions can only be generated by the presence of a will and reason. They denied that inanimate matter could have any kind of will or reason.

Ibn Rushd discussed the arguments put forward by al-Ghazālī regarding the size of the universe and the corruption of the Sun and tried to show that these arguments were faulty. Obviously, Ibn Rushd relied completely on Aristotelian views and syllogism. He tried in vain, as far as I can see, to convince his readers that the arguments of al-Ghazālī were not valid, since his thinking went outside of the Aristotelian framework. This might be true and might have convinced a limited circle of thinkers, but not those outside it, and surely not the contemporary scientists and philosophers. The views presented by Ibn Rushd concerning these two problems would have been acceptable within the context of pre-Galilean physics, but certainly not in astrophysics and modern cosmology.

CHAPTER SEVEN

Neo-*Kalām*: A Possible Transformation of Traditional Islamic Thought

Equipped with penetrative thought and fresh experience the world of Islam should courageously proceed to the work of reconstruction before them. This work of reconstruction, however, has a far more serious aspect than mere adjustment to modern conditions of life.

Muhammad Iqbal

IN THE INTRODUCTORY CHAPTER to this volume, I presented the basic doctrines upon which the views of Islamic *kalām* with respect to the natural world are based. Those doctrines I have called the "principles of *daqīq al-kalām*". For a long time, these principles contradicted the philosophical substratum of classical physics—the pre-twentieth century physics and classical cosmology—namely, the notion of an eternal universe and the concept of deterministic nature. To the contrary, such principles are now found to be in agreement with the spirit of the basic concepts and views of modern physics, namely, relativity and quantum physics. As there is no recognizable philosophy of modern physics, the principles of *kalām* might be eligible to present a foundation for a new full-fledged philosophy of modern natural sciences.

In the five chapters that followed the introduction of the principles of *daqīq al-kalām*, I have presented a few examples of applications of those principles in an endeavor to show their strength in presenting sound arguments on current issues in science and religion debates. Five topics were discussed: law and order in the universe, causality, divine action, space and time, and finally, in the previous chapter, I have given examples of arguments presented by al-Ghazālī and Ibn Rushd on the size of the universe and the fate of the Sun.

Living in a world where the value of science is becoming more and more relevant for societal as well as individual progress, it becomes a rather important task to revive a rational approach and to try to realize a scientifically viable system of thought in the organization of modern Islamic thinking. Thus, we now need to discuss the possibility for such a venture to be realized in a practical program that may substantially contribute to transforming Islamic thought and successfully accomplishing a realm of new ideas and directions. The aim is to establish a systematic approach that may lead to a reformulation of current theology and the interpretations of the truth of Islam. Such a transformation is surely necessary for any reformulation that aims at modernizing scholastic thinking, as well as that of the wider public, and at a more lucid involvement in the modern world. Despite the great cultural wealth of Islam, the Islamic world, and particularly the Arab world, is very late in pursuing a proper approach to modern life and civilization. This goal might appear to be a sort of wishful thinking, but history of thought tells us that many revolutionary ideas started out as dreams, later culminating in real movements and achieving profound transformation. In this chapter, I will glimpse at the possibilities for *daqīq al-kalām* to provide a philosophical basis for a new *kalām*, one which will in turn constitute the "mother theory" for developing a transformation in Sharia law and in Islamic thought in general.

For any dream to turn into reality, the obstacles hindering its realization have to be identified accurately and the work needed to remove those obstacles should be performed by proper and efficient means. The main impediment to realizing a transformation of Islamic thought into a new era lies in the fact that the traditional teachings are now many centuries old. These old teachings are persistent, almost rooted in the Islamic subconscious, despite the fact that the whole world has changed. In many cases, these teachings may not reflect the true facts of Islam, but are a sort of ideology that was adopted by religious clerics under the influence of the ruling regimes only to later become a fundamental part of public beliefs. That ideology belongs to age-old concepts, interpretations, and methodologies that are no longer relevant in our modern time. Accordingly, a refreshing of Islamic thought is strongly needed at this stage in the world's development in order to enable Muslims to contribute positively to the progress of mankind.

Islam has its own character and the good thing about the legacy of Islam is that its main authentic sources are available and have been preserved, in many cases, with a high degree of authenticity. The teachings of the Qur'an and the narrations of the Prophet Muhammad (peace be upon him) contain great value that humanity should not miss out on. However, those teachings of the Qur'an and the hadiths have suffered in some cases, throughout the history of Islam, from misunderstandings, misinterpretations, and from the wrong implementation.

The present task for Muslim scholars and public leadership is to reconsider the facts of Islam from its original sources and to formulate a system of thought that can serve to develop Islamic society in order to achieve real progress and improvement. The understanding of the basic tenets of Islam has to be renewed and, instead of employing age-old methodologies, we need to grasp those original tenets within a framework which is compatible with the original aims of the Islamic message. This message is summarized in the verse which says, "We have not sent you (Muhammad) except as a mercy for all mankind" (Qur'an 21:107). So, let us revive this concept of mercy and apply it to all of humanity so that Islam is used to achieve this goal and not as an ideology for terror and war.

Violence and Islam

The incidents of international violence that have been carried out during the last two decades by some groups who claim their acts as a defense of the Muslim nation have left severe scars on international geopolitics and have caused a retaliation that went far beyond the need to suppress those isolated fanatical movements. Two major Islamic countries (Afghanistan and Iraq) have been destroyed and left in wreckage with their people left divided and immersed in bloodshed. Other Muslim countries have also been badly affected by the new strategies of the West and its impositions of security requirements that contribute more and more to setting back public opinion of Muslims, breeding hatred, and culminating in an unbalanced "clash of civilizations", instead of a dialogue of civilizations. The bad traits of both sides, the Western imperialism and the Islamic dogma, have dominated. Those strategies can by no means lead to peace and prosperity in the world.

In an essay, Abdal Hakim Murad (Tim Winter)[1] has blamed Western postmodernism and so-called Qutbism (after Sayyid Qutb, the Egyptian Islamic activist) for generating such a criminal reaction as suicide bombing. But, one should not underestimate the serious effect of the cultural background that contributes to this attitude among terrorist groups. The misinterpretation of some traditional Islamic beliefs about life and people who subscribe to other faiths, and the misconception that the vicious acts of suicide bombers are the honorable acts of martyrs, which will be rewarded with a joyful life after death, are all to blame too. There are many absurdities that have been planted in the minds of people belonging to certain cultures that would encourage terrorist acts provoked by the suffering of those people as a result of the aggression of Western powers. In many cases, people, whether in the West or the East, are driven by influential ideologies that go beyond reason. These acts have been experienced in Afghanistan and Iraq. Innocent people in those invaded countries were brutally tortured, raped, and beaten to death for no reason other than a hatred implanted by ideologies. The sectarianism that became embedded in Iraq following the American invasion has caused continuous bloodshed between Sunni and Shiʿi. At the moment, this conflict could expand into a third world war in the Islamic world. The damage and severe wounds caused to Iraqi society might need many decades to heal. For this purpose, the peoples of the West and the East are required to do their homework, to revitalize the good tenets found in their cultures, and to bring into action the good of their respective traditions and spirits.

The value of human life as defined in the Qur'an is very high; it is clearly stated that whoever kills an innocent, it is as if he has killed all of mankind (5:32). It is a dogmatic and incorrect understanding of Islam, and miseducation in religious concepts by some sects, that has produced such an ugly ideology which degrades the value of someone who does not subscribe to Islamic belief. Furthermore, this backward ideology and prevailing misinterpretation of the truth of Islam are compounding a situation of underdeveloped societies ruled by ruthless dictators and religious dogma. For this reason, a reformation of Islamic thought becomes a strongly needed goal in order to achieve a transformed way of thinking that may help Muslim societies to deal with their problems reasonably and efficiently. However, there are several serious obstacles that may hinder the transformation process. I can identify here the following:

(1) The consideration of the hadiths (alongside the Qur'an) as a prime source for Islamic beliefs and the deduction of Sharia law without taking into consideration the historical circumstances surrounding them or the fact that they were narrated during ideal conditions at the time of the Prophet. No one seems to pay attention to the fact that the approved sources of the hadiths, in the official collections, were chosen selectively on ideological grounds in many cases.

(2) The assumption that the best understanding of Islam was only achieved in the remote past by our predecessors (the Salaf) and that our understanding in the present day cannot supersede that, irrespective of the advancement in our knowledge of the world compared with that of the Salaf.[2]

(3) The assumption that the optimum interpretations and commentaries of the Qur'an were given by the Salaf and that they cannot be replaced by any better understanding, despite the fact that the available traditional interpretations of some verses of the Qur'an are actually in disagreement with the literal meaning of the Arabic.

(4) The domination of the narrated texts and thoughts over rational facts in the mentality of most Muslims. These narrations have been given sacred

status, despite the fact that most of them do not enjoy enough authenticity to be part of the true legacy of the Prophet. As such, this deeply rooted method of dealing with religious matters will present the biggest stumbling block in achieving a successful transformation in Islamic thought.

It was very depressing for me to find that one of my students had decided to leave the astronomy course that he had been so keenly attending at first, because he suspected that modern astronomy might corrupt his religious beliefs. This student was studying Islamic Sharia, for whom the course was originally intended. The problem is that a backward way of teaching, along the lines mentioned above, persists among many religious leaders, especially in Saudi Arabia.

In physics, the inertia of a body prevents any change, whether in a state of rest or of motion. Similarly, any transformation of thought within a society can be expected to find some natural resistance to change. Yet, in the realm of thought, two factors are at play: the *inertia* and the *means*. The resistance to change will surely be greater if new ideas are introduced from external or alien sources. This might explain why Greek philosophy did not flourish in Muslim societies and why it was soon confined to small circles once al-Ghazālī had presented his arguments refuting the philosophical approach, using the doctrines of *kalām* as a rival to philosophy. This historical example is very important, since it teaches us many lessons. It was not the genius of al-Ghazālī alone which defeated philosophy in the Islamic world, but it was the fact that its rival, *kalām*, was far more in harmony with the Islamic mind than the doctrines of Aristotle. From this example we can learn that the chance of success is much greater for a change in thought when it is initiated from within that mindset and culture itself. On the other hand, we also learn from the rise and the downfall of *kalām* that, when religiously structured thoughts turn to politics, they are deemed to fail because of the genuine difference between the tactics required by politics and the strategies assumed by religion. It is known that *kalām* was initially considered to be a novel and genuine Islamic trend of thought by which the basic doctrines of creed were rationally understood. This is why originally *kalām* was considered to be one of the two pillars of Islamic thought: *uṣūl al-dīn*, by which the fundamentals of belief are justified, complemented by *uṣūl al-fiqh*, by which Sharia laws are deduced. However, once *kalām* became the subject of political aggravation, it lost its popularity and was discarded by the public as well as by successive rulers and jurisprudents who suffered as a result of the political imposition of *jalīl al-kalām* deductions. Consequently, *kalām* was deserted and the wealth of *daqīq al-kalām* passed away with the junk of the *jalīl*.

I should stress again that social systems are different from physical systems, in that they require change to come from a force within and not from the outside. A change which is externally imposed may cause a reaction, not an interaction. This might explain why Western influence on Islamic societies over the last two centuries, intending to bring about modernization and a transfer of thought, has failed. The failure of Napoleon's campaign in Egypt and Syria is just one example. Despite employing the best intellects of France, wearing the Islamic turban, and coordinating with prominent clerics, Napoleon failed to buy the cooperation of the Egyptians. Many other attempts had a similar fate, because they were trying to impose rules and lifestyles which were incompatible with the traditions of the society. For a change to take place in a society, one needs to see interaction, not reaction. For this reason, a successful transformation of Muslim society must be brought about from within the Islamic tradition itself, not from outside.

Historical Attempts

For historical reasons related to the clash between the fundamentalist theologians and the Muʿtazila, the exchange of *kalām* arguments was prohibited by the state at the beginning of the eleventh century. The Abbasid Caliph al-Qādir Billāh (r. 991–1031) issued an edict historically known as the Qādirī document, by which he defined the basics of Islamic belief and asked the nation to follow them. The statement warned that those who did not abide by its stipulations would face severe punishment. A look at the prevailing circumstances at that time shows that this statement targeted several social and religious issues. On the one hand, it was aimed at ending the social unrest brought about by the spreading argument between Muʿtazili and Sunni theologians (the Ashʿaris); such argumentation developed into clashes at certain incidents, including the mutual accusation of deceipt and *kufr* between the two sides. The second aim was to reorganize Islamic theological trends into a well-defined mainstream and thereby avoid much of the confusion and deviation that took Islamic beliefs far away from the original Qur'anic stipulations and the teachings of the Prophet. Yet, this historic move by Caliph al-Qādir resulted in some undesirable consequences for Islamic theology and Islamic thought in general. The main effect was causing a setback for the rational trend in Islam. This resulted in inhibiting innovative thinking and confined intellectual achievement to certain stagnated venues. Consequently, much of the intellectual work produced during the period that followed was mainly concerned with revisions and commentaries of old manuscripts. Although the Qādirī document, as it is known, was a good move intended to restore social peace and to align the abundance of thoughts, it was also a victory for dogma and resulted in spreading a state-designed "formal Islam", one very much limited to the narrated basic principles and the old literal commentaries of the Qur'an that are engulfed in old understanding and interpretation. This resulted in a state of stagnation developing over a very long time, and which has been the dominating influence on Islamic thought until now. It is known that the Qādirī document was formulated by Hanbali advisers in the Caliph's court, which is why most public belief moved in this direction from then on.

Although the Qādirī document adopted by successive governments was very much in conformity with Hanbali attitudes, nevertheless they could not predominate in the Islamic world because of the much stronger positions held by the Hanafis and Shafiʿis. The Sufi groups were much more acceptable to people and consequently the Sufi outlook was more dominant during the twelfth century and the centuries that followed. The Sufi approach went to extremes in terms of spiritual practice, to the extent of deviating from basic Islamic teachings, and went on to be much disfavored by the traditional clergy until Ibn Taymiyya (1263–1328) was able to establish a philosophical base and scholastic curricula for a more radical Sunni Islam. The teaching of this cleric gradually became the predominant faith in the Middle East and North Africa. But, as the ordinary people of urban regions like to live life in a more practical manner, their religious practices became much more lenient. This brought back traditional Islamic trends with a Sufi touch into the lives of people in the Middle East, mainly in Syria, Palestine, Jordan, Iraq, and the Arabian Peninsula (now Saudi Arabia). The movement of Muḥammad ibn ʿAbd al-Wahhāb (1703–92) was launched in collaboration with a local ruler of the region of Najd in the Arabian Peninsula. This collaboration resulted in the establishment of the Kingdom of Saudi Arabia, which adopted the Wahhabi understanding of Islam.

The Western Renaissance, the scientific revolution, and the transformation of thought which took place in Europe during the eighteenth and nineteenth centuries became the subject of long debates among Muslim elites. The aim was to access such a change and to decide how to react to the consequent Western influence. From the beginning of the nineteenth century, efforts by some learned Muslim scholars were made to understand the change that was taking place in the West. Muḥammad ʿAlī (1769–1849), the famous ruler of Egypt, sent forty students to study in France. Some important books on topics of literature, natural sciences, and philosophy were translated. In order to be able to compete with the West, Muslim scholars began to examine Islamic disciplines and question their methods. New Qur'anic exegesis dealing with those verses that have scientific relevance appeared. An example of this is Ṭanṭāwī Jawharī's commentary of the Qur'an called *al-Jawāhir*. Islamic law codification according to modern civil law took place and in Islamic jurisprudence (*fiqh*) some new studies appeared. The idea of revitalizing Islamic *kalām* came up and some Muslim scholars found that *kalām* would be the best framework through which to achieve a major transformation in the mentalities and lives of Muslims all over the world. Most of these scholars realized that *kalām* provides the basis for an original Islamic methodology that can preserve the basics of Islamic belief and at the same time enable the assessment, evaluation, and adoption of rational trends in Islamic thought. Yet, these scholars realized that the "old *kalām*" would be inadequate to achieve a transformation in Islamic thought and Muslim society toward the new era of modern scientific and philosophical achievements. Sait Özervarlı[3] has written a good review of the attempts to revitalize *kalām*; here, I will give a short summary of the views that were presented by some of those scholars.

At the end of the nineteenth century, a number of Muslim scholars expressed their hopes of revitalizing Islamic *kalām* in order to address current issues of Islamic life. Works under such titles as *ʿIlm al-kalām al-jadīd* (in Arabic and Persian) and *Yeni ʿilm-i kalām* (in Ottoman Turkish) were used to propose this revitalization. In Ottoman Turkey, ʿAbd al-Laṭīf Ḫarpūtī (1842–1916), who was a professor of *kalām* in Darülfünun (now Istanbul University), wrote a book on the history of *kalām* in which he suggested revising the old *kalām*:

> Just as early *mutakallimūn* reacted to Aristotelian philosophy selectively, today's *mutakallimūn* should study modern thoughts accurately and choose according to Islamic principles what is necessary from them so that a new contemporary *ilm-i kalām* can be established.[4]

Clearly, with these words Ḫarpūtī has identified his approach and suggested that Muslims should deal with modern thoughts selectively. This kind of approach might not lead to a generative system of thought unless originally based on a theory of *kalām* that provides the infrastructure according to which we can make our selections.

İsmāʿīl Hakḳī İzmirlī (1868–1946) contributed substantially to attempts to revitalize *kalām*. He wrote a book entitled *Yeni ʿilm-i kalām* (*New science of* kalām) in which he set out a plan to revise Islamic theology. According to İzmirlī, al-Bāqillānī's *kalām* was replaced by Fakhr al-Dīn al-Rāzī's because of its inadequacy, but now al-Rāzī's *kalām* has become inadequate and should too be replaced, since it no longer meets the needs at our modern age. To him, post-Ghazālī *kalām* depended on Aristotelian philosophy and the emergence of new problems has made it necessary for Muslim scholars to develop a new *kalām* based on contemporary needs and more in harmony with philosophy. İzmirlī argued that our formal theology (in Ottoman, *resmī ʿilm-i kalām*) has lost its scientific foundations. Thus, it should change to be in conformity with new philosophical theories and develop in accordance with the needs of the age.[5] The basic thesis of İzmirlī's proposal was classical philosophy's loss of validity over the preceding three centuries. Since the Islamic message needs to be understood by earlier and later generations, an outdated scholastic method should not be used to explain its doctrines. So, in his *Yeni ʿilm-i kalām*, he considered scientific methodology and employed both formal and modern logic. Yet he did not include natural sciences in his book in order to avoid complexity and turning it into philosophy. According to him, Muslim theologians ought to approach modern thought carefully and adopt suitable new methods, while refusing the methodological premises of the classical Muslim theologians. He concluded by suggesting that, if a change does not occur in Islamic theology, the Islamic message will not satisfy people intellectually.

In Egypt, the forerunner for the revitalization of *kalām* was the famous Imam Muḥammad ʿAbduh (1849–1905). On criticizing the *kalām* studies of his time, ʿAbduh stressed that only a few scholars had access to the books written by the great early theologians such as al-Ashʿarī, al-Māturīdī, al-Bāqillānī, or al-Isfarāʾīnī; students of *kalām*, he said, read only much later books by post-Ghazālī theologians:

> Those studying *kalām* were not dealing with problems of theology but were only working on understanding, with difficulty, the literal meaning of hard formulations within the text. In other words they were summarizing passages without any real ability to distinguish between correct and incorrect information.[6]

ʿAbduh correctly recognized that reading textbooks alone was not enough for those who wanted to be theologians, because, he said, the science of *kalām* is clearly related to the observation of nature and is based on well-established logical arguments. ʿAbduh also accused post-Ghazālī theologians of accepting the philosophical doctrines of their age without really examining their validity and accuracy.

Muḥammad Farīd Wajdī (1875–1954) followed ʿAbduh in his trend of seeing the harmony between science and religion and also tried to open the way for changes in *kalām*. Through his numerous writings, he strongly resisted the ideas imbued in Western materialism. He wrote his book *al-Islām fī ʿaṣr al-ʿilm* (*Islam in the age of science*) in order to defend the claim that Islam was not an obstacle to science, but rather a supporter and advocate of science; in it he stressed that in scientific discoveries and rational truths there would be nothing to oppose Islamic principles, and he strived in his book to show this.

In India, perhaps it was Syed Ahmad Khan (1817–98) who first used the concept of a "new *kalām*". According to Khan, to merely claim that Islam is not contradictory to science is not satisfactory at all. Therefore, he proposed a new *ʿilm al-kalām* based on a modern methodology:

> Today we need, as in former days, a modern *ilm al-kalām* by which to either render futile the tenets of modern science or [show them to be] doubtful, or bring them into harmony with the doctrines of Islam.[7]

Shiblī Nuʿmānī (1857–1914), a disciple of Khan, stressed the need for a new *kalām* with his book *ʿIlm al-kalām*,[8] which he wrote in a style different from the traditional books, criticizing the use of lengthy introductions concerned with logical terms and philosophical details. Instead, he argued that an author of *kalām* must aim at a simple and clear style of explanation to satisfy both the heart and mind. Shiblī argued that, since *kalām* is a methodological science that attempts to define and explain Islamic doctrine, not only must late Ashʿari theologians such as al-Ghazālī or al-Rāzī be seen as theologians (*mutakallimūn*), but also Mawlānā Jalāl al-Dīn Rūmī (d. 1273) and other Sufi philosophers who presented Islam in a spiritual method. Shiblī insisted that the *kalām* books written in his time, especially in India, Egypt, and Syria, were not in accordance with the needs of the age because some of them were based on the post-Ghazālī method while others were only copies of Western philosophical thought. It is important to note that Shiblī did not support the abdication of the historical, ethical, and social legacies of religion in general, nor of Islam in particular, in contemporary studies. In his "new *kalām*", Shiblī suggested that some of the traditional topics, such as the creation of the Qur'an, whether the attributes of God are part of His essence, and whether human action affects belief or not, should be avoided. Shiblī criticized Ashʿaris for not having emphasized the role of reason sufficiently and for denying deterministic causality. Instead, he adopted the scientific findings and mechanistic determinism of the philosophy of classical physics.

Muhammad Iqbal (1877–1938) wrote in his famous book *The Reconstruction of Religious Thought in Islam* that the Qur'an accepts changes in life and supports experimentation and observation over logical reasoning. Iqbal proposed that future theologians of Islam should recognize old concepts and theories, such as those related to atoms and indeterminacy, in order to bring *kalām* and modern science more in line with each other. This is the point where Iqbal's wish meets my aim of revitalizing *daqīq al-kalām*. Obviously, Iqbal was aware of Einstein's theory of relativity and the studies of atomic structure that brought forth criticism of causality. Therefore, his conjecture was surely based on the findings of modern physics, even though he was not a specialized physicist.

Transformation from Within

During the nineteenth and the twentieth centuries, there were several attempts to transform Islamic society. Many modern thinkers tried to propose revisions to the systems of thought and called for modernization. A wide spectrum of reformists and movements suggested changes to the structure of Islamic thought; these can be classified in three categories:

(1) *The Salafi Movements.* These movements claim the adoption of the traditional teachings of Islam as narrated by the Prophet and his followers. The basic trend is to follow the main sources of Sharia represented by the Qur'an and the hadiths. This includes the Wahhabi movement originated by Muḥammad ibn ʿAbd al-Wahhāb, which called upon Muslims to negate Sufi beliefs and practices (mysticism) and to give up subscription to traditional Sunni religious authorities (*taqlīd*), namely the Maliki, Hanafi, Shafiʿi, and Hanbali schools. However, Salafi movements constitute a wide spectrum of ideologies; some have even adopted elements of Sufi tradition, such as the Mahdi movement in Sudan and the Sanussi movement in Libya. The Muslim Brotherhood movement, which was founded by Ḥasan al-Bannāʾ (1906–49), is one variant of a modernized Salafi movement.

(2) *The Liberal Movements.* This includes the attempts of Jamāl al-Dīn al-Afghānī (1838–97) in Egypt and ʿAbd al-Raḥmān al-Kawākibī (1855–1902) in Syria and Egypt to establish a new orientation for Islamic thought by which Muslims would deal with the Western civilization selectively to adopt the achievements and ideas which did not contradict the original teachings of Islam. Muḥammad ʿAbduh, a cleric and a disciple of al-Afghānī, along with Muḥammad Rashīd Riḍā (1865–1935) and Muṣṭafá ʿAbd al-Rāziq (1885–1947), continued on the same line, but was not able to have much influence on the traditional approach to Sharia. The reason for the poor influence of these movements, in my opinion, lies in the fact that they could not propose a consistent view and methodology in the form of a general theory to deal with the legacy of Islam. Most of their proposals were scattered calls for the introduction of rational thinking and employing scientific methodologies without suggesting a new system of thought. ʿAbduh and his followers were accused by traditionalists as being members of a Masonic group, which badly affected their reputations.

(3) *The Secular Movements.* During the last few decades, some scholars have tried to introduce new methodologies in studying the Qur'an. These methodologies are based on Western theories in linguistics and hermeneutics. The

famous names of these scholars include Ṭāhā Ḥusayn (1889–1973), Amīn al-Khūlī (1895–1966), and Salāma Mūsá (1887–1958). More recently, Muslim scholars such as Mohammed Arkoun (1928–2010), Naṣr Ḥāmid Abū Zayd (1943–2010), Tayeb Tizini (1934–), and Muḥammad ʿĀbid al-Jābirī (1936–2010) critically discussed Islamic thought and proposed revisions of the old views. These attempts could not achieve much influence in the Islamic world for one good reason—that its frame of reference was in Western philosophies and methodologies—and this is a very sensitive point when it comes to studies related to the Qur'an or the Sharia. In addition, their arguments were not convincing, as they seem to have ignored some of the basics of Islamic belief, dealing with the Qur'an independently of any consideration of its divine source. These strategies are deemed to fail in influencing Islamic thought and mentality.

Targeting the need to establish a methodology for a new understanding of the Qur'an, a Syrian engineer called Muḥammad Shahrūr published a book in 1990 under the title *al-Kitāb wa al-Qurʾān*. In this book, Shahrūr tried to identify the differences between some terms which are usually considered synonymous, such as *al-kitāb*, *al-furqān*, and *al-qurʾān*, with several other terms which he considered from a linguistic perspective. However, he did not seem to be consistent in his methodology, as he made selective choices of the terms as they had been written in the Qur'an. It is unfortunate that his work has mistakenly been considered by some authors to be a "highly original book"[9] and was praised by Western authors, when a closer look at the details of his work shows that most of his analyses are flawed and most of his conclusions are wrong. In this respect, Shahrūr is a layman in Arabic linguistics, as he has misunderstood expressions to have different meanings in different parts of the Qur'an, whereas those different terms are actually describing the same things by their different aspects. The Qur'an is a *qurʾān* (recitation), as it is a sacred readable text, and it is a *kitāb* (book), as it contains stipulations (orders) of the Sharia, and it is a *furqān*, as it separates truth from mendacity. As far as I can see, Shahrūr's unfounded claims and superficial interpretations will quickly disappear despite the support and propaganda provided to his books.

Islamization of Knowledge

The "Islamization of knowledge" is a phrase which describes attempts and approaches to recast various fields of modern thought in an Islamic perspective. The claim is that modern knowledge in the social, political, and natural sciences is cast in a Western mold based on materialistic perspectives and that it serves interests which are far from Islamic tenets. This goal was announced in the First Conference on Muslim Education held in Mecca in 1977, where it was said that, "The task before us is to recast the whole legacy of human knowledge from the standpoint of Islam. In concrete terms, we must Islamize the disciplines in accordance with the Islamic vision".[10] This announcement did not gain much momentum, despite the great efforts made by the conveners of that conference, namely, Syed Muhammad Naquib al-Attas (1931–) and Ismaʿīl al-Farūqī (1921–86), who were very enthusiastic about the project. Later, the International Institute of Islamic Thought (IIIT) was established to implement such aims, but unfortunately no clear working methodology is known, other than wishful thinking, for the declared goals of the Islamization of knowledge.

The reason, I find, for the failure of the Islamization of knowledge proposal was its lack of a philosophical basis. Beautiful dreams and passionate aims, though necessary, cannot guarantee success in such cases. The Islamization proposal did not have the profound vision by which intellectuals can be nucleated to work on a genuinely innovative program that achieves its aims. This is why the conference was no more than a debate between conflicting views which could not find common ground, except in the aim of revitalizing the role of the Muslim nation (*umma*) within contemporary international civilization.

The system of knowledge is like a tree; we see the colorful and beautiful symmetrical upper part, but we do not pay much attention to the lower parts, the roots, which are necessary for the sustainment of the tree's life. Likewise, some Muslims look at the deeds of Islam and the social impact that it could have once adopted in the life of individuals and societies and they become eager to implement these ideals without nourishing the roots of these deeds.

Renowned characters such as Professor Abdus Salam, Seyyed Hossein Nasr, and Ziauddin Sardar objected, at least partially, to the concept and the suggested methodology. I would agree with the late Professor Abdus Salam in identifying science as being an outcome which is independent of any religion or belief. It is the implementation of science and its application which might be tinged with special religious and philosophical beliefs. However, when we analyze the philosophical basis of certain scientific assumptions, we may find that there is a kind of character within those assumptions that subscribes to certain beliefs. This might be clear in social sciences, as they involve many assumptions and analyses which depend on underplaying philosophies and views; nonetheless, one can find examples from natural sciences too. For example, to assume that the universe is eternal embeds the assumption that there is no creator or that God is the universe itself. That is why Stephen Hawking questioned the place for the creator once he found that the universe is non-singular (has no beginning) in time. In another example, to assume that the laws of nature work independently would be eliminating divine action, except, perhaps, for coordinating the action of such laws. Nevertheless, a theist science need not enroll divine action in every step of natural processes, it suffices to assume that necessity is at play with the available possibilities and that the outcome of the action of natural laws is indeterministic. To summarize, I would say that introducing Islamic tenets into science can be made possible if an underlying philosophy is found to furnish a background for the views. In this case, *daqīq al-kalām* is qualified to play such a role. Problems in natural as well as social sciences and the arts can be analyzed, studied, and interpreted in the light of the principles of *daqīq al-kalām*. Accordingly, a wealth of knowledge that has a common and consistent basis might be formed, which will then constitute a coherent knowledge that reflects an Islamic contribution to civilization.

Obviously, science and scientific knowledge is not an ideology and should not be set in ideological molds, whether Marxist, Islamic, or otherwise. Knowledge should satisfy four basic requirements to be called "scientific": it should be explanatory, consistent, verifiable (or falsifiable), and predictive. Knowledge that does not explain anything or is in self-contradiction, or is not verifiable, cannot be called "scientific knowledge". On the other hand, predictability is a strong element in any theory, as it can be used as a direct means of verification. Accordingly, the "Islamization of knowledge" should contribute to the meaningful content of scientific knowledge and enhance one or more of the elements in its structure, otherwise it would be a useless exercise sought in vain.

The Scientific Miracle of the Qur'an

Faced with advancements in science and technology, some Muslim intellectuals rediscovered the Qur'an through verses which point to natural phenomena and events. These intellectuals tried to give a modern scientific interpretation for those sacred verses, claiming that the Qur'an had predicted these discoveries fourteen centuries ago, an observation which they called the "scientific miracle of the Qur'an". In many cases, these attempts at interpretation were performed by unspecialized people who had only a vague understanding of scientific truth. Consequently, they made mistakes in representing scientific facts and, in some cases, they presented pseudoscience.

From an Islamic point of view, the Qur'an is the word of Allah, revealed from the divine knowledge and cast into Arabic. Since Arabic words, like in any other language, are meaningfully limited, this allows for interpretation within the available meanings of the words. For this reason, the wording of some verses might seem obscure and might allow for different interpretations. This is what made different exegeses of the Qur'an possible in the first place. Synonyms of the same word may bear different meanings and these meanings can only be studied within the context of the subject matter of the verse. For this reason, the possible meanings of a verse are not open to random interpretation, but are constrained by several factors, most important of which is lingual consistency and internal uniformity. Lingual consistency might be easily achieved through the wide spectrum of synonyms available in Arabic, but internal uniformity is more difficult to achieve; for this task, we need to look throughout the Qur'an for all those verses containing the same word. For example, the word "heaven" is mentioned 120 times in the Qur'an and points to several different meanings, including clouds, and the word "heavens" appears in the Qur'an 190 times. A study aimed at finding the astronomical designation for these two words has concluded that, while the word "heaven" (singular) can be understood as pointing to a few different meanings, the word "heavens" (plural) is obscure and cannot be taken to point to any limited set of terms that we can designate in our current knowledge of astronomy or cosmology.[11]

But, does the Qur'an contain scientific miracles? That is to say, does the Qur'an contain descriptions which point to scientifically meaningful knowledge? According to Islamic belief, the Qur'an is a miracle by its own merits; it is the word of Allah revealed to the Prophet Muhammad with a divine choice of words. It was narrated by the Prophet and written under his supervision. So, when in certain verses the Qur'an describes natural phenomena, it is not surprising to find some Muslims contemplating about it. However, such contemplations and reflections should be performed by specialized people in order to avoid presenting pseudoscience or unfounded claims. Laypeople should take these signs as ratifying the power of Allah, the beauty and consistency of His creation, but not derive science from it. A specialized scientist who is well acquainted with Arabic may reflect on those subtle verses in order to look for scientific viability, not to prove or disprove the Qur'an since we can always claim that science is incomplete, but also to look for alternatives to those available from the claimed discoveries of science. Such an exercise was performed by one of my students, who questioned the reality of the claim that the cosmic microwave background radiation (CMB) leads to an ever-expanding universe. This claim was based on the finding that the universe is spatially flat and, according to the Friedman models, a spatially flat universe should continue expanding forever. Such a result is in sheer contradiction with the stipulations of the Qur'an, which says that the heavens will collapse one day (21:104). Since the same observations of the CMB confirmed the presence of a non-zero cosmological constant, my student considered a flat spacetime plugging in a cosmological constant, constructing the Einstein field equations and solving it. Our result shows an oscillating universe that starts from a non-singular Planck-sized space expanding to reach a maximum radius and then collapsing into a state similar to the one it started with. So, the conclusion was that a flat universe with a non-zero cosmological constant would allow a collapsing phase once a specific value of the cosmological constant is made possible.[12] Obviously, all this is speculative, since the fate of the universe is far from being known with any degree of certainty. However, such a mathematical exercise, which was implicitly provoked by an apparent contradiction between the Qur'an and the findings of science, was certainly not futile. Moreover, the Qur'an presents descriptions of the day when the Sun will collapse, providing the knowledgeable reader with such a stunning picture of Earth, the Moon, and the stars that one can hardly deny its factual value when compared with descriptions provided by current astrophysicists. Therefore, it is not fair to completely ignore the value of the scientific signs pointed to in the Qur'an. But, we should always remember that these signs are not presented to construe astrophysical knowledge and develop theories but to encourage believers to contemplate nature and become more confident in the word of Allah. Some other signs are presented to attract the attention of non-believers to discover that the Qur'an is truly the divine word. This, I see, is the true meaning of the "miracle of the Qur'an".

The Approach

Two important factors play essential roles in the successful transformation of Islamic thought: first, the change should be made from within Islamic thought itself and, second, it should be based on a strong philosophical basis stemming from original Islamic sources.

My proposal for effecting a transformation of Islamic society is based on revitalizing *kalām* so that it might become an efficient methodology for analysis and deduction in religion and modern Islamic thought. I suggest this should be done in two stages. First, we should revitalize *daqīq al-kalām* with the aim of using this tradition of thought to represent the Islamic view of nature and science. The fact that the principles of *daqīq al-kalām* are in conformity with concepts of modern physics and cosmology would enable us to achieve such a goal without much trouble. Second, once the principles and the methodology of *daqīq al-kalām* are established, some essential problems in natural sciences, social sciences, religion, and the arts have to be analyzed and studied according to the new methodology. Questions such as the epistemological value of science, determinism, and causality in the natural world, biological evolution, the design argument, and many others might be discussed and analyzed within the context of neo-*kalām* interfacing with scientific fact to develop a worldview that shares the achievements of modern science. This might be initiated by some sample case studies to demonstrate the effectiveness and efficiency of the new methodology and principles.

Once *daqīq al-kalām* finds a firm ground in scholastic studies, other questions such as divine action, consciousness, free will, and predestination can be studied on the foundation provided by the earlier studies of *daqīq al-kalām*. No doubt these studies will be an essential step for delving into topics of *jalīl al-kalām*, which is much more subtle. In the light of the findings of a new *jalīl al-kalām*, questions of Sharia law can be discussed and proper rules can be deduced. The sources of Sharia which are adopted in my approach are: the Qur'an, the authentic and applicable hadiths, and the intellect (*ʿaql*). These three sources are to be used in deducing all the doctrines of *ʿaqīda* and all Sharia laws.

No doubt, the above ambitious proposal needs a huge collective effort that may be implemented over several decades, but all of this can start by establishing a small institute for fundamental studies in Islam. After all, the road of a thousand miles starts with a single step. The most important thing is that the vision should be clear and that the concepts and principles should always form a consistent package that can be used to analyze specific workable examples, providing solutions that are reasonable, while being in conformity with the stipulations of the original sources of Islam.

I believe that, if one can develop a trend for change that motivates critical thinking and proposes an efficient scheme for dealing with the revision of Islamic thought, which includes Islamic Sharia, then real transformation might be initiated. To be successful, this transformation should stem from the original sources of Islam and thus should preserve the mission of Islam and develop it into a workable modern system of thought.

When deciding on a revitalization of *kalām*, there are a number of vital issues that must be considered. First, we should take into consideration that *kalām* was not traditionally favored and that it was considered to be a disreputable subject. Most traditional theologians who appeared in the fourteenth century and later considered the *kalām* discourse to be distorting the facts of Islam and a potential danger that might cause a person to leave Islam and become a *kāfir*. This attitude is still widespread among Muslims nowadays and I confess that I have faced difficulties in discussing issues in *daqīq al-kalām* with some scholars who were brought up according to traditional beliefs. Second, we should take into consideration that the practical failures of some scholarly efforts during the nineteenth century, and the early decades of the twentieth, were partially due to the fact that they were not acquainted with modern scientific knowledge, and consequently they could not harmonize the truth of Islam with science. Examples are ʿAbduh in Egypt, and Khan and Shiblī Nuʿmānī in India. Facts of quantum physics, relativity, and modern biology were unknown to those scholars and consequently they adopted the concepts of classical physics and their limited knowledge of other natural sciences, so they either could not practically implement their claims of a harmony between science and Islam, as was the case with ʿAbduh, or they adopted the concepts of the mechanistic world of classical physics and assumed deterministic causality, which is in contradiction with the concepts of Islam, as in the case of Shiblī Nuʿmānī.

The new approach suggested for the transformation of Islamic thought opens the way for a well-founded methodology of theological development: *ijtihād*, which has been nearly banned from the discussions of fundamental trends of jurisprudence. Those fundamental trends concern the resources of Sharia, the rules of accepting and rejecting narrations of hadiths, the rules of interpreting verses of the Qur'an dealing with Sharia rules, and the rules of deducing the law. This is a pivotal point in establishing new trends in Islamic jurisprudence.

Some thinkers and reformists of our modern times were captivated by the methodology of the Salaf and their understanding of the terms of the Qur'an and hadiths, including some deliberate or accidental mistakes that they committed in those interpretations. We should not allow ourselves to be so captivated; we should not accept their methodology in full; we should also allow for whatever we find to be truthful. For this purpose, we should be able to provide strong arguments from the Qur'an, the Arabic, and the use of reason, using the common grounds of agreement, to support the fact that our approach maintains the originality of Islamic teaching as delivered by the message of the Prophet Muhammad.

The introduction of new trends should take into consideration the affirmed facts of Islam, on both the spiritual and the practical level, and of course we should be careful not to create a new religion by deducing Sharia laws through misinterpreting the Qur'an or hadiths and taking the words out of context. Such an unusual approach causes more confusion in Islamic thought, as is the case with Syrian engineer Muḥammad Shahrūr's exploit, which is deemed to fail and will find no echo within the social Islamic sphere. I find it a shame to support such an unfounded approach, since it goes far beyond the meaning of the Arabic words spoken in the Qur'an. To identify some examples of synonymous words such as *kitāb* and *qurʾān* and to say that they do not point to the same meaning is certainly acceptable, and to deny that some verses of the Qur'an supersede others in their legislative power (by *naskh*) might be acceptable too, and to claim that there is no clear order for the stoning of sins in the Qur'an is also acceptable, but to deny some basic laws which have been clearly stipulated is a sheer distortion of basic Islamic teachings and is certainly a slippery slope.

The main goal for the transformation in Islamic thought is to revitalize the good and valuable tenets of Islam and put them into practice. The sources of Islam provide the capable researcher with enough support for this endeavor and there is plenty of room for the reformation of legal as well as social trends, though the latter might be much more difficult to uphold.

One of the major topics of old *kalām* was the question of the divine attributes. This was one of the main sources of disagreement and conflict among the *mutakallimūn* themselves, as well as with other theologians. For this reason, a new understanding of divinity is required. Allah is described in the Qur'an as He whom *nothing resembles*, yet He is the one who hears and sees (38:11). This means that the reality of the divine stands in His existence and His ability to act. God's perception of a matter goes beyond our comprehension, since He is not a material entity, and therefore we cannot expect that He perceives through any physical means. Thus, these attributes must be taken a priori and should not be subjected to rational analysis. However, we are directly concerned with divine action. To understand the development of the world, our lives, and our destinies with the presence of divine action requires that we analyze and understand how God acts through His creation. This is why the Qur'an has called upon us to contemplate creation and to question how it was all started. Such an understanding will help us to comprehend the mechanism of the development of the physical world and may help us to understand our destiny. Here analytic theology plays a role, where our understanding of this creation may help us very much to understand how re-creation in the next life would be possible. If we adopt the re-creation principle as a general rule, then it would be easy to envisage how the next form of life might be much different from this one. For example, the moment that we cease to be alive, our souls may be re-created in another world. This assumption does not necessarily entail the many-worlds hypothesis, because the world into which the soul transfers is strictly non-physical. To summarize, I would say that, while the topic of divine action in the world is of interest for neo-*kalām*, the issues concerning the divine attributes are not a matter for philosophical interest, but one to be taken metaphorically and that need not be studied any further. Nevertheless, spiritual experience should be allowed room in neo-*kalām*, as it constitutes a vital part of Islamic teaching and religious practice. The rational acknowledgment of spiritual experience can always be understood through the fact that there is always much to learn about our soul and the world that might go beyond our limited current knowledge. That is to say, spiritual experience is something that cannot be denied, as it is a real feeling obtained through the interaction of our senses with the environment and our mind. Therefore, it cannot be but an integrated part of our consciousness, which might extend far beyond our direct experience.

Subjects to Encounter

There are some essential subjects that one would encounter once embarking on a serious transformation program in Islamic thought. The first is to define clearly the sources from which rules of belief and laws are to be derived. The second is to define how to deal with such sources and validification that such deductions would require. Here I will take a glimpse at this subtle topic in order to draw out the main aspects of the change that is sought.

The Sources of Sharia

An important part of Islamic thought is concerned with Sharia law and these are the core rules by which Muslims practice their everyday lives both individually and jointly in groups. At present, we have a great store of thoughts that have accumulated over many centuries of deduction and work on Sharia laws. These include the foundational works of the Sunni fundamentalists who laid the basis of Islamic jurisprudence, namely Imam Mālik, Abū Ḥanīfa, al-Shāfiʿī, Aḥmad ibn Ḥanbal, Ibn Ḥazm, and their followers al-Ashʿarī and al-Māturīdī, and also the later traditionalists al-Ghazālī, al-Shāṭibī, Ibn Taymiyya, and their students. According to the Hanafi rules, the main sources for deducing the law are the Qur'an, the hadiths, *qiyās* (the use of analogical reasoning in legislations), and *ijmāʿ* (the consensus of jurisprudents, the *ʿulamāʾ*). Al-Shāfiʿī considered *qiyās* to be a part of *ijtihād* (the innovative deduction of the law), and he also considered the *ijmāʿ* of the Companions of the Prophet as a strong source for deducing laws. Al-Shāfiʿī believed the practice of the Prophet's Companions and their opinions concerning law to be a source of higher priority than *qiyās*.

In our modern era, and considering the previous experience of Muslims and the huge changes in knowledge and lifestyle, we can confidently say that we need new deductions for Sharia laws and for this purpose the sources can be defined as:

(1) the Qur'an;
(2) the authentic Sunna;
(3) the intellect (reason).

In our time, there are established institutions representing the public in different forms and by different means. Parliaments are the political organ for representing people, civil society organizations play a role in serving the interests of society, and next to this a council of *ʿulamāʾ* can also be established to draw up Sharia laws, which should then be subjected to the endorsement of parliament. The collective efforts of all of these in an organized society ought to flourish into the proper representation of public interest, which means *ijmāʿ* in practice. Through this collaboration, an Islamic society would be able to adopt Sharia laws and put them into practice in a civilized way. However, a system for deducing law from the sources should be established so that fruitful results can be obtained. In early Islamic history, specifically during the reign of ʿUmar ibn al-Khaṭṭāb, several important debates took place where the practice of *ijmāʿ* happened through an assembly of Muslim leaders. One of these occasions concerned the problem of land distribution in Iraq, which had been confiscated from the Persian regime, where the decision was taken to keep the land in the ownership of the central Islamic government and not to reallocate it to individuals who had participated in the conquest. The other occasion was deciding who should lead the fighters in the main battle against the Persians, where ʿUmar himself suggested that he should be the leader, but his suggestion was rejected by the assembly out of fear that the sudden loss of the Caliph in battle might cause a fatal setback to the Muslim side. The details of such incidents are mentioned by famous historians such as al-Ṭabarī.

Metaphor in the Qur'an

Metaphor is one of the serious issues to be discussed in Islamic *kalām* and it was the Muʿtazila who first suggested that some content of the Qur'an should be understood in a metaphorical way. Ibn Khaldūn[13] gave detailed accounts of the arguments put forward by the Muʿtazila and other groups in connection with the metaphoric interpretation of the Qur'an. Among these are the divine attributes, the descriptions of heaven/s and hell, and the punishments and rewards which are described in many physical terms. This raises several questions: How do we deal with a metaphorical statement in the Qur'an? What rules should be followed to uncover the true meanings of such statements? Ibn Rushd considered that whatever in the Qur'an appeared to be in conflict with scientific knowledge should be considered a metaphor and should be subjected to rational interpretation (*taʾwīl*). This suggestion would have attributed to the Qur'an the scientific knowledge of the time, and so, as we know scientific knowledge is mutable, the suggestion by Ibn Rushd cannot be taken seriously.

A metaphor is identified as a word or phrase which describes an object or action to which it is not literally applicable. Such a metaphor should then be understood by its implicit meaning, which is mostly contextual. For example, when it is said "The hand of Allah is above their hands" (Qur'an 48:10), it should be understood to mean that the power of Allah is supporting them. Similarly comes the question which has caused much debate; where the Qur'an says "and His Throne was on the water" (11:07), it is again a metaphor describing that His kingdom was based on water, and since water is the basis for life, accordingly one may understand that the Throne of Allah is life itself, as He is known by us through life. Such an understanding is more acceptable now that we realize water is a very essential component of life. Similarly, the reward in paradise and punishment in hell should now be understood as something that takes place in another world, which might be non-physical, since the literal descriptions given in the Qur'an do not apply to our physical properties. Moreover, the next life is always described as happening in another form and in a different world, so it would not be in any sense strange to describe paradise, hell, reward, and punishment as metaphors for the state of life after death. Scientifically, there are many alternative suggestions for imagining possible other non-physical worlds in which at least some of the identified peculiarities can be realized. For example, a space-like world can accommodate eternity in the absence of time, and so forth. Such matters can be discussed in much more detail and a reasonable picture might be obtained. On the other hand, joy, amusement, sorrow, and depression are all psychological feelings, so it might happen that our entities in other worlds might not be presented in material form anyway. Nevertheless, the concept of life after death remains a matter of belief.

The Sunna of the Prophet

The Sunna of the Prophet Muhammad is composed of his narrations (hadiths) and his established acts. This part of Islamic heritage is almost well preserved, however its value in respect of authentication might differ from one system of judgment to another. The traditional method is to look through the sources of narration and apply an authentication test or to investigate the sequence of narrators following the prime narrator, who is normally one of the Companions of the Prophet. According to Sunni Muslims, all of the Companions are primarily considered to be authentic and just, therefore there is no question of defects concerning them.

The Prophet Muhammad has taught his followers almost everything in life. The contemporary followers watched and recorded nearly every aspect of his life and narrated it to subsequent generations. Obviously, some of the behavior of the Prophet was to do with his own personal life, habits, choices, or tastes, which means it was part of his personal character. Others were his teachings that aimed at organizing individuals and society to carry out their lives in the most effective ways. Nevertheless, most Muslims do not differentiate between what was a particular characteristic of the Prophet and what was a part of his religious teachings. It is unfortunate that the Sunna was taken to be part of the religious duties of Muslims and that it should be followed as if it is the order of God. This has caused much concern for Muslims, to the extent that, in some cases, the Sunna was thought to supersede the Qur'an. For this reason, although the punishment of having illegal intercourse, for example, is limited by the Qur'an to a hundred lashes, Muslim clerics insist on applying death by stoning to the married offender. They claim that the act of the Prophet supersedes the stipulations of the Qur'an. In another example, we find that the Qur'an left open the allocations for the *zakāt* tax, such an important element in the organization of society and the state. This might be understood as a *tolerance* in Islamic law necessitated by the suitability of the condition in each case; such allocations can only be defined by the needs of the society at a given place and a given time, thus they were left open. However, the clerics insist on applying the same allocations that were practiced during the time of the Prophet, with some differences between them. Several other examples can be furnished too. Such practices of the Sunna have constrained the freedom to organize the economic and social life of society within unnecessarily tight limits.

A serious review of the Sunna is needed in order to reclaim the true understanding of the Qur'an, not forgetting, for instance, that the Prophet himself had instructed his Companions not to write down his teachings other than the Qur'an. An inane explanation is normally given for the instructions of the Prophet on this issue, claiming that it was prescribed only to avoid mixing the Qur'an with Sunna. This revision of the Sunna should cover the authentication rules, the basis of assessing hadiths, and the role of reason in justifying the Sunna. These issues can only be dealt with within a well-defined neo-*kalām* framework.

NOTES

CHAPTER ONE: *DAQĪQ AL-KALĀM*: A POSSIBLE ROLE IN SCIENCE AND RELIGION DEBATES

1. William Lane Craig, *The Kalām Cosmological Argument* (London and Basingstoke: Macmillan Press, 1979), 17.

2. ʿAlī ibn Muḥammad al-Jurjānī, *Kitāb al-taʿrīfāt* (Beirut: Maktabāt Lubnān, 1407/1987), 155.

3. Ibid., 96.

4. *Merriam-Webster OnLine*, s.v. "science", accessed 28 January 2015, <http://www.merriam-webster.com/dictionary/science>.

5. Throughout this book, I have mostly relied on the translations of Muhammad Muhsin Khan and Muḥammad Taqī al-Dīn al-Hilālī, but sometimes I have added my own touches.

6. Azim Kidwai and C.H. Lai, eds., *Ideals and Realities: Selected Essays of Abdus Salam*, 3rd ed. (Singapore: World Scientific, 1989).

7. Some people may think that this is not a request but an order. I argue that it should be understood as a request rather than an order, since God is explaining why we should read "in the Name of God, the Creator".

8. Kees Versteegh, *The Arabic Linguistic Tradition*, Landmarks in Linguistic Thought, vol. 3 (London and New York: Routledge, 1997), 4.

9. Houari Touati, *Islam and Travel in the Middle Ages*, trans. Lydia G. Cochrane (Chicago: University of Chicago Press, 2010), 51.

10. Yaʿqūb ibn Isḥāq al-Kindī, *Rasāʾil al-Kindī al-falsafīyya*, 2 vols., ed. M.ʿA.H. Abū Rīda (Cairo: Dār al-Fikr al-ʿArabī, 1372/1953). My translation.

11. Franz Rosenthal, "Al-Kindi als Literat", *Orientalia* 11 (1942): 262–88.

12. Peter Adamson, *Al-Kindi* (New York: Oxford University Press, 2007); Peter Adamson, "Abu Maʿshar, al-Kindi and the Philosophical Defense of Astrology", *Recherches de philosophie et théologie médiévales* 69 (2002): 245–70.

13. Harry Austryn Wolfson, *The Philosophy of the Kalām* (Cambridge, MA: Harvard University Press, 1976), 2.

14. For some details about these sects, see Wilferd Madelung, *Religious Schools and Sects in Medieval Islam* (London: Variorum Reprints, 1985).

15. Ian Barbour, *Religion and Science: Historical and Contemporary Issues* (London: SCM Press, 1998), 100.

16. Craig, *Kalām Cosmological Argument*.

17. Ibn Khaldūn, *The Muqaddimah: An Introduction to History*, trans. Franz Rosenthal (New York: Pantheon Books, 1958).

18. By "all-discrete", I mean a comprehensive theory of atomism by which all entities are thought to be atomized.

19. Richard Walzer, "Early Islamic Philosophy", in *The Cambridge History of Later Greek and Early Medieval Philosophy*, ed. A.H. Armstrong (Cambridge: Cambridge University Press, 1970), 648.

20. Craig, *Kalām Cosmological Argument*, 17, and references therein.

21. My emphasis of the word "with" is important here, since the *mutakallimūn* asserted that both space and time were created along with matter and everything else in the world. So, any existence of space and time before the creation of the world cannot be conceived of.

22. Wolfson discussed at length the meaning of *lā min shayʾ* in connection with the concept of the nonexistent (*al-maʿdūm*), which was proposed by the Muʿtazila presenting different views about this concept. See Wolfson, *Philosophy of the Kalām*, 359–72.

23. The meaning of "accident" in this context is any attribute which might be associated with a body, such as color, smell, hardness, motion, rest, etc.

24. This explains why the Islamic atomism had to be different from the Greek atomism, a question that has upset Harry Wolfson. See Wolfson, *Philosophy of the Kalām*, 472–86.

25. Shlomo Pines, *Studies in Islamic Atomism*, trans. Michael Schwarz, ed. Tzvi Langermann (Jerusalem: The Magnes Press, 1997).

26. Wolfson, *Philosophy of the Kalām*.

27. An indeterministic event is any event that may or may not happen despite the availability of all of its necessary conditions, whereas a deterministic event is any event which must happen once all the necessary conditions are made available. When we say deterministic we mean naturally deterministic without assuming the intervention of God.

28. Abū Ḥāmid al-Ghazālī, *The Incoherence of the Philosophers*, trans. Michael E. Marmura (Provo, UT: Brigham Young University Press, 2000).

29. Averroes, *Tahafut al-Tahafut (The Incoherence of the Incoherence)*, trans. Simon Van Den Bergh (London: Trustees of the E.J.W. Gibb Memorial, 1954).

30. Averroes, *The Philosophy and Theology of Averroes* [*Faṣl al-maqāl*], trans. Mohammed Jamil al-Rahman (Baroda: A.G. Widgery, 1921).

31. Maimonides (d. 1204), or Mūsā ibn Maymūn, was a Jewish philosopher from Córdoba during the Islamic era. Some argue he was influenced by Muslim philosophers such as Ibn Sīnā, Ibn Rushd, and al-Fārābī. See Moses Maimonides, *The Guide for the Perplexed*, trans. Michael Friedländer, 2nd ed. (London: Routledge & Kegan Paul Ltd., 1904).

32. Mohammed Basil Altaie, "The Scientific Value of Daqīq al-Kalām", *Journal of Islamic Thought and Scientific Creativity* 4, no. 2 (1994): 7–18.

33. For a detailed account on this terminology, see Pines, *Studies in Islamic Atomism*. It is also of importance to point out that the term "substance" (as originally defined within Greek philosophy) does not accurately correspond to the Islamic atom. There are some basic differences between the Greek atom and the Islamic atom (see Wolfson, *Philosophy of the Kalām*, 471–2).

34. It is sometimes claimed that the *jawhar* is a magnitudeless entity (see Wolfson, *Philosophy of the Kalām*, 472), but in fact this identification is not unanimous, since, although Muʿtazila considered the *jawhar* to be magnitudeless, Ashʿaris considered it to have some magnitude; see Abū al-Maʿālī al-Juwaynī, *Kitāb al-shāmil fī uṣūl al-dīn*, ed. ʿAlī Sāmī Nashshār (Alexandria: Munshaʾat al-Maʿārif, 1388/1969), 159.

35. Mohammed Basil Altaie, "Atomism According to Mutakallimūn", *Etudes Orientales* 23/24 (2005): 49–90.

36. Wolfson, *Philosophy of the Kalām*, 466.

37. Pines, *Studies in Islamic Atomism*.

38. The best account for this doctrine is given in al-Juwaynī, *Kitāb al-shāmil*, 159.

39. This view resonates with what the philosophy of quantum theory stipulates according to the interpretation of the Copenhagen school; see Max Jammer, *The Philosophy of Quantum Mechanics: The Interpretations of Quantum Mechanics in Historical Perspective* (New York: Wiley-Interscience, 1974).

40. However, this does not mean that the *mutakallimūn* rejected causal relation or the existence of cause and effect, rather they believed in these only to the extent that they would reflect our own logic, rather than having the role of full control of nature. This is perhaps one of the most misunderstood problems of *kalām*.

41. See, for example, Abū Bakr al-Bāqillānī, *Kitāb al-tamhīd al-awāʾil wa talhīṣ al-dalāʾil*, ed. ʿImād al-Dīn Aḥmad Ḥaydar (Beirut: Muʾassasat al-Kutub al-Thaqāfiyya, 1407/1987).

42. Mohammed Basil Altaie, "Time in Islamic Kalām" (conference paper, Einstein, God and Time, University of Oxford, 11–13 September 2005).

43. The concepts of space and time in Arabic are given in many general as well as specialized dictionaries: see, for example, al-Jurjānī, *Kitāb al-taʿrīfāt*, s.vv. "*al-zaman*", "*al-makan*".

44. The best reference for these terms is Ibn Ḥazm's *al-Fiṣal*, where he explicitly states this point of view with many interesting details. For example, he says: "They (the philosophers) say that absolute space and absolute time is not what we have defined previously because they are not invariant". See ʿAlī ibn Aḥmad ibn Ḥazm, *Kitāb al-fiṣal fī al-milal wa al-ahwāʾ wa al-niḥal*, ed. Muḥammad ibn ʿAbd al-Karīm al-Shahrastānī (Egypt: Muʾassasat al-Khānjī, 1383/1964), 75.

45. The different views of *mutakallimūn* over this concept of motion are presented in more detail in al-Ashʿarī's *Maqalāt*. See Abū al-Ḥasan al-Ashʿarī, *Maqālāt al-Islāmiyyīn wa ikhtilāf al-muṣallīn*, ed. H. Ritter (Wiesbaden: Franz Steiner, 1980), 322–23.

46. Jammer, *Philosophy of Quantum Mechanics*, 259.

47. According to Zeno of Elea (490–430 BC), if we assume that a finite distance between two points is infinitely divisible, then a moving body will never be able to cover this distance, since it should cover half of it first and then cover half of that half, and so on ad infinitum. This problem is also shown in the arrow and the tortoise paradoxes.

48. Karl R. Popper, *The Myth of the Framework: In Defence of Science and Rationality*, ed. Mark A. Notturno (London and New York: Routledge, 1996).

49. In his book *The Logic of Scientific Discovery*, Popper devoted a chapter to discussing the assumptions of quantum theory, specifically Heisenberg's uncertainty principle. He attempted to eliminate the metaphysical element from those assumptions by inverting Heisenberg's program. Later, it seems that Popper retracted his claim on eliminating Heisenberg's uncertainty limit upon criticisms from Einstein and others over his thought experiment. See Karl R. Popper, *The Logic of Scientific Discovery* (New York: Basic Books, 1959), 238.

50. Hawking and Hartle have already found that the universe could have been in a state of an infinitely extending imaginary time before the big bang. See James B. Hartle and Stephen W. Hawking, "Wave Function of the Universe", *Physical Review D* 28, no. 12 (1983): 2960.

51. Stephen Hawking, "Black Holes and the Information Paradox" (lecture, GR17: 17th International Conference on General Relativity and Gravitation, Dublin, Ireland, 18–24 July 2004).

52. The series called Scientific Perspectives on Divine Action, edited by Robert John Russell *et al.*, contains the following titles jointly published by the Vatican Observatory, Vatican City State, and the Center for Theology and the Natural Sciences, Berkeley, CA: Robert John Russell, Nancey Murphy, and C.J. Isham, eds., *Quantum Cosmology and the Laws of Nature*, vol. 1 (1993); Robert John Russell, Nancey Murphy, and Arthur Peacocke, eds., *Chaos and Complexity*, vol. 2 (1995); Robert John Russell, William R. Stoeger, S.J., and Francisco J. Ayala, eds., *Evolutionary and Molecular Biology*, vol. 3 (1998); Robert John Russell *et al.*, eds., *Neuroscience and the Person*, vol. 4 (1999); Robert John Russell *et al.*, eds., *Quantum Mechanics*, vol. 5 (2001).

53. Craig, *Kalām Cosmological Argument*.

54. Christoph Lameter, "Divine Action in the Framework of Scientific Knowledge" (PhD thesis, Fuller Theological Seminary, Newark, CA, 2004).

CHAPTER TWO: LAWS OF NATURE AND LAWS OF PHYSICS

1. "Nature is a concept with two major sets of inter-related meanings, referring on the one hand to the things which are natural, or subject to the normal working of 'laws of nature', or on the other hand to the essential properties and causes of those things to be what they naturally are, or in other words the laws of nature themselves." For a quick reference, see: <http://en.wikipedia.org/wiki/Nature_(philosophy)>

2. Paul Davies, *The Mind of God: The Scientific Basis for a Rational World* (London: Simon and Schuster, 1992), 73.

3. Davies, *The Mind of God*, 91–2.

4. David C. Lindberg, *The Beginnings of Western Science* (Chicago: University of Chicago Press, 1992).

5. Edward Grant, "Celestial Orbs in the Latin Middle Ages", *Isis* 78 (1987): 153–73.

6. Aristotle, *Metaphysics* 12.1072b4.

7. *Oxford English Dictionary*, 3rd ed., s.v. "laws of nature".

8. I have read in the book of Hibat Allāh ibn Malkā al-Baghdādī (1087–1165), entitled *al-Muʿtabar fī al-Ḥikma*, statements about motion similar to those of Descartes. Centuries before Galileo, Ibn Malkā made it clear that free-falling bodies would have the same velocity if dropped in a vacuum.

9. John Henry, "Metaphysics and the Origins of Modern Science: Descartes and the Importance of Laws of Nature", *Early Science and Medicine* 9 (2004): 73–114.

10. Daniel Garber, "God, Laws, and the Order of Nature: Descartes and Leibniz, Hobbes and Spinoza", in *The Divine Order, the Human Order, and the Order of Nature: Historical Perspectives*, ed. Eric Watkins (New York: Oxford University Press, 2013), 48.

11. Thomas Hobbes, *Elements of Philosophy*, cited in Garber, "God, Laws, and the Order of Nature", 52.

12. Pierre Laplace, *A Philosophical Essay on Probabilities*, trans. F.W. Truscott and F.L. Emory (New York: Dover, 1951). Emphasis added.

13. Frank E. Manuel, *The Religion of Isaac Newton*, The Fremantle Lectures 1973 (Oxford: Clarendon Press, 1974), 28.

14. Lee Smolin, *The Trouble with Physics: The Rise of String Theory, the Fall of a Science and What Comes Next* (Boston: Houghton Mifflin, 2006).

15. David Deutsch, "Quantum Theory, the Church-Turing Principle and the Universal Quantum Computer", *Proceedings of the Royal Society A* 400 (1985): 97.

16. Davies, *The Mind of God*, 108.

17. Otto Neugebauer, *The Exact Sciences in Antiquity*, 2nd ed. (New York: Dover Publications, 1969), 33.

18. Ibid., 36.

19. This was expressed by Steven Weinberg during an interview with Richard Dawkins. It is available here: "Voices of Science: Steven Weinberg", Discussions with Richard Dawkins: Episode 2, YouTube video, 1:14:17, posted by "Muon Ray", 25 August 2012, <https://www.youtube.com/watch?v=EGL8SesIo6Y>.

20. Richard Feynman, *The Character of Physical Law* (Cambridge, MA: M.I.T. Press, 1985), 75.

21. Albert Einstein, "Physics and Reality" (1936), in *Ideas and Opinions*, trans. Sonja Bargmann (New York: Bonanza, 1954), 292.

22. Albert Einstein, *Physics and Reality* (New York: Philosophical Library, 1987), 131.

23. Stephen Hawking and Leonard Mlodinow, *The Grand Design* (New York: Bantam Books, 2010), passim.

24. Lawrence M. Krauss, *A Universe from Nothing: Why There is Something Rather Than Nothing* (New York: Free Press, 2012), passim.

25. See, for example, Davies, *The Mind of God*, 49.

26. See, for example, Stephen Hawking and George F.R. Ellis, *The Large Scale Structure of Space-Time* (Cambridge and New York: Cambridge University Press, 1973).

27. See Murat Özer and M.O. Taha, "A Model of the Universe Free of Cosmological Problems", *Nuclear Physics B* 287 (1987): 776–96; Mohammed Basil Altaie and U. al-Ahmad, "A Non-Singular Universe with Vacuum Energy", *International Journal of Theoretical Physics* 50 (2011): 3521–8.

28. This is something Einstein is supposed to have said on his deathbed.

29. Nancy Cartwright, *How the Laws of Physics Lie* (Oxford: Clarendon Press; New York: Oxford University Press, 1983).

30. We should take into consideration that Einstein's understanding of God was very much related to the total order of the universe. Therefore, his rejection of a god that plays dice is an outcry against indeterminism in nature.

31. Einstein was quoted toward the end of his life as saying, "I want to know how God created this world . . . I want to know His thoughts, the rest are details". Quoted in Timothy Ferris, *Coming of Age in the Milky Way* (New York: Morrow, 1988), 177. Perhaps he had such a privilege, but only at the very moment that he died.

32. Sean Carroll, "Why (Almost All) Cosmologists Are Atheists", *Faith and Philosophy* 22, no. 5 (2005): 622–35.

33. Nancy Cartwright, "No God; No Laws", in Dio, la Natura e la Legge: God and the Laws of Nature, ed. E. Sindoni and S. Moriggi (Milan: Angelicum-Mondo X, 2005), 183–90.

34. Ibid.

CHAPTER THREE: CAUSALITY: AN ISLAMIC PERSPECTIVE

1. Qāḍī Abū al-Ḥasan ʿAbd al-Jabbār, *Al-Muḥīṭ bi al-taklīf*, ed. Omar Sayed Azmi (Cairo: Al-Dār al-Miṣrīyya li al-Ta'līf wa al-Tarjama, 1384/1965), 101. My translation.

2. Craig, *Kalām Cosmological Argument.*

3. Carl Hoefer, "Causal Determinism", in *The Stanford Encyclopedia of Philosophy*, ed. Edward N. Zalta, Stanford University, Winter 2008, <http://plato.stanford.edu/archives/win2008/entries/determinism-causal/>.

4. Al-Bāqillānī, *Kitāb al-tamhīd*, 61.

5. See the original hadith in the collections of al-Bukhārī (*Saḥīḥ Bukhārī* 846 and 1038) and Muslim (*Saḥīḥ Muslim* 71).

6. James A. Sanders, *Canon and Community: A Guide to Canonical Criticism* (Philadelphia: Fortress Press, 1984).

7. Wolfson, *Philosophy of the Kalām*, 519.

8. Ibid., 559.

9. Al-Ghazālī, *Incoherence of the Philosophers*, 170. This point will be discussed further when we discuss al-Ghazālī's problem with causality below.

10. Mohammed Basil Altaie, *Daqīq al-kalām: al-ru'ya al-islāmiyya li falsafa al-ṭabīʿa* [*Daqīq al-kalām*: the Islamic approach to natural philosophy] (Irbid: ʿĀlam al-Kutub al-Ḥadīth, 1431/2010), 227–51.

11. Mohammed Basil Altaie, A. Malkawie, and M. Sabbarini, "Causality in Islamic Kalām and in Modern Physics", *Jordan Journal of Islamic Studies* 8, 2A (2012): 7–37. Arabic.

12. In Islamic tradition, Allah is described by ninety-nine "attributes" or "names". For example, "the Creator", "the Sustainer", "the Merciful", "the Forgiving".

13. Philosophical studies and analysis of these types of causal relationships are very rare; even Wolfson in his book (*The Philosophy of the Kalām*) did not elaborate much on these terms. However, the original sources that I mentioned in the text above provide very useful details and give some examples which help to understand the differences (see Altaie, *Daqīq al-kalām*, 168–85).

14. Qāḍī ʿAbd al-Jabbār, *Muhīṭ bi al-taklīf*, 101. My translation.

15. Wolfson, *Philosophy of the Kalām*, 559–78.

16. Abū al-Ḥusayn al-Khayyāṭ, *Kitāb al-intiṣār*, ed. H.S. Nyberg, trans. Albert N. Nader (Beirut: Les lettres orientales, 1376/1957), 48.

17. Pines, *Studies in Islamic Atomism*, 31.

18. Muḥammad ibn ʿAbd al-Karīm al-Shahristānī, *Kitāb al-milal wa al-niḥal* (Cairo: Mu'assasat al-Ḥalabī, 1388/1968), 65–8.

19. Qāḍī ʿAbd al-Jabbār, *Muhīṭ bi al-taklīf*, 385.

20. Ibn Ḥazm, *Kitāb al-fiṣal*, 58–9.

21. Ibn Ḥazm, *Kitāb al-fiṣal*, 39.

22. Al-Ghazālī, *Incoherence of the Philosophers*, 166.

23. Ibid., 167.

24. Ibid., 168.

25. Ibid., 171.

26. Ibid.

27. Ibid., 174.

28. Al-Ghazālī, *Miʿyār al-ʿilm fī fan al-manṭiq* (Cairo: Kirdistan al-ʿIlmiyyāt, 1329/1911), 74.

29. Ibid.

30. Al-Ghazālī, *Deliverance from Error (al-Munqidh min al-Dalāl)*, trans. Richard J. McCarthy, S.J. (Boston: Twayne, 1980), 10.

31. Frank Griffel, *Al-Ghazālī's Philosophical Theology* (Oxford and New York: Oxford University Press, 2009).

32. Averroes, *Tahafut al-Tahafut*, 587.

33. Ibid., 584.

34. Ibid., 587.

35. Wolfson, *Philosophy of the Kalām*, 551–8.

36. Laplace, *A Philosophical Essay on Probabilities*. Emphasis added, p. 4.

37. Walter W. Rouse Ball, "Pierre Simon Laplace (1749–1827)", in *A Short Account of the History of Mathematics*, 4th ed. (New York: Dover Publications, 2003).

38. Stephen Hawking, "Information Preservation and Weather Forecasting for Black Holes" (lecture, Fuzz or Fire Workshop, The Kalvi Institute for Theoretical Physics, Santa Barbara, CA, August 2013), preprint available at arXive: 1401.5761v1, accessed 22 June 2013.

39. Erwin Schrödinger, "Die Gegenwärtige Situation in der Quantenmechanik [The Present Situation in Quantum Mechanics]", *Naturwissenschaften* 33 (November 1935).

40. Albert Einstein, B. Podolsky, and N. Rosen, "Can Quantum-Mechanical Description of Physical Reality Be Considered Complete?", *Physical Review* 47 (1935): 777–80.

41. Gilbert Grynberg, Alain Aspect, and Claude Fabre, *Introduction to Quantum Optics: From the Semi-Classical Approach to Quantized Light* (New York: Cambridge University Press, 2010). In this book, many experiments are described in which the pure quantum aspects of light and particles are exposed.

42. David Bohm, *Quantum Theory* (New York: Prentice-Hall, 1951).

43. John Archibald Wheeler and Wojciech Hubert Zurek, *Quantum Theory and Measurement* (Princeton: Princeton University Press, 1983), 139.

44. John S. Bell, *Speakable and Unspeakable in Quantum Mechanics: Collected Papers on Quantum Philosophy* (Cambridge: Cambridge University Press, 1988).

45. Cited in Gerald James Holton, "Einstein's Scientific Program: The Formative Years", in *Some Strangeness in the Proportion: A Centennial Symposium to Celebrate the Achievements of Albert Einstein,* ed. Harry Woolf (Reading, MA: Addison-Wesley Pub. Co., 1980), 65.

46. $t=0$, the moment of the creation, called time singularity, is a moment before which nothing can be realized. But once we find that there is no $t=0$, that is to say that the universe has really existed eternally, there can be no real $t=0$ and consequently there will be no beginning for the universe. Hawking and Hartle could only show that the universe may have existed for unlimited imaginary time before $t=0$. This imaginary time, however, is non-physical, as it is unmeasurable, and therefore we cannot talk about a physically existing universe.

47. Stephen Hawking, *A Brief History of Time* (New York: Bantam, 1988), 141.

48. Adolf Grünbaum, "The Pseudo-Problem of Creation in Physical Cosmology", *Philosophy of Science* 56, no. 3 (1989): 373–94.

49. Adolf Grünbaum, "Creation as a Pseudo-Explanation in Current Physical Cosmology", *Erkenntinis* 35 (1994): 233–54.

50. Paul Davies, *God and the New Physics* (London: Penguin Books, 1990), 35. Emphasis in the original.

51. See, for example, the article by Steven Weinberg, "Without God", *The New York Review of Books*, 25 September 2008.

52. F. Jamil Ragep, "When Did Islamic Science Die (and Who Cares?)", *Viewpoint: The Newsletter of the British Society for History of Science*, no. 85 (February 2008): 1–3; Macksood Aftab, "Ghazali, Islamophobia, and the Myth of Islamic Decline", *Macksood A. Aftab* (blog), December 2013, <http://www.muslimphilosophy.com/aftab/myth-of-islamic-decline/>.

53. Mehdi Golshani, "Quantum Theory, Causality and Islamic Thought", in *The Routledge Companion to Science and Religion*, ed. James W. Haag, Gregory R. Peterson, and Michael L. Spezio (London: Routledge, 2012), 179.

54. Mohammad Hashim Kamali, "Causality and Divine Action: The Islamic Perspective", Ghazali.org, accessed 26 June 2015, <http://www.ghazali.org/articles/kamali.htm>.

55. Ibid.

56. For a detailed technical consideration, see Mohammed Basil Altaie, "Re-Creation: A Possible Interpretation of Quantum Indeterminism", in *Matter and Meaning*, ed. Michael Fuller (Newcastle upon Tyne: Cambridge Scholar Publishing, 2010), 21; available at arXive: quant-ph/0907.3419v1.

CHAPTER FOUR: DIVINE ACTION FROM A MODERN ISLAMIC PERSPECTIVE

1. Christoph Lameter, "Divine Action in the Framework of Scientific Knowledge", PhD thesis, Fuller Theological Seminary, Newark, CA, 2004.

2. See, for example, Nicholas T. Saunders, "Does God Cheat at Dice? Divine Action and Quantum Possibilities", *Zygon* 35, no. 3 (2000): 517–44; John Polkinghorne, "The Metaphysics of Divine Action", in *Chaos and Complexity*, Scientific Perspectives on Divine Action, vol. 2., ed. Robert John Russell, Nancey Murphy, and Arthur Peacocke (Vatican City State: Vatican Observatory; Berkeley, CA: Center for Theology and the Natural Sciences, 1995), 147–56.

3. Paul Davies admits this fact but he says it is a matter of semantics. See Davies, *God and the New Physics*, 35.

4. Steven Weinberg in a debate with John Polkinghorne at the SSQ symposium "Science and the Three Monotheisms: A New Partnership?", Granada, Spain, 23–5 August 2002.

5. Al-Ghazālī, *Incoherence of the Philosophers*, 166, 17th discussion on causality and miracles.

6. See al-Ghazālī, *On Divine Predicates and Their Property*, ed. and trans. ʿAbd al-Raḥmān Abū Zayd (Lahore: Sh. Muhammad Ashraf, 1990), 1.

7. Wolfson, *Philosophy of the Kalām*; Majid Fakhry, "Philosophy and Theology", in *The Oxford History of Islam,* ed. John L. Esposito (Oxford: Oxford University Press, 1999), 269–304.

8. See, for example, Muḥyiddīn ibn ʿArabī, *The Tree of Being: Shajarat al-kawn: An Ode to the Perfect Man*, trans. Shaykh Tosun Bayrak al-Jerrahi al-Halveti (Cambridge: Archetype, 2005).

9. See al-Ghazālī, *Incoherence of the Philosophers*, 55.

10. As shown in Chapter Two (Laws of Nature and Laws of Physics), there is a fundamental difference between both terms. Such a difference is mostly overlooked in the scientific literature.

11. See Chapter One in this volume.

12. See, for example, al-Ashʿarī, *Maqālāt al-islāmiyyīn.*

13. See Pines, *Studies in Islamic Atomism*; Wolfson, *Philosophy of the Kalām*, ch. 4.

14. Al-Ashʿarī, *Maqālāt al-islāmiyyīn*, 358.

15. Al-Bāqillānī, *Kitāb al-tamhīd*, 38.

16. See the introductory part of this volume for substantiated references.

17. Lameter, "Divine Action".

18. Robert John Russell, Philip Clayton, Kirk Wegter-McNelly, and John Polkinghorne, eds., *Quantum Mechanics*, Scientific Perspectives on Divine Action, vol. 5. (Vatican City State: Vatican Observatory; Berkeley, CA: Center for Theology and the Natural Sciences, 2001).

19. Nancey Murphy, *Beyond Liberalism and Fundamentalism: How Modern and Postmodern Philosophy Set the Theological Agenda* (Valley Forge, PA: Trinity Press, 1996), 62.

20. Lameter, "Divine Action", 2.

21. Erwin Schrödinger, "Quantisierung als Eigenwertproblem (Erste Mitteilung)", *Annalen der Physik* 79, no.4 (1926): 361.

22. Paul Dirac, "The Quantum Theory of the Electron", *Proceedings of the Royal Society A* 117 (1928): 610.

23. Richard P. Feynman, Robert B. Leighton, and Matthew Sands, *The Feynman Lectures on Physics*, vol. 1 (Reading, MA: Addison-Wesley, 1965), 16-5.

24. Max Born, "Zur Quantenmechanik der Stoßvorgänge [Quantum Mechanics of Collision]", *Zeitschrift für Physik* 37 (1926): 863–7.

25. The asterisk (*) symbolizes a complex conjugate and the total probability is the integral all over the allowed space.

26. Werner Heisenberg, "Über quantentheoretische Umdeutung kinematischer und mechanischer Beziehungen", *Zeitschrift für Physik* 33 (1925): 879–93; "Über quantentheoretische Kinematik und Mechanik", *Mathematische Annalen* 95 (1926): 683–705.

27. Max Born, Werner Heisenberg, and P. Jordan, "Zur Quantenmechnik II", *Zeitschrift für Physik* 35 (1926): 557–615.

28. John von Neumann, *Mathematical Foundations of Quantum Mechanics*, trans. Robert T. Beyer (Princeton: Princeton University Press, 1955).

29. Alain Aspect, "Quantum Mechanics: To Be or Not to Be Local", *Nature* 446 (2007): 866–7.

30. For a detailed account of *kalām* atomism, see Wolfson, *Philosophy of the Kalām*, ch. 4. In this context it is useful to mention that the *mutakallimūn* profoundly adopted the notion of re-creation on a conceptual level and it led them to recognize that natural events were indeterministic. See also Mohammed Basil Altaie, "Islamic Kalām: A Possible Role in Contemporary Science and Religion Dialogue", *Annals of the Sergiu Al-George Institute of Oriental Studies* 11 (2007): 95–109.

31. Quoted in Jammer, *Philosophy of Quantum Mechanics*, 57.

32. Mikio Namiki and Saverio Pascazio, "Quantum Theory of Measurement Based on the Many-Hilbert-Space Approach", *Physics Report* 232, no. 6 (1993): 301–411.

33. Josef M. Jauch, "The Problem of Measurement in Quantum Mechanics", in *The Physicist's Conception of Nature*, ed. Jagdish Mehra (Boston: D. Reidel Publishing Co., 1973), 684.

34. Albert Einstein, "Physics and Reality", *Journal of the Franklin Institute* 221, no. 3 (1936): 349.

35. Max Born, *The Born–Einstein Letters, 1916–1955: Friendship, Politics and Physics in Uncertain Times* (New York: Walter and Co.; London: Macmillan, 1971), 10.

36. David Bohm, "A Suggested Interpretation of the Quantum Theory in Terms of 'Hidden' Variables, I and II", *Physical Review* 84 (1952): 166–79.

37. Frederik Jozef Belinfante, *A Survey of Hidden Variables Theories* (Oxford: Pergamon Press, 1973).

38. John S. Bell, "On the Einstein Podolsky Rosen Paradox", *Physics* 1 (1964): 195–200.

39. Hugh Everett, III, "Relative State Formulation of Quantum Mechanics", *Reviews of Modern Physics* 29 (1957): 454–62.

40. Ibid.

41. Ibid.

42. John A. Wheeler, "Assessment of Everett's 'Relative State' Formulation of Quantum Theory", *Reviews of Modern Physics* 29 (1957): 463–5.

43. Neill Graham, "The Everett Interpretation of Quantum Mechanics" (PhD thesis, University of North Carolina at Chapel Hill, 1970); Bryce S. DeWitt and Neill Graham, eds., *The Many-Worlds Interpretation of Quantum Mechanics: A Fundamental Exposition by Hugh Everett, III, with Papers by J.A. Wheeler, B.S. DeWitt, L.N. Cooper and D. Van Vechten, and N. Graham* (Princeton: Princeton University Press, 1973).

44. Altaie, "Re-Creation"; Altaie, *Daqīq al-kalām*.

45. *Oxford English Dictionary*, 2nd ed., s.v. "miracle".

46. John Polkinghorne, *Reason and Reality: The Relationship Between Science and Theology* (London: SPCK, 1993), 1.

47. William G. Pollard, *Chance and Providence: God's Action in a World Governed by Scientific Law* (New York: Charles Scribner's Sons; London: Faber and Faber, 1958), 104–5.

48. Ibid., 114–15.

49. Ibid., 86–8.

50. John Polkinghorne, "God's Action in the World" (J.K. Russell Fellowship Lecture, Pacific School of Religion Chapel, Berkeley, CA, 6 April 1990).

51. Ibid.

52. Ibid.

53. In this respect, one might consider the arguments given by Nancy Cartwright in her book *How the Laws of Physics Lie.*

54. In reference to Davies, *The Mind of God.*

55. This is what Einstein was reported to have said on his deathbed.

56. Nancey Murphy, "Divine Action in the Natural Order", in *Chaos and Complexity*, Scientific Perspectives on Divine Action, vol. 2., ed. Robert John Russell, Nancey Murphy, and Arthur Peacocke (Vatican City State: Vatican Observatory; Berkeley, CA: Center for Theology and the Natural Sciences, 1995), 325–57.

57. James T. Cushing, *Philosophical Concepts in Physics: The Historical Relation between Philosophy and Scientific Theories* (Cambridge: Cambridge University Press, 1998), 307–15.

58. Quoted in Cushing, *Philosophical Concepts*, 307.

59. F. David Peat, *From Certainty to Uncertainty: The Story of Science and Ideas in the Twenty-First Century* (Washington, DC: Joseph Henry Press, 2002), 61–9.

60. Polkinghorne, "The Metaphysics of Divine Action", 147–156.

61. Ibid., 148.

62. Ibid.

63. Werner Heisenberg, *Physics and Philosophy: The Revolution in Modern Science* (New York: Harper & Row, 1958; repr., New York: Prometheus, 1999), 132–33.

64. Hawking and Hartle have already found that the universe could have been in a state of an infinitely extending imaginary time before the big bang.

65. Hawking, "Black Holes and the Information Paradox".

CHAPTER FIVE: SPACE, TIME, AND *KALĀM*

1. St. Augustine, *Confessions and Enchiridion*, trans. Albert C. Outler (Grand Rapids, MI: Christian Classic Ethereal Library, 2000), ch. 11, no. 11.

2. St. Augustine, *Confessions*, ch. 11, no. 13.

3. I have emphasized the word "real" since Hawking and Hartle have proved that the universe could have existed in an imaginary time before coming into being.

4. St. Augustine, *Confessions*, ch. 11, no. 14.

5. Aristotle, *Physics*, trans. P.H. Wicksteed and F. Cornford (Cambridge, MA: Harvard University Press, 1929), 4.11.219a.

6. Aristotle, *Physics*, 4.11.219b2.

7. Aristotle, *Physics*, 4.11.219b.

8. Isaac Newton, *The Principia: Mathematical Principles of Natural Philosophy* (London: Snowball Publishing, 2010), 6.

9. Max Jammer, *Concepts of Space: The History of the Concepts of Space in Physics*, 2nd ed. (Cambridge, MA: Harvard University Press, 1969), 102.

10. Ibid.

11. For an accurate presentation of the concepts of space and time in the theory of relativity, see Michael Friedman, *Foundations of Space-Time Theories: Relativistic Physics and Philosophy of Science* (Princeton: Princeton University Press, 1983).

12. Edwin F. Taylor and John A. Wheeler, *Exploring Black Holes* (New York: Addison-Wesley Longman, 2000), G-11.

13. Al-Jurjānī, *Kitāb al-taʿrīfāt*, s.v. *al-makān.*

14. Al-Juwaynī, *Kitāb al-shāmil*, 156.

15. Al-Jurjānī, *Kitāb al-taʿrīfāt*, s.v. *al-khalaʾ*.

16. Al-Ḥasan ibn Aḥmad Ḥibn Mattawayh, *Kitāb al-tadhkira fī aḥkām al-jawāhir wa al-aʿrāḍ* (Cairo: Dār al-Thaqāfa, n.d.), 116–24.

17. Al-Jurjānī, *Kitāb al-taʿrīfāt*, s.v. *al-zaman.*

18. Jammer, *Concepts of Space*, 65.

19. Ibid.

20. Maimonides, *Guide for the Perplexed*, 122

21. Ibid.

22. We might have to consider the assumption of re-creation here in order to resolve the problem consistently. The trajectory will never be the same, even for identical particles, since it is born anew every time it is re-created. As such, every particle has its own trajectory.

23. Lev Davidovich Landau and Evgenii Mikhailovich Lifshitz, *Quantum Mechanics: Non-Relativistic Theory*, vol. 3, 2nded. (Oxford: Pergamon Press, 1965).

24. Jammer, *Concepts of Space*, 67.

25. Ibid., 68.

26. *Encyclopaedia of Islam*, 2nd ed., s.v. "Ibn Ḥazm".

27. Roger Arnaldez, "Ibn Hazm", Islamic Philosophy Online, trans. Miriam Rosen, 27 June 2015, <http://www.muslimphilosophy.com/hazm/ibnhazm.htm>.

28. Ibn Ḥazm, *Kitāb al-fiṣal*, 57–8.

29. Ibid., 58.

30. For more details, see Altaie, *Daqīq al-kalām*, 76–84.

31. Ibn Ḥazm, *Kitāb al-fiṣal*, 61.

32. Ibid., 57.

33. Ibid.

34. Ibid., 62.

35. Ibid., 22.
36. Ibid., 73.
37. Ibid., 61.
38. Al-Ghazālī, *Incoherence of the Philosophers*, 32.
39. In the original Arabic text it is called "spatial dimension" (*buʿd makānī*).
40. In the original Arabic text it is called "time dimension" (*buʿd zamānī*).
41. Ibid., 31.
42. Al-Ghazālī, *Incoherence of the Philosophers*, 33–4.
43. Ibid., 35.

CHAPTER SIX: CASES FROM OLD DEBATES: THE SIZE OF THE UNIVERSE AND THE FATE OF THE SUN

1. Al-Ghazālī, *Incoherence of the Philosophers*, 1–2.
2. Ibid., 2.
3. Ibid., 3.
4. Ibid., 48.
5. Noel M. Swerdlow and Otto E. Neugebauer, *Mathematical Astronomy in Copernicus's "De revolutionibus"* (New York: Springer-Verlag, 1984).
6. Mohammed Basil Altaie and M.K. al-Zuʾbī, "The Concept of Heaven and Heavens in the Qur'ān and Modern Astronomy", *Jordanian Journal of Islamic Studies* 4, no. 3 (2008): 223–49.
7. Craig, *Kalām Cosmological Argument.*
8. Considering time as a dimension on equal footing with space is a fundamental concept that was introduced, in modern times, by Albert Einstein through his theory of relativity. The three known spatial dimensions were integrated with the time dimension to form the spacetime continuum.
9. No doubt, the notion that time only existed along with the creation of the world was part of the propositions of St. Augustine in his *Confessions.*
10. Al-Ghazālī, *Incoherence of the Philosophers*, 37. Clearly in his question al-Ghazālī is talking here about God's absolute power, arguing for the possibility of having a universe that is larger or smaller than its known size. The argument is equally the same as if he had said it would have been possible that the universe was created larger or smaller by one or more cubits. The allowance for such a possibility confirms that he was convinced by such a possibility, though he did not provide a natural reason for it.
11. Ibid.
12. Ibid., 38.
13. Grünbaum, "Creation as a Pseudo-Explanation".
14. Al-Ghazālī, *Incoherence of the Philosophers*, 35.

15. Averroes, *Tahafut al-Tahafut*, 66.
16. Ibid., 65.
17. Ibid.
18. Ibid., 66.
19. See Chapter Five in this volume on space, time, and *kalām*.
20. See Edwin Hubble, "The Problem of the Expanding Universe". *American Scientist* 30, no. 2 (1942), 99–115.
21. Al-Ghazālī, *Incoherence of the Philosophers*, 35.
22. Ibid., 33
23. I could not find a clear citation for Galen regarding this, but surely the general idea is known to be part of the Greek philosophical doctrines? See, for example, S. Marc Cohen, Patricia Curd, Charles David, and Chanel Reeve, eds., *Readings in Ancient Greek Philosophy: From Thales to Aristotle*, 3rd ed. (Indianapolis, IN: Hackett, 2005).
24. Al-Ghazālī, *Incoherence of the Philosophers*, 49.
25. Ibid.
26. Ibid.
27. Averroes, *Tahafut al-Tahafut*, 84.
28. Ibid., 85.
29. Ibid.
30. Ibid.
31. Ibid., 86.
32. Although it is not so for the conservation of energy, as the concept of energy was unknown at the time.
33. See Weinberg, "Without God".
34. Al-Ghazālī, *Incoherence of the Philosophers*, 64.
35. Ibid., 4.
36. Ibid., 6.
37. Ibid.
38. Al-Bāqillānī, *Kitāb al-tamhīd*, 64.
39. Ibid., 66.
40. Ibid., 75.

CHAPTER SEVEN: NEO-*KALĀM*: A POSSIBLE TRANSFORMATION OF TRADITIONAL ISLAMIC THOUGHT

1. Abdal Hakim Murad, *Bombing Without Moonlight: The Origins of Suicidal Terrorism* (Bristol: Amal Press, 2008).
2. The term "Salaf" refers to the first communities of Muslims. Not to be confused with the modern "Salafi" movement.

3. M. Sait Özervarlı, "Attempts to Revitalize Kalām in the Late 19th and Early 20th Centuries", *The Muslim World* 89, no. 1 (1999): 90–105.

4. ʿAbd al-Laṭīf Ḫarpūtī, *Tarīkh-i ʿilm-i kalām* (Istanbul: n.p., 1332/1914), 111.

5. İsmāʿīl Hakḳī İzmirlī, *Islam'da felsefe: Yeni ʿilm-i kalām*, Sebilurrashād XIV/344:43 (1333/1915).

6. Syed Ahmad Khan, "Lecture on Islam", trans. Christian W. Toll, in *Sayyid Ahmad Khan. A Reinterpretation of Islamic Theology* (Karachi: Oxford University Press, 1979).

7. Muhammad ʿAbduh, *Al-Islam wā al-Naṣraniyya* (Cairo: n.p., 1953–54), 139.

8. Shiblī Nuʿmānī, *ʿIlm al-kalām* (Karachi: n.p., 1348/1929).

9. Nidhal Guessoum, *Islam's Quantum Question: Reconciling Muslim Tradition and Modern Science* (London: I.B. Tauris, 2011).

10. Ziauddin Sardar, *Desperately Seeking Paradise: Journey of a Skeptical Muslim* (London: Granta Books, 2004), 201.

11. Altaie and al-Zuʾbī, "Heaven and Heavens in the Qurʾān", 223–49.

12. Munīr Darādka, "A Collapsing Flat Universe" (MSc thesis, Yarmouk University, 2009).

13. Ibn Khaldūn, *Muqaddimah*.

BIBLIOGRAPHY

ʿAbduh, Muḥammad. *al-Islām wa al-Naṣrāniyya*. Cairo: n.p., 1953–54.

Adamson, Peter. "Abu Maʿshar, al-Kindi and the Philosophical Defense of Astrology". *Recherches de philosophie et théologie médiévales* 69 (2002): 245–70.

———. *Al-Kindi*. New York: Oxford University Press, 2007.

Aftab, Macksood. "Ghazali, Islamophobia, and the Myth of Islamic Decline". *Macksood A. Aftab* (blog). Accessed 26 June 2015. <http://www.muslimphilosophy.com/aftab/myth-of-islamic-decline/>.

Altaie, Mohammed Basil. "Atomism According to Mutakallimūn". *Etudes Orientales* 23/24 (2005): 49–90.

———. *Daqīq al-kalām: al-ruʾya al-Islāmiyya li falsafa al-ṭabīʿa* [*Daqīq al-Kalām*: The Islamic approach to natural philosophy]. Irbid: ʿĀlam al-Kutub al-Ḥadīth, 1431/2010.

———. "Islamic Kalām: A Possible Role in Contemporary Science and Religion Dialogue". *Annals of the Sergiu Al-George Institute of Oriental Studies* 11 (2007): 95–109.

———. "Re-Creation: A Possible Interpretation of Quantum Indeterminism". In *Matter and Meaning*, edited by Michael Fuller, 21–37. Newcastle upon Tyne: Cambridge Scholar Publishing, 2010. Available at arXive: quant-ph/0907.3419v1.

———. "The Scientific Value of Daqīq al-Kalām". *Journal of Islamic Thought and Scientific Creativity* 4, no. 2 (1994): 7–18.

———. "Time in Islamic Kalām". Conference paper presented at Einstein, God and Time, University of Oxford, 11–13 September 2005.

Altaie, Mohammed Basil, and U. al-Ahmad. "A Non-singular Universe with Vacuum Energy". *International Journal of Theoretical Physics* 50 (2011): 3521–8.

Altaie, Mohammed Basil, and M.K. al-Zuʾbī. "The Concept of Heaven and Heavens in the Qurʾān and Modern Astronomy". *Jordanian Journal of Islamic Studies* 4, no. 3 (2008): 223–49.

Altaie, Mohammed Basil, A. Malkawie, and M. Sabbarini. "Causality in Islamic Kalām and in Modern Physics". *Jordanian Journal of Islamic Studies* 8, 2A (2012): 7–37. Arabic.

BIBLIOGRAPHY

Aristotle. *Physics*. Translated by P.H. Wicksteed and F. Cornford. Cambridge, MA: Harvard University Press, 1929.

Arnaldez, Roger. "Ibn Hazm". Islamic Philosophy Online. Translated by Mirriam Rosen. Accessed 27 June 2015. <http://www.muslimphilosophy.com/hazm/ibnhazm.htm>.

al-Ashʿarī, Abū al-Ḥasan. *Maqālāt al-islāmiyyīn wa ikhtilāf al-muṣallīn*. Edited by H. Ritter. Istanbul: Devlet Matbaası, 1347–48/1929–30.

Aspect, Alain. "Quantum Mechanics: To Be or Not to Be Local". *Nature* 446 (2007): 866–7.

Averroes. *The Philosophy and Theology of Averroes* [*Faṣl al-maqāl*]. Translated by Mohammed Jamil al-Rahman. Baroda: A.G. Widgery, 1921.

———. *Tahafut al-Tahafut (The Incoherence of the Incoherence)*. Translated by Simon Van Den Bergh. London: Trustees of the E.J.W. Gibb Memorial, 1954.

al-Bāqillānī, Abū Bakr. *Kitāb al-tamhīd al-awāʾil wa talkhīṣ al-dalāʾil*. Edited by ʿImād al-Dīn Aḥmad Ḥaydar. Beirut: Muʾassasat al-Kutub al-Thaqāfiyya, 1407/1987.

Barbour, Ian. *Religion and Science: Historical and Contemporary Issues*. London: SCM Press, 1998.

Belinfante, Frederik Jozef. *A Survey of Hidden Variables Theories*. Oxford: Pergamon Press, 1973.

Bell, John S. "On the Einstein Podolsky Rosen Paradox". *Physics* 1 (1964): 195–200.

———. *Speakable and Unspeakable in Quantum Mechanics: Collected Papers on Quantum Philosophy*. Cambridge: Cambridge University Press, 1988.

Bohm, David. "A Suggested Interpretation of the Quantum Theory in Terms of 'Hidden' Variables, I and II". *Physical Review* 84 (1952): 166–79.

———. *Quantum Theory*. New York: Prentice-Hall, 1951.

Born, Max. *The Born–Einstein Letters, 1916–1955: Friendship, Politics and Physics in Uncertain Times*. New York: Walter and Co.; London: Macmillan, 1971.

———. "Zur Quantenmechanik der Stoßvorgänge [Quantum Mechanics of Collision]". *Zeitschrift für Physik* 37 (1926): 863–7.

Born, Max, Werner Heisenberg, and P. Jordan. "Zur Quantenmechnik II". *Zeitschrift für Physik* 35 (1926): 557–615.

al-Bukhārī, Muḥammad ibn Ismāʿīl. *al-Jāmiʿ al-ṣaḥīḥ al- mukhtaṣar*. Edited by Muṣṭafā al-Bughā. Beirut: Dār Ibn Kathīr, 1407/1987.

Carroll, Sean. "Why (Almost All) Cosmologists Are Atheists". *Faith and Philosophy* 22, no. 5 (2005): 622–35.

Cartwright, Nancy. *How the Laws of Physics Lie*. Oxford: Clarendon Press; New York: Oxford University Press, 1983.

———. "No God; No Laws". In *Dio, la Natura e la Legge: God and the Laws of Nature*, edited by E. Sindoni and S. Moriggi, 183–90. Milan: Angelicum-Mondo X, 2005.

Cohen, S. Marc, Patricia Curd, Charles David, and Chanel Reeve, eds. *Readings in Ancient Greek Philosophy: From Thales to Aristotle*. 3rd ed. Indianapolis, IN: Hackett, 2005.

Craig, William Lane. *The Kalām Cosmological Argument*. London and Basingstoke: Macmillan Press, 1979.

Cushing, James T. *Philosophical Concepts in Physics: The Historical Relation between Philosophy and Scientific Theories*. Cambridge: Cambridge University Press, 1998.

Darādka, Munīr. "A Collapsing Flat Universe". MSc thesis, Yarmouk University, 2009.

Davies, Paul. *God and the New Physics*. London: Penguin Books, 1990.

———. *The Mind of God: The Scientific Basis for a Rational World*. London: Simon and Schuster, 1992.

Dawkins, Richard. "Voices of Science: Steven Weinberg". Discussions with Richard Dawkins: Episode 2. YouTube video, 1:14:17. Posted by "Muon Ray", 25 August 2012. <https://www.youtube.com/watch?v=EGL8SesIo6Y>.

Deutsch, David. "Quantum Theory, the Church-Turing Principle and the Universal Quantum Computer". *Proceedings of the Royal Society A* 400 (1985): 97–117.

DeWitt, Bryce S., and Neill Graham, eds. *The Many-Worlds Interpretation of Quantum Mechanics: A Fundamental Exposition by Hugh Everett, III, with Papers by J.A. Wheeler, B.S. DeWitt, L.N. Cooper and D. Van Vechten, and N. Graham*. Princeton: Princeton University Press, 1973.

Dirac, Paul. "The Quantum Theory of the Electron". *Proceedings of the Royal Society A* 117 (1928): 610–24.

Einstein, Albert. "Physics and Reality". In *Ideas and Opinions*. Translated by Sonja Bargmann. New York: Bonanza, 1954.

———. "Physics and Reality". *Journal of the Franklin Institute* 221, no. 3 (1936): 349–82.

———. *Physics and Reality*. New York: Philosophical Library, 1987.

Einstein, Albert, B. Podolsky, and N. Rosen. "Can Quantum-Mechanical Description of Physical Reality Be Considered Complete?". *Physical Review* 47 (1935): 777–80.

Everett, III, Hugh. "Relative State Formulation of Quantum Mechanics". *Reviews of Modern Physics* 29 (1957): 454–62.

Fakhry, Majid. "Philosophy and Theology". In *The Oxford History of Islam,* edited by John L. Esposito, 269–304. Oxford: Oxford University Press, 1999.

Ferris, Timothy. *Coming of Age in the Milky Way*. New York: Morrow, 1988.

Feynman, Richard. *The Character of Physical Law*. Cambridge, MA: M.I.T. Press, 1985.

Feynman, Richard P., Robert B. Leighton, and Matthew Sands. *The Feynman Lectures on Physics*, vol. 1. Reading, MA: Addison-Wesley, 1965.

Friedman, Michael. *Foundations of Space-Time Theories: Relativistic Physics and Philosophy of Science*. Princeton: Princeton University Press, 1983.

Garber, Daniel. "God, Laws, and the Order of Nature: Descartes and Leibniz, Hobbes and Spinoza". In *The Divine Order, the Human Order, and the Order of Nature: Historical Perspectives*, edited by Eric Watkins, 45–66. New York: Oxford University Press, 2014.

al-Ghazālī, Abū Ḥāmid. *Deliverance from Error (al-Munqidh min al-Dalāl)*. Translated by Richard J. McCarthy, S.J. Boston: Twayne, 1980.

———. *The Incoherence of the Philosophers*. Translated by Michael E. Marmura. Provo, UT: Brigham Young University Press, 2000.

———. *Miʿyār al-ʿilm fī fan al-manṭiq*. Cairo: Kirdistan al-ʿIlmiyyāt, 1329/1911.

———. *On Divine Predicates and their Property*. Edited and translated by ʿAbd al-Raḥmān Abū Zayd. Lahore: Sh. Muhammad Ashraf, 1990.

Golshani, Mehdi. "Quantum Theory, Causality and Islamic Thought". In *The Routledge Companion to Science and Religion*, edited by James W. Haag, Gregory R. Peterson, and Michael L. Spezio, 179–90. London: Routledge, 2012.

Graham, Neill. "The Everett Interpretation of Quantum Mechanics". PhD thesis, University of North Carolina at Chapel Hill, 1970.

Grant, Edward. "Celestial Orbs in the Latin Middle Ages". *Isis* 78 (1987): 153–73.

Griffel, Frank. *Al-Ghazālī's Philosophical Theology*. Oxford and New York: Oxford University Press, 2009.

Grünbaum, Adolf. "Creation as a Pseudo-Explanation in Current Physical Cosmology". *Erkenntinis* 35 (1994): 233–54.

———. "The Pseudo-Problem of Creation in Physical Cosmology". *Philosophy of Science* 56, no. 3 (1989): 373–94.

Grynberg, Gilbert, Alain Aspect, and Claude Fabre. *Introduction to Quantum Optics: From the Semi-Classical Approach to Quantized Light*. New York: Cambridge University Press, 2010.

Guessoum, Nidhal. *Islam's Quantum Question: Reconciling Muslim Tradition and Modern Science*. London: I.B. Tauris, 2011.

Ḫarpūtī, ʿAbd al-Laṭīf. *Tarīkh-i ʿilm-i kalām*. Istanbul: n.p., 1332/1914.

Hartle, James B., and Stephen W. Hawking. "Wave Function of the Universe". *Physical Review D* 28, no. 12 (1983): 2960.

Hawking, Stephen. *A Brief History of Time*. New York: Bantam, 1988.

———. "Black Holes and the Information Paradox". Lecture at GR17: 17th International Conference on General Relativity and Gravitation, Dublin, Ireland, 18–24 July 2004.

———. "Information Preservation and Weather Forecasting for Black Holes". Lecture at Fuzz or Fire Workshop, The Kalvi Institute for Theoretical Physics, Santa Barbara, CA, August 2013. Preprint available at arXive: 1401.5761v1, accessed 22 June 2013.

Hawking, Stephen, and George F.R. Ellis. *The Large Scale Structure of Space-Time*. Cambridge and New York: Cambridge University Press, 1973.

Hawking, Stephen, and Leonard Mlodinow. *The Grand Design*. New York: Bantam Books, 2010.

Heisenberg, Werner. *Physics and Philosophy: The Revolution in Modern Science*. New York: Prometheus, 1999. First published 1958 by Harper & Row.

———. "Über quantentheoretische Kinematik und Mechanik". *Mathematische Annalen* 95 (1926): 683–705.

———. "Über quantentheoretische Umdeutung kinematischer und mechanischer Beziehungen". *Zeitschrift für Physik* 33 (1925): 879–93.

Henry, John. "Metaphysics and the Origins of Modern Science: Descartes and the Importance of Laws of Nature". *Early Science and Medicine* 9 (2004): 73–114.

Hoefer, Carl. "Causal Determinism". In *The Stanford Encyclopedia of Philosophy*, edited by Edward N. Zalta. Stanford University, Winter 2008. <http://plato.stanford.edu/archives/win2008/entries/determinism-causal/>.

Holton, Gerald James. "Einstein's Scientific Program: The Formative Years". In *Some Strangeness in the Proportion: A Centennial Symposium to Celebrate the Achievements of Albert Einstein*, edited by Harry Woolf, 57–76. Reading, MA: Addison-Wesley Pub. Co., 1980.

Hubble, Edwin. "The Problem of the Expanding Universe". *American Scientist* 30, no. 2 (1942), 99–115.

Ibn ʿArabī, Muḥyiddīn. *The Tree of Being: Shajarat al-kawn: An Ode to the Perfect Man*. Translated by Shaykh Tosun Bayrak al-Jerrahi al-Halveti. Cambridge: Archetype, 2005.

Ibn Ḥazm, ʿAlī ibn Aḥmad. *Kitāb al-fiṣal fī al-milal wa al-ahwāʾ wa al-niḥal*. Edited by Muḥammad ibn ʿAbd al-KarIm al-Shahrastānī. Egypt: Muʾassasat al-Khānjī, 1383/1964.

Ibn Khaldūn. *The Muqaddimah: An Introduction to History*. Translated by Franz Rosenthal. New York: Pantheon Books, 1958.

Ḥībn Mattawayh, al-Ḥasan ibn Aḥmad. *Kitāb al-tadhkira fī aḥkām al-jawāhir wa al-aʿrāḍ*. Cairo: Dār al-Thaqāfa, n.d.

Ibn Rushd *see* Averroes.

İzmirlī, İsmāʿīl Haḳḳī. *Islam'da felsefe: Yeni ʿilm-i kalām*. Sebilurrashād XIV/344:43. 1333/1915.

al-Jabbār, Qāḍī Abū al-Ḥasan ʿAbd. *Al-Muḥīṭ bi al-taklīf*. Edited by Omar Sayed Azmi. Cairo: Al-Dār al-Miṣrīyya li al-Taʾlīf wa al-Tarjama, 1384/1965.

Jammer, Max. *Concepts of Space: The History of the Concepts of Space in Physics*. 2nd ed. Cambridge, MA: Harvard University Press, 1969.

———. *The Philosophy of Quantum Mechanics: The Interpretations of Quantum Mechanics in Historical Perspective*. New York: Wiley-Interscience, 1974.

Jauch, Josef M. "The Problem of Measurement in Quantum Mechanics". In *The Physicist's Conception of Nature*, edited by Jagdish Mehra, 684–6. Boston: D. Reidel Publishing Co., 1973.

al-Jurjānī, ʿAlī ibn Muḥammad. *Kitāb al-taʿrīfāt*. Beirut: Maktabāt Lubnān, 1407/1987.

al-Juwaynī, Abū al-Maʿālī. *Kitāb al-shāmil fī uṣūl al-dīn*. Edited by ʿAlī Sāmī Nashshār. Alexandria: Munshāʾat al-Maʿārif, 1388/1969.

Kamali, Mohammad Hashim. "Causality and Divine Action: The Islamic Perspective". Ghazali.org. Accessed 26 June 2015. <http://www.ghazali.org/articles/kamali.htm>.

Khan, Syed Ahmad. "Lecture on Islam". In *Sayyid Ahmad Khan. A Reinterpretation of Islamic Theology*, translated by Christian W. Troll. Karachi: Oxford University Press, 1979.

al-Khayyāṭ, Abū al-Ḥusayn. *Kitāb al-intiṣār*. Edited by H.S. Nyberg. Translated by Albert N. Nader. Beirut: Les lettres orientales, 1376/1957.

Kidwai, Azim, and C.H. Lai, eds., *Ideals and Realities: Selected Essays of Abdus Salam*. 3rd ed. Singapore: World Scientific, 1989.

al-Kindī, Yaʿqūb ibn Isḥāq. *Rasāʾil al-Kindī al-falsafiyya*. 2 vols. Edited by M.ʿA.H. Abū Rīda. Cairo: Dār al-Fikr al-ʿArabī, 1372/1953.

Krauss, Lawrence M. *A Universe from Nothing: Why There is Something Rather Than Nothing*. New York: Free Press, 2012.

Lameter, Christoph. "Divine Action in the Framework of Scientific Knowledge". PhD thesis, Fuller Theological Seminary, Newark, CA, 2004.

Laplace, Pierre. *A Philosophical Essay on Probabilities*. Translated by F.W. Truscott and F.L. Emory. New York: Dover, 1951.

Landau, Lev Davidovich, and Evgenii Mikhailovich Lifshitz. *Quantum Mechanics: Non-Relativistic Theory*, vol. 3. 2nd ed. Oxford: Pergamon Press, 1965.

Lindberg, David C. *The Beginnings of Western Science*. Chicago: University of Chicago Press, 1992.

Madelung, Wilferd. *Religious Schools and Sects in Medieval Islam*. London: Variorum Reprints, 1985.

Maimonides, Moses. *The Guide for the Perplexed*. Translated by Michael Friedländer. 2nd ed. London: Routledge & Kegan Paul Ltd., 1904.

Manuel, Frank E. *The Religion of Isaac Newton*. The Fremantle Lectures 1973. Oxford: Clarendon Press, 1974.

Marmura, Michael E., ed. *Islamic Theology and Philosophy*. New York: State University of New York Press, 1984.

Murad, Abdal Hakim. *Bombing Without Moonlight: The Origins of Suicidal Terrorism*. Bristol: Amal Press, 2008.

Murphy, Nancey. "Divine Action in the Natural Order". In *Chaos and Complexity*, Scientific Perspectives on Divine Action, vol. 2, edited by Robert John

Russell, Nancey Murphy, and Arthur Peacocke, 325–57. Vatican City State: Vatican Observatory; Berkeley, CA: Center for Theology and the Natural Sciences, 1995.

———. *Beyond Liberalism and Fundamentalism: How Modern and Postmodern Philosophy Set the Theological Agenda*. Valley Forge, PA: Trinity Press, 1996.

Muslim, Ibn al-Ḥajjāj. *al-Musnad al-ṣaḥīḥ al-mukhtaṣar bi naql al-ʿadl ʿan al-ʿadl ilā Rasūl Allāh*. Edited by Muḥammad Fu'ād ʿAbd al-Bāqī. 5 vols. Beirut: Dār Iḥyā' al-Turāth al-ʿArabī, n.d.

Namiki, Mikio, and Saverio Pascazio. "Quantum Theory of Measurement Based on the Many-Hilbert-Space Approach". *Physics Report* 232, no. 6 (1993): 301–411.

Neugebauer, Otto. *The Exact Sciences in Antiquity*. 2nd ed. New York: Dover Publications, 1969.

Newton, Isaac. *The Principia: Mathematical Principles of Natural Philosophy*. London: Snowball Publishing, 2010.

Nuʿmānī, Shiblī. *ʿIlm al-kalām*. Karachi: n.p., 1348/1929.

Özer, Murat, and M.O. Taha. "A Model of the Universe Free of Cosmological Problems". *Nuclear Physics B* 287 (1987): 776–96.

Özervarlı, M. Sait. "Attempts to Revitalize Kalām in the Late 19th and Early 20th Centuries". *The Muslim World* 89, no. 1 (1999): 90–105.

Peat, F. David. *From Certainty to Uncertainty: The Story of Science and Ideas in the Twenty-First Century*. Washington, DC: Joseph Henry Press, 2002.

Pines, Shlomo. *Studies in Islamic Atomism*. Translated by Michael Schwarz. Edited by Tzvi Langermann. Jerusalem: The Magnes Press, 1997.

Polkinghorne, John. "God's Action in the World". J.K. Russell Fellowship Lecture, Pacific School of Religion Chapel, Berkeley, CA, 6 April 1990.

———. *Reason and Reality: The Relationship Between Science and Theology*. London: SPCK, 1993.

———. "The Metaphysics of Divine Action". In *Chaos and Complexity*, Scientific Perspectives on Divine Action, vol. 2, edited by Robert John Russell, Nancey Murphy, and Arthur Peacocke, 147–56. Vatican City State: Vatican Observatory; Berkeley, CA: Center for Theology and the Natural Sciences, 1995.

Pollard, William G. *Chance and Providence: God's Action in a World Governed by Scientific Law*. New York: Charles Scribner's Sons; London: Faber and Faber, 1958.

Popper, Karl R. *The Logic of Scientific Discovery*. New York: Basic Books, 1959.

———. *The Myth of the Framework: In Defence of Science and Rationality.* Edited by Mark A. Notturno. London and New York: Routledge, 1996.

Ragep, F. Jamil. "When did Islamic Science Die (and Who Cares?)". *Viewpoint: The Newsletter of the British Society for History of Science*, no. 85 (February 2008): 1–3.

Rosenthal, Franz. "Al-Kindi als Literat". *Orientalia* 11 (1942): 262–88.

Rouse Ball, Walter W. "Pierre Simon Laplace (1749–1827)". In *A Short Account of the History of Mathematics*. 4th ed. New York: Dover Publications, 2003.

Russell, Robert John, Philip Clayton, Kirk Wegter-McNelly, and John Polkinghorne, eds. *Quantum Mechanics*, Scientific Perspectives on Divine Action, vol. 5. Vatican City State: Vatican Observatory; Berkeley, CA: Center for Theology and the Natural Sciences, 2001.

Russell, Robert John, Nancey Murphy, and C.J. Isham, eds. *Quantum Cosmology and the Laws of Nature*, Scientific Perspectives on Divine Action, vol. 1. Vatican City State: Vatican Observatory; Berkeley, CA: Center for Theology and the Natural Sciences, 1993.

Russell, Robert John, Nancey Murphy, Theo C. Meyering, and Michael A. Arbib, eds. *Neuroscience and the Person*, Scientific Perspectives on Divine Action, vol. 4. Vatican City State: Vatican Observatory; Berkeley, CA: Center for Theology and the Natural Sciences, 1999.

Russell, Robert John, Nancey Murphy, and Arthur Peacocke, eds. *Chaos and Complexity*, Scientific Perspectives on Divine Action, vol. 2. Vatican City State: Vatican Observatory; Berkeley, CA: Center for Theology and the Natural Sciences, 1995.

Russell, Robert John, William R. Stoeger, S.J., and Francisco J. Ayala, eds. *Evolutionary and Molecular Biology*, Scientific Perspectives on Divine Action, vol. 3. Vatican City State: Vatican Observatory; Berkeley, CA: Center for Theology and the Natural Sciences, 1998.

St. Augustine. *Confessions and Enchiridion.* Translated by Albert C. Outler. Grand Rapids, MI: Christian Classic Ethereal Library, 2000.

Sanders, James A. *Canon and Community: A Guide to Canonical Criticism.* Philadelphia: Fortress Press, 1984.

Sardar, Ziauddin. *Desperately Seeking Paradise: Journey of a Skeptical Muslim.* London: Granta Books, 2004.

Saunders, Nicholas T. "Does God Cheat at Dice? Divine Action and Quantum Possibilities". *Zygon* 35, no. 3 (2000): 517–44.

Schrödinger, Erwin. "Die Gegenwärtige Situation in der Quantenmechanik [The Present Situation in Quantum Mechanics]". *Naturwissenschaften* 33 (November 1935).

———. "Quantisierung als Eigenwertproblem (Erste Mitteilung)". *Annalen der Physik* 79, no.4 (1926): 361–76.

al-Shahristānī, Muḥammad ibn ʿAbd al-Karīm. *Kitāb al-milal wa al-niḥal*. Cairo: Muʾassasat al-Ḥalabī, 1388/1968.

Smolin, Lee. *The Trouble with Physics: The Rise of String Theory, the Fall of a Science and What Comes Next*. Boston: Houghton Mifflin, 2006.

Swerdlow, Noel M., and Otto E. Neugebauer. *Mathematical Astronomy in Copernicus's "De revolutionibus"*. New York: Springer-Verlag, 1984.

Taylor, Edwin F., and John A. Wheeler. *Exploring Black Holes*. New York: Addison-Wesley Longman, 2000.

Touati, Houari. *Islam and Travel in the Middle Ages*. Translated by Lydia G. Cochrane. Chicago: University of Chicago Press, 2010.

Versteegh, Kees. *The Arabic Linguistic Tradition*. Landmarks in Linguistic Thought, vol. 3. London and New York: Routledge, 1997.

von Neumann, John. *Mathematical Foundations of Quantum Mechanics*. Translated by Robert T. Beyer. Princeton: Princeton University Press, 1955.

Walzer, Richard. "Early Islamic Philosophy". In *The Cambridge History of Later Greek and Early Medieval Philosophy*, edited by A.H. Armstrong, 642–669. Cambridge: Cambridge University Press, 1970.

Weinberg, Steven. "Without God". *The New York Review of Books*. 25 September 2008.

———. Debate with John Polkinghorne at the SSQ symposium "Science and the Three Monotheisms: A New Partnership?", Granada, Spain, 23–5 August 2002.

Wheeler, John A. "Assessment of Everett's 'Relative State' Formulation of Quantum Theory". *Reviews of Modern Physics* 29 (1957): 463–5.

Wheeler, John Archibald, and Wojciech Hubert Zurek. *Quantum Theory and Measurement*. Princeton: Princeton University Press, 1983.

Wolfson, Harry Austryn. *The Philosophy of the Kalām*. Cambridge, MA: Harvard University Press, 1976.

INDEX

Lightning Source UK Ltd.
Milton Keynes UK
UKHW041414280219
338200UK00001B/135/P

9 789948 025276